Hard Money - Soft Outcomes

Evaluating and Managing the IT Investment

Edited by Barbara Farbey, David Targett and Frank Land

ALFRED WALLER LIMITED
Henley on Thames
In association with UNICOM

Published by
Alfred Waller Limited, Publishers
Orchards, Fawley, Henley on Thames, Oxon RG9 6JF

First published 1995

British Library Cataloguing in Publication Data
A Catalogue record for this book is available from the British Library

ISBN 1 872474 23 3

Printed and bound in Great Britain by the Lavenham Press, Suffolk

Contents

1 Introduction

Barbara Farbey and David Targett
Centre for Research into Strategic Information Systems, School of Management, University of Bath, UK
Frank Land
London School of Economics, UK

1. BACKGROUND

This book grew out of two seminars on evaluating and managing the IT investment, run by UNICOM Seminars Ltd. in January and November of 1992. The papers in this collection update and extend the seminar papers.

In the first seminar, chaired by Leslie Willcocks, the overarching theme was the evaluation and management of the IT investment across the lifetime of IT-based systems. The contributions covered the creation of a strategic investment climate for IT, the processes of evaluation, alternative techniques for evaluation and the control of IT investment, most particularly with respect to risk.

The second meeting, chaired by Barbara Farbey, took as its focus the concern of senior management as to the real value of their IT investment. The papers and discussion addressed three related issues: business, people and action. Its basic propositions were that

- IT serves business ends. The evaluation and management of IT must take into account the nature and purpose of the business, its objectives and its business practices.
- the evaluation and management of IT must concern itself with the interests, objectives, actions and satisfactions of the people who are affected by it – the stakeholders
- the evaluation and management of IT must serve as a basis for action. To do this they need to provide information which enables timely and decisive action. Equally, the managers of IT investment must be ready to take up and use the information provided. Even the best evaluation procedures will be wasted if there are no active benefits management procedures in place.

Contributions covered a range of methods and practical experience. They reported many complex organisational issues raised by evaluation and the process of evaluation.

2. A NEW FOCUS

But if a week is a long time in politics, two years is aeon in Information Systems.

Whilst not wishing to lose any of the lessons learned in the two seminars, the points about process, people and action which were well-made then and are still valid today, the focus in this collection is different again.

It is about a particular tension: the tension between the hard, usually quantitative discourse of formal evaluations and evaluation methodologies and the much softer issues which have their roots in organisations as human creations.

From this different perspective, the hard, quantitative results of an evaluation are as Coombs writes, 'only one of the inputs to the process of judgment and bargaining which eventually makes the decisions.' Getting that input right is important: many of the chapters in this book describe different methodologies with varying capabilities for providing numbers, assuring the process and adapting to context. Coping with the softer issues is however just as vital, as Targett writes 'the [broader organisational] issues constitute the soft shell which is wrapped around the hard centre. The shell may be thicker than the centre.'

The chapter organisation reflects the later perspective. The early chapters introduce some of the problems currently being experienced with evaluation. In Chapter 2, Galliers, having due regard to the concern of senior management over their IT investment, appeals for a more appropriate process, suggesting a "Business Systems Strategy" in place of an 'IT strategy.' By Business Systems Strategy, he means to refer to the integration of IT with business strategy formulation and business planning. Dimensions to consider are: people, processes, structure, culture and technology. In Chapter 3 Coombs notes the increasing integration of IT and business strategies. He strongly emphasises the importance of political 'readings' and the interests which people have in shaping and re-shaping organisational goals and structures.

The following chapters are essentially methodological, suggesting techniques and principles on which evaluation might be based. In Chapter 4 Birch and McEvoy present a method for coping with risk. In Chapter 5 Connolly makes a plea that costs are not considered in isolation from benefits, or from the influences which determine expenditure levels. In Chapter 6 Coleman takes a cold look at the limits of financial analysis and moves on to an approach which takes into account risks and intangibles. Leyton in Chapter 7 strongly emphasises the inter-relatedness of problems in IT which are often considered separately. He pleads for a balanced approach and a move away from financial measures where they are too simplistic.

In Chapter 8 Rowsell-Jones stresses the need for personal accountability for benefit realisation and the importance of commitment stemming from a shared perspective of key issues. He also notes some of the circumstances and attitudes which get in the way. Among these are a coercive management style, a rigid functional hierarchy, issues of 'class' (in Britain in the 1990s!) and quite fundamentally, a lack of priority preventing business management putting in the time required to manage the project. Chapter 9 ends the section with Heduan's practical study of the experience of one very large organisation in appraising IT projects, during a time of immense organisational and environmental change. Interestingly he suggests the possibility of a Knowledge Based system to assist in the management of IT investment, although he notes soberly that 'organisations must accept that there is no magic solution.'

IT projects are often, perhaps increasingly, large, complex and multi-faceted. In Chapter 10 Willcocks and Griffiths tackle the problem of risk in large-scale projects. In Chapter 11 Keen's case study of digital imaging in health care captures the predicament of would-be evaluators in a case where the outcomes are simply not foreseeable. As he writes, 'To ask about the value of a particular technology today is one thing; to ask about its value in a changed climate three or five years hence is quite another.' He notes a number of possibilities for evaluation including interview, observation and documentary analysis; treating the implementation of the system as an exercise in R&D or in other words to concentrate attention on the 'successful creation of a new product.' One strategy which Keen develops is to look to established evaluation methodologies, in particular to goal-free and the so-called Fourth Generation evaluation (4GE). From these he develops an iterative process of Recursive Evaluation. In Chapter 12 Willcocks, Lacity and Fitzgerald report their work on outsourcing. The delicate complexity of the relationship between user and vendor lead them to advocate the use of formal, short-term contracting in outsourcing relationships.

Many of the themes, issues and contradictions brought out in the earlier sections of the book resurface in the later chapters. The clash between strategy which may be best left fuzzy and investment which must be firm, or as he says it 'crisp', is the theme of Powell's paper in Chapter 13. He argues 'The very purpose of methodologies is to bring order and consistency to a system development process. Conversely the trend in strategy is to retreat from rigorous definition and to avoid imposing such constraints.'

In Chapter 14, Targett homes in on the importance of what he calls 'soft shell' evaluation. His case is that the meaning of evaluation has been too narrowly construed as referring to the 'quantification of well defined benefits with the sole objective of getting the project over organisational fences.' He calls for a broader vision of evaluation encompassing strategic, financial and social issues, arguing that as IS covers greater areas of the organisation and has impacts at all levels from strategic to tactical, the importance of the soft shell evaluation will increase. Targett captures directly another theme, present in different ways through many of the contributions, and that is the role played by evaluation as itself an organisational activity. He concludes 'If, as seems probable, evaluation influences implementation success then it may also be inevitable that without evaluation projects are more likely to fail.'

The last chapter is by way of conclusion and reflection on IT evaluation as it stands in 1994. In Chapter 15, Farbey summarises the outstanding themes and develops further some of the quieter ones. Taking a cut across the papers as a whole, she extracts some common themes, showing that evaluation has many purposes, that the objects of evaluation vary and noting the implications of what has been written for methods and method development.

The evaluation of IT is not a new problem. It is as old as IT itself. But given the pace of technological innovation, the unfolding appreciation of how and where and for what purposes the technology can be used coupled with the ever-changing business environment, there are always going to be new twists to the old story.

2 Rethinking IT evaluation in the context of business systems strategy

Robert D Galliers
Warwick Business School, University of Warwick

1. BACKGROUND

Why is it that senior executives in British companies have identified cost containment as the single major issue they face in dealing with Information Technology (IT)? (Grindley, 1992, p.7; 1993, p.8)

Back in July 1991, the Price Waterhouse/*Computing* Opinion Survey reported that the highest rated issue associated with the management of IT had changed for the first time in four years. At this point in time we saw 'cost containment' taking over from 'integrating IT', and this has remained as the top issue – and extended its lead – since then. 'Taking over' is probably not quite the right expression, however, because the two issues are very much interlinked. As one respondent to the July 1991 survey put it:

> "We need to reduce overall costs by 30% to 40%, and use the remaining 60% to 70% to focus on the core needs of the business. We want to simplify architectures, reduce infrastructure, increase systems development, and reduce operational expenses." (Grindley, 1992)

There is considerable anecdotal and empirical evidence that might help to answer the question posed in introducing this chapter. For example, Sir Denys Henderson, Chairman of ICI is quoted as saying:

> "I still worry enormously, both about the amount we spend on IT and the increasing difficulty of justifying that expense in terms of the bottom line." (Grindley, 1991)

Henderson's concerns regarding the rising expenditure on IT are borne out by figures recently released which indicate that despite declining cost-performance ratios for IT estimated to be as much as 30% *per annum* (Scott Morton, 1991), expenditure on IT, far from falling, has actually increased – *in real terms* – over the past eight years or so. (Grindley, 1992, p.4; 1993, p.4) Estimates vary, but it is often suggested that the amount spent on IT is around 2% of turnover annually.

(Weill and Olson, 1989; Willcocks, 1992)

When these concerns are considered in the light of the current adverse economic conditions, and other evidence that has come to light in recent years, it is no wonder that executives are becoming increasingly concerned to have real evidence of value for money from their IT investments. This 'other evidence' includes the point that there is apparently no correlation between the amount invested in IT and general business performance (Hochstrasser, 1987) and that it is often the case that there is an absence of agreement as to what the IT investment is actually supposed to achieve in business terms, let alone adequate procedures by which such benefits may be identified and/or measured (Bayne, 1991).

There is even more recent evidence to suggest that, despite the large sums of money involved, those firms that do attempt to evaluate their IT investments (and this is by no means all firms), tend to use the simpler financial criteria rather than the more sophisticated techniques such as net present value (NPV), internal rate of return (IRR) or profitability index (PI). (Ballantine *et al.*, 1994) While accounting techniques have been called into question as being inappropriate for IT investment assessment – given the unforeseen nature of the business benefits often involved (e.g. Willcocks, 1992), this argument tends to be based on an assessment of the more simple techniques, rather than the more sophisticated ones.

In addition, the recent research (Ballantine *et al.*, 1994) also suggests that IT investments are considered on an individual basis. Conversely, the concept of considering investments of a synergistic nature as a 'bundle' rather than as individual, isolated investments within a 'bundle', is gaining considerable ground in accounting circles. (Hendricks *et al.*, 1992; Miller and O'Leary, 1994)

In the light of the above, it would seem that, perhaps, Information Systems practitioners and academics may have been 'barking up the wrong tree' with regard to IT investment assessment. This chapter attempts to rethink the topic of IT evaluation in a broader context, specifically utilising Business Systems Strategy (BSS) as a basis for appropriate and on-going assessment and learning.

2. GOAL SETTING

A typical process associated with the introduction of IT into an organisation might be illustrated as in Figure 2.1. It may well be the case that the key business benefits expected from such investment are unknown, or at best are only dimly perceived. Nevertheless, and particularly in situations where senior management are inclined to abrogate responsibilities in this regard to the IS function, decisions are made to introduce IT systems.

Because of the lack of agreement concerning the business benefits to be had from the investment, the monitoring of its impact takes place in a kind of vacuum and, generally speaking, this also takes place in isolation from related projects, as

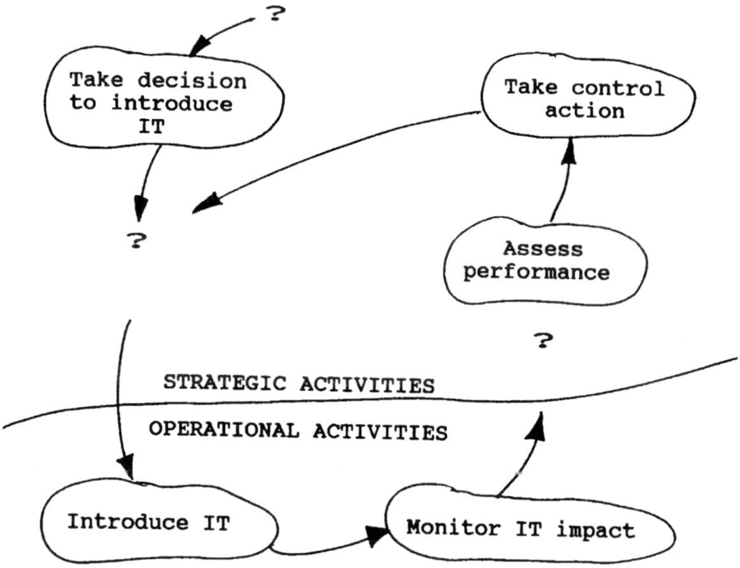

Figure 2.1 Introducing IT: a typical process (Source: amended from Galliers, 1993).

we have seen. Even if control action is attempted (e.g. because of some unease about the benefits that have actually accrued, or because of some unforeseen negative impact), such control action again takes place in somewhat undirected fashion because clear targets remain unset and the investment is viewed in isolation.

Given the analysis thus far, it will come as no surprise that the central message of this paper is fairly simple and can be stated in two parts:

1. Understand what it is you are trying to achieve through the use of IT, and then attempt to measure whether or not the desired effect has occurred.
2. Attempt to assess the impact of related IS/IT projects as a whole, rather than as individual investments.

Of course, in reality, this is not quite as simple as it may first appear: how can you be sure that it is the introduction of IT that has had the desired effect, as opposed to some other combination of factors? The complexity is further apparent when the introduction of IT systems is considered in the context of socio-technical change, with consequential impacts on organisational arrangements and the very nature of the business processes themselves. (e.g. Venkatraman, 1991) This is illustrated by a variation on Leavitt's (1965) so-called 'diamond', as depicted in

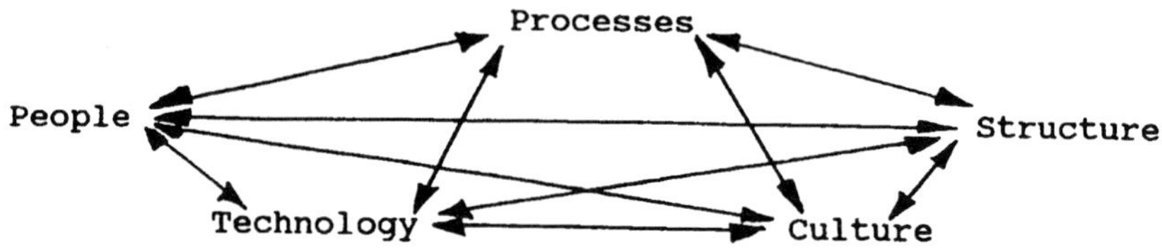

Figure 2.2 Amended version of Leavitt's (1965) Diamond.

Figure 2.2. Any change in one of the factors will have a consequential impact on other aspects of the broader sociotechnical system.

While IT evaluation is, of course, a more complex issue than simply measuring against predefined targets, periodic review of actual performance, based on criteria that are appropriate for one's own circumstances, combined with the kind of 'double-loop learning' advocated by, for example, Argyris and Schön (1978), will have a cumulative impact on one's ability to sense whether linked IT investments – *and their associated organisational changes* – are providing value for money or not.

So, how might we go about understanding the role of IT in improving business performance, so that we might then identify appropriate performance measures to enable this review to take place? Again, the answer at first sight seems simple enough, actually carrying this out in practice is apparently more difficult.

The answer, as the title of this chapter implies, is to institute an on-going business systems strategy and review process, which will be described in more detail in the section that follows.

3. INSTITUTING A BUSINESS SYSTEMS STRATEGY AND REVIEW PROCESS

Before this process is described, however, it is perhaps advisable first to say something about the form of words being used. It is more common to hear the expression 'Information Systems Planning' or 'Information Systems Strategy', or some combination of these terms in this context. 'Business Systems Strategy' is used in preference, however, as it is meant to imply that there is more to this process than the mere identification of IT systems for development. The process should not simply be linked, however closely, with the Business Planning and Strategy Formulation process, but *integrated* with it and the Strategy Implementation process as well. The outputs, as indicated in the section above, include business and organisational change, rather than simply ideas for IT applications. Indeed, from this perspective, Information Systems themselves are seen as human activity systems (Checkland, 1981; Checkland and Scholes, 1990), rather than some purely technological entity.

A reasonably comprehensive definition of Business Systems Strategy is provided in Figure 2.3. Note that it contains reference (after Earl, 1989) to:

- an *information* strategy
- an *information technology* strategy
- an *information management* strategy
- a *change management/implementation* strategy, and
- an on-going process of *evaluation and review*,

and is illustrated in Figure 2.4.

As indicated in Figure 2.4, the Business Systems Strategy process should be able to answer the questions:

- *why?* (i.e. why is it that the business strategy is appropriate, given our current

---

Business Systems Strategy is that on-going management task[1] that is concerned with integrating information systems considerations into the business planning and strategy formulation process, and with providing a direct link between this and, e.g., information technology acquisition decisions and the applications development process. More specifically, it involves the identification of:

- current and future information, information systems, and information technology requirements and priorities, in line with organisational objectives and responsibilities (including the ability to question the appropriateness of the business strategy and the assumptions upon which this is based);
- possibilities provided by advances in IT for improved competitiveness (or organisational survival!), in line with environmental circumstances (eg., competitor activity, market trends, changing customer requirements) and organisational strengths (and weaknesses);
- the risks associated with, and resource/ organisational implications of, alternative IS plans (including human resource considerations such as skill requirements);
- corporate, as well as individual/discrete, information needs, which in turn enables decisions to be made regarding the composition of corporate systems (databases, distributed systems, networks), appropriate end-user developed systems, and the corporate information systems architecture.
- appropriate measures of performance that enable on-going evaluation and review which in turn provides an indication of the impact of the process on business performance.

[1]Business systems strategy, as seen from this perspective, is a corporate management responsibility, not simply an information systems management task. While it is crucially dependent on the input from, and guidance of the IT Director (or equivalent) and other IS/IT professionals, it should be viewed as an integral part of the business strategy process, in much the same way as, for example, financial planning.

Figure 2.3 Business systems strategy definition (Source: Amended from Galliers, 1987b, p230).

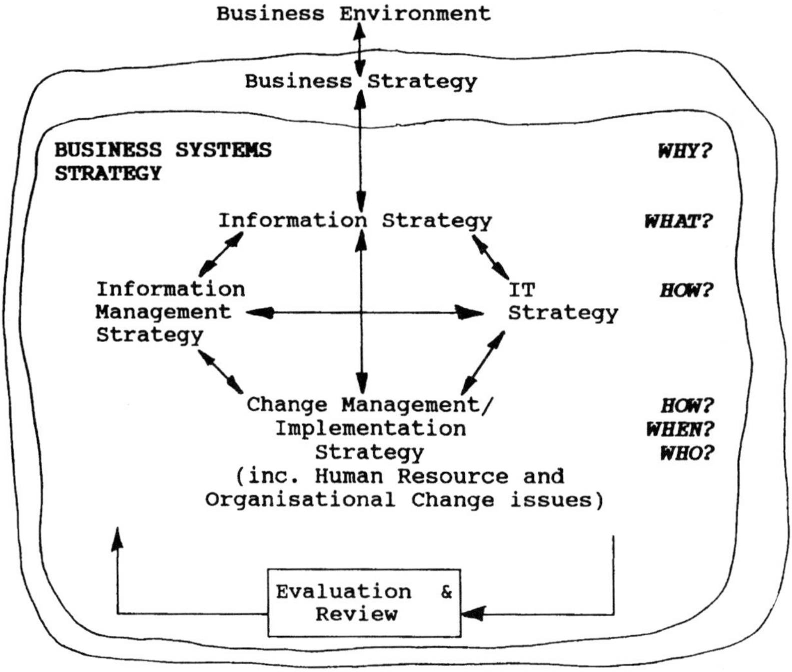

Figure 2.4 Business systems strategy formulation, implementation and review (Source: amended from Galliers, 1991;1992a, and Earl, 1989, pp63-64)

circumstances and the nature of the business environment?)

- *what*? (i.e. what information is necessary to question the assumptions on which our business strategy is based? and what information is necessary to enable key business processes and decisions to be undertaken?)
- *how*? (i.e. how might we utilise IT to provide this information and improve the efficacy of our business processes? and how might we organise our IS services to enable the business systems strategy to be carried out efficaciously?)
- *when*? (i.e. when should required IT projects be undertaken? in what order? within what timescale?)
- *who*? (i.e. who should be involved? who should be responsible? what skills are required or need to be developed?).

An attempt has been made to depict the process of Business Systems Strategy formulation and implementation as but one aspect of Business Strategy – not necessarily a central aspect, but very much a crucial one. It should also be viewed as an on-going activity, rather than a one-off or *ad hoc* process.

4. THE CRUCIAL ROLE OF TARGETS IN BUSINESS SYSTEMS STRATEGY

Figure 2.4 also attempts to illustrate (i) the potential impact of IT projects on business processes and organisational boundaries, by stressing the need to manage change; (ii) information analysis based on *required* business processes in line with business objectives, rather than on *existing* ways of doing business, and (iii) the on-going nature of the process, which is crucially reliant on evaluation and review. The latter aspect is illustrated further by Figure 2.5, which uses the same format as Figure 2.1. Note, however, the introduction of targets, utilising the concept of critical success factors (CSFs) (Rockart, 1979), and their corollaries, critical failure factors (CFFs), i.e. those factors likely to have a major negative impact on organisational performance, and critical assumptions (CAs), i.e. those taken-

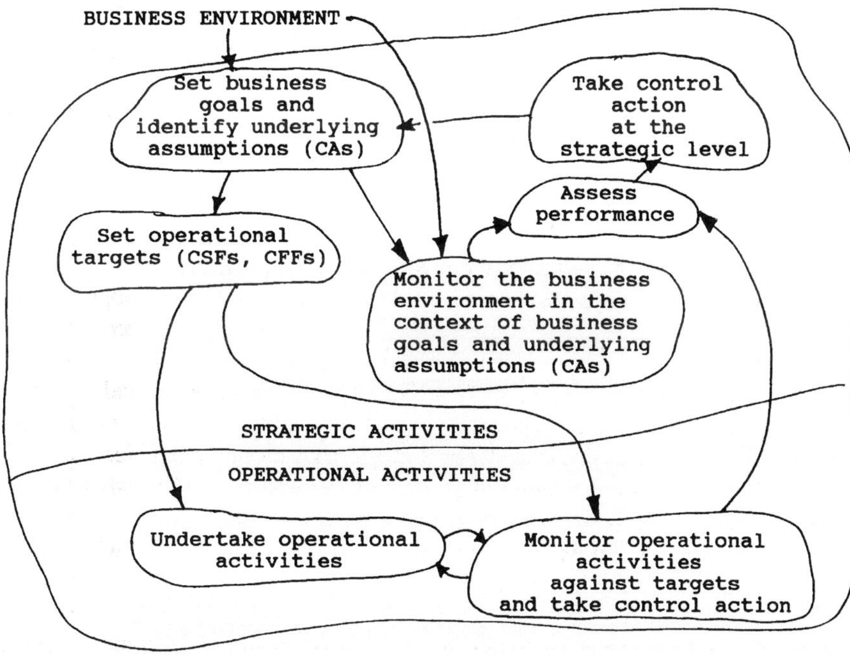

Figure 2.4 Management control activity: a more appropriate process (Source: Galliers, 1993 – amended from Galliers, 1987b, p301)

for-granted assumptions upon which business strategy is based and which if, in the event, prove to be false would render the strategy inappropriate. (Galliers, 1993)

Neither Figures 2.4 or 2.5 should be viewed as being entirely deterministic, however. Strategies are both deterministic and emergent (Mintzberg and Waters, 1985); outcomes will be both intended and unintended. The monitoring and control process is meant to take both these perspectives into account.

5. REVIEWING THE BUSINESS SYSTEMS STRATEGY PROCESS

It is important to take account of appropriate targets in the kind of process depicted in Figure 2.5. For example, in the context of Business Systems Strategy, the viewpoints of different stakeholder groups regarding what constitutes a successful outcome might well differ.

Given the wide range of approaches to Business Systems Strategy (as illustrated in Table 2.1), it is important that we have some means of identifying the kind of approach that is going to produce the best outcome for our purposes.

The first question to ask in reviewing Business Systems Strategy – as with any IT project – is 'what do we want to achieve?' Strange as it may seem, there is often a variety of answers to this question – even in the same organisation! For

Table 1 Earl's Classification of strategic information systems planning approaches (Source: amended from Earl, 1990)

APPROACH	*FEATURES*
Technology Driven	The development of IT architectures as a foundation for expected application needs.
Method Driven	The use of techniques (often a consultant's methodology) to identify IS needs by analysing business processes and objectives.
Resource Driven[a]	The objective is to establish IT capital and expense budgets to satisfy approved projects – this is often essentially a 'wish list' approach.
Business Led	Business plans are analysed to identify where IS/IT is most critical to meeting those plans.
Thematic[b]	Development of key themes for IS/IT investment derived from a consensus view of priorities established by a group of senior executives.

[a]Earl uses the term 'Administrative' to describe the 'Resource driven' approach.
[b]Earl uses the term 'Organisation Led' to describe the 'Thematic' approach.

example, when asked what the single most important outcome from the process is, senior executives, middle managers and IS/IT executives often have different ideas on the matter. In earlier research (Galliers, 1987a), it was found that the most common answer to the question from each group was as given in Table 2.2.

As might be expected from the introduction to this chapter, senior executives expect to gain greater control over IT initiatives generally, and are currently looking for cost containment. Middle ranking executives appear to be more interested in seeing the implementation of information systems that directly support their part of the business. Conversely, Information Systems Managers, often overburdened with requests that cannot be met because of limited resources and faced with a rapidly changing business and technological environment, are frequently looking for some degree of certainty and clarity in their world. An agreed plan with clear priorities goes some way to fulfilling this dream!

In addition, it may be that the desired outcomes will vary according to the use IT is put to in different organisations, and their relative experience and expertise (cf. the 'stages of growth' concept of, for example, Nolan, 1979; Earl, 1989; and Galliers and Sutherland, 1991).[2]

While motivations will differ from one organisation (or manager) to the next, whatever the situation, it is important to clarify with key stakeholder groups what it is they are looking for from the planning process. Different approaches are likely to be more or less successful simply on the basis of those outcomes that are considered to be most appropriate from different perspectives.

Arising from the research described above (Galliers, 1987a), an outline table (Table 2.3) has been produced which lists some of the most often stated motivations for Business Systems Strategy, and attempts an assessment of different types of approach in the context of these alternatives. Again, it is likely that other motivations or desired outcomes will be evident in any particular organisation. The idea is for the table to be used as a basis for asking questions and assessing alternatives, rather than for providing cast-iron answers as to the appropriate choice of approach.

Table 2.2 Differing viewpoints as to key outcomes of the business systems strategy process

Management Group	*Single Most Important Outcome of Business Systems Strategy*
Senior Management	Improved Control over IS
Middle Management	Improved Quality of IS (to meet *their* needs)
IS Management	Agreed plan/priorities for IS

[2] It is helpful to apply such 'stages of growth' models as part of the Business Systems Strategy process since this helps to give some indication as to the implementation issues associated with desired strategies.

Table 2.3 Choosing appropriate business systems strategy approaches based on stakeholder motivations (Source: amended from Galliers, 1991, p63). Extent of coverage: * minor, ** reasonable; *** major

		BSS Orientation[3]	
Motivation	*IT*	*Organisation*	*Environment*
Efficiency, cost reduction	**	**	*
Effectiveness	*	***	**
Improved products, services	*	**	***
Applications portfolio	*	***	**
IT acquisitions	***	*	*
IT architecture	***	*	*
Database architecture	***	**	*
Information architecture	*	***	*
Competitive, strategic IS	*	**	***
Improved management/ IS relations	*	**	**
Resourcing decisions	**	**	*
Human resource considerations	**	**	**
Business process redesign	*	**	**

[3] 'Business Systems Strategy Orientation' relates to the type of approach being considered, i.e. whether the focus is on the technology itself (isolated), or on matters internal to the organisation (reactive), or on the business environment (proactive).

6. SUCCESSFUL IT PROJECTS BEGIN WITH A SUCCESSFUL BUSINESS SYSTEMS STRATEGY

In general, despite the range of motivations discussed above, there are some commonly agreed aspects to Business Systems Strategy that, while not guaranteeing success, contribute to it. It is perhaps unfortunate that it seems that current practice is, as often as not, deficient in these very same aspects! As a result, successful IT projects remain elusive in many organisations. Table 2.4 provides a partial list of those factors that appear to contribute to successful Business Systems Strategy formulation and may be used in the review process.

One word of warning, however: while the preceding arguments are useful in preparing for IT projects, there is no universal panacea for IT success. It takes a great deal of effort and the willingness of colleagues to contribute to discussions, take on responsibilities to see things through and to approach the challenges posed with an open mind and flexible attitude. Business Systems Strategy is a useful basis for IT evaluation, and the on-going evaluation and review, which is an essential feature of it, provides a means by which organisations can learn to be

Table 2.4 Some factors that contribute to successful business systems strategies (Source: Galliers, 1991, p63)

- gaining appropriate *commitment* to, and *involvement* in IS Planning on the part of senior and middle management
- paying due regard to the *implementation*, as well as formulation, process
- *reviewing* and *assessing* the benefits and actual outcomes of the IS Planning process, taking account of the differing motivations and expectations of different stakeholders
- *integrating* IS considerations into the business strategy process.

successful with their IT investments. For too long we have tended to perceive IT evaluation in terms of individual projects or investment decisions. The suggestion here is to incorporate evaluation into the Business Systems Strategy process on an on-going basis and to evaluate related IT investments together in the context of wider change (cf. Figure 2.2) and changing business imperatives.

REFERENCES

Argyris. C & Schön, D (1978) *Organizational Learning: A Theory of Action Perspective.* Addison-Wesley, Reading, MA

Ballantine, J, Galliers, R D and Stray, S (1994) Information Systems/Technology Investment Decisions – The Use of Capital Investment Appraisal Techniques in Organisations, Warwick Business School Research Papers, No. 105, February

Bayne, T (1991) Unpublished MBA Dissertation, Warwick Business School, University of Warwick. (Cited in Galliers, 1992a, *op cit.*)

Checkland, P B (1981) *Systems Thinking, Systems Practice.* Wiley, Chichester

Checkland, P and Scholes, J (1990) *Soft Systems Methodology in Action.* Wiley, Chichester

Earl, M J (1989) *Management Strategies for Information Technology.* Prentice-Hall, New York

Galliers, R D (1987a) Information Systems Planning in the United Kingdom and Australia – A Comparison of Current Practice. In P I Zorkoczy (ed.), *Oxford Surveys in Information Technology*, **4**, Oxford University Press, Oxford, pp223-255

Galliers, R D (ed.) (1987b) *Information Analysis: Selected Readings.* Addison-Wesley, Wokingham

Galliers, R D (1991) 'Strategic Information Systems Planning: Myths, Reality and Guidelines for Successful Implementation' *European Journal of Information Systems*, **1**(1), pp55-64

Galliers, R D (1992a) 'Information Technology – Management's Boon or Bane?' *Journal of Strategic Information Systems*, **1**(2), March, pp50-56

Galliers, R D (1992b) 'Integrating Information Systems into Business: Research at Warwick Business School', *International Journal of Information Management*, **12**, pp160-163

Galliers, R D (1993) 'Towards a Flexible Information Architecture: Integrating Business Strategies, Information Systems Strategies and Business Process Redesign' *Journal of*

Information Systems, **3**(3), July, pp199-213

Galliers, R D and Sutherland, A R (1991) 'Information Systems Management and Strategy Formulation: The 'Stages of Growth' Model Revisited' *Journal of Information Systems*, **1**(2), pp89-114

Grindley, K (ed.) (1991) *Information Technology Review 1991/92*. Price Waterhouse, London

Grindley, K (ed.) (1992) *Information Technology Review 1992/93*. Price Waterhouse, London

Grindley, K (ed.) (1993) *Information Technology Review 1993/94*. Price Waterhouse, London

Hendricks, J A, Bastian, R C and Sexton, T L (1992) Bundle monitoring of strategic projects, *Management Accounting*, pp31-35

Hochstrasser, B (1987) *Does Information Technology Slow You Down?* Kobler Unit, Imperial College, London

Leavitt, H J (1965) Applying Organizational Change in Industry: Structural, technical and humanistic approaches. In: J G March (ed), *Handbook of Organizations*, Rand McNally, Chicago

Miller, P and O'Leary, T (1994) Accounting, 'Economic citizenship' and the spatial reordering of manufacture, *Accounting, Organisations and Society*, **19**(1), pp15-43

Mintzberg, H and Waters, J A (1985) Of strategies, deliberate and emergent, *Strategic Management Journal*, **6**, pp257-272

Nolan, R L (1979) 'Managing the Crises in Data Processing' *Harvard Business Review*, **57**(2), March-April

Rockart, J F (1979) 'Chief Executives Define Their Own Data Needs' *Harvard Business Review*, **57**(2), March-April. (Also in Galliers (ed.) (1987a), *op cit*., pp267-289)

Scott Morton, M S (ed.) (1991) *The Corporation of the 1990s: Information Technology and Organizational Transformation*. Oxford University Press, Oxford

Venkatraman, N (1991) 'IT-Induced Business Reconfiguration' In Scott Morton (1991), *op cit*., pp122-158

Weill, P and Olson, M (1989) Managing investment in IT, *MIS Quarterly*, **13**(1), pp3-17

Willcocks, L (1992) Evaluating information technology investments: research findings and reappraisal, *Journal of Information Systems*, **2**(4), pp243-268

3 IT systems and changes in organisational culture

Professor Rod Coombs
Manchester School of Management, UMIST

1. INTRODUCTION

Major IT system changes in organisations are almost invariably now bound up with changes in the culture of those organisations. This trend can be seen reflected in two general principles concerning the role of IT in modern organisations which are now becoming 'received wisdom' for the most experienced practitioners and users of IT in our larger companies. These are:

1. IT systems no are longer simply used in the supporting and auxiliary functions within a business or organisation. They are increasingly a major feature of the actual *product or service* provided, or of the delivery system.
2. IT is no longer simply *automating* existing business processes; it is increasingly *transforming* them, involving more radical changes in products, organisational structures, work-roles and patterns of relationships between firms.

To put it more succinctly, IT systems do not simply change the way you do business, they can change the business you do!

But although people may recognise *intellectually* that IT system development will involve them in major business change, and that therefore it should really be seen as just that – a major business change – there is still a tendency at the *practical* level to place too much emphasis and too many expectations on the narrower technological issues. This is often a consequence of the fact that it sometimes seems a lot easier to agree and progress technical projects than to clarify and agree on major organisational and business changes. But this can lead to significant conflict further down the line when there is an attempt to answer questions about returns on investment in IT, because there is conflict over just what factors properly deserve a place in the numerator and denominator of the cost-benefit calculation. Are the business changes, both positive and negative, genuinely attributable to the IT project or not?

These problems are, to a considerable extent, the underlying causes of the current 'crisis of confidence' in the relations between IT professionals and business users. So far, the years of the IT revolution have, paradoxically, been characterised by rates of economic growth and productivity lower than those of the pre-computer years of the 'long boom' during the 1950s and 1960s. At the level of the individual company using IT in its business activities, one finds scepticism in equal measure with expectation. For many boards of directors, large IT projects frequently appear to be frighteningly expensive, difficult to justify in conventional cost-benefit terms, capable of creating enormous mishaps, and yet impossible to pull out of. IT practitioners get much of the blame. Sometimes it seems that the technological potential increases, the claimed business advantages multiply, and the boxes get cheaper and cheaper; but the budget and the headcount still rise, the benefits seem elusive, and the strategic direction of the IT investment and development programmes becomes ever more of an organisational battleground.

2. AN EXAMPLE OF NOT RECOGNISING CULTURAL CHANGE

Here is an example of one company's experience which illustrates problems of this type. The company, which we have given a false name to save its blushes, was researched extensively over many years by a group of my colleagues in the Manchester School of Management at UMIST, co-ordinated by Professor David Knights.

Pensco is an insurance and pensions company with a substantial IT function. With the new Social Security Act in 1988, new business opportunities were created for Pensco, and it decided to develop a new pensions product. The IT department in Pensco was engaged to play a major part in the pensions product development, since significant new IT applications had to be written to provide the product.

At the same time, however, the company was anxious to improve the level of customer service for existing products, and wanted to make substantial changes to the IT systems to achieve this. Indeed, the overwhelming feature of previous IT development in Pensco was its subordination to technological or administrative driving factors. Consequently, the IT function found itself under pressure from two separate groups in the company to develop new product-related IT systems and new administrative systems simultaneously. This lead to a battle.

The IT function responded by saying that they did not have the capacity, and that anyway, there were substantial technical difficulties involved in trying to achieve these two major IT changes at the same time. At board level, sponsors of both projects refused to back down, and the board itself abdicated from making a choice. So the IT function backed down and reluctantly accepted both charges. Both projects proceeded and were finished *on schedule*, but the quality of the outcomes were privately judged by most of those involved to be much lower than desired, and less than could have been achieved if a better strategic compromise had been struck. The IT strategy of Pensco had, in effect, been the battleground upon which groups within Pensco fought over, and in a sense discovered, the fact that they were experiencing a collective cultural change. The change was from a traditional insurance company driven by actuaries, administrators and technologists, into a more market-oriented company driven by product lines and product innovation. This did not become fully clear to those concerned until quite late in the process; for much of the time, they thought they were simply changing their IT systems!

3. CULTURAL CHANGE AND STRATEGIC CHANGE

The Pensco cases illustrates the principle that when IT 'touches' the core cultural characteristics of an organisation it can have galvanic effects. One interesting and vital consequence of these changes in the role of IT from supporting player to starring role, is that there has been an increase in the need to treat IT as a major feature of the *genuinely strategic* discussions which take place within organisations. Both providers and users of the Information Services Function now take it for granted that, as a very minimum, we should use business strategy as the starting point for the derivation of IT strategy. Indeed, as time goes on, some organisations are finding that the distinction between IT strategy and business strategy is becoming less sharp.

Instead of 'aligning' IT strategy with business strategy it is increasingly a question of *integrating* these strategies. Financial service companies such as Pensco are probably at the leading edge of this trend, but the lesson is increasingly relevant for other sectors.

One consequence of this increasing integration of IT strategy and overall business strategy is that the character of IT strategies is changing. Instead of having 'weak' agendas which focus mainly on aligning the IT application portfolio with the business structure, strategies are increasingly likely to have 'strong' agendas which are concerned with how IT will gain or sustain competitive advantage. Of course, this is very exciting for IT professionals because their position in the corporate pecking order can be enhanced. In fact, it is remarkable to note in passing how easily the new position of IT Director has been institutionalised in many companies. As a student of technology management in the wider domains of technology outside IT, I can only marvel at the fact that R&D directors have struggled to reach the same status in UK companies for more than 30 years, and failed more often that they have succeeded.

So the IT function is migrating towards the 'core' strategic agenda of the firm, but this raises two major problems which are shared by IT professionals and the other senior management groups in the firm. However, they may not always be seen as shared, but rather as the subject of argument and attribution of 'blame' for perceived failures. These problems are:

- Finding acceptable ways of justifying expenditure on IT. This is a major problem, and generates many organisational conflicts and disputes between IT professionals, consultants, and users. There are two polar approaches. The first is to treat IT investment like other investments and attempt to measure a financial return. Now perhaps this can be attempted in 'automation' situations – where existing business processes are simply changed from paper-based to IT based – but it does not have a good record in applications which are genuinely 'transformation' situations. In these circumstances, which are more and more common, it seems to me to be more appropriate to see the IT investment as part of a broader (and risky) attempt to re-engineer major features of an organisations's structure and goals. The Pensco example given above is, in some senses, illustrative of this argument. In this (transformative) context, perhaps you can only justify IT retrospectively by pointing to the actual performance of the whole business activity of which the IT is a part. Or more generally, by looking at other instances of similar combined IT and organisational change programmes and their current benefits. Again, there are parallels here with some firms' attitude to R&D expenditure. But this second approach is difficult because the idea of clearly demonstrating a financial return is deeply rooted in Anglo-Saxon business culture and hard to resist. What is more, the natural suspicions which IT users have about the motives, candour, and covert agendas of IT professionals makes them unwilling to let them be excused the rigours of cost-justifying their investment proposals, especially when other groups are not so excused. So, with these suspicions and potential functional rivalries, organisational politics begins to rear its head, and this takes us to the second problem which comes from IT's migration towards the core strategic agenda of the firm.

- The second problem for IT of having become 'strategic' is that the formulation and implementation of any strategy (whether business, IT, or an integration of the two) is intrinsically political (in the sense of *organisational* politics). But, you might object, surely this is too cynical a view; yes, we know that politics is always lurking beneath the surface in organisations, but surely that is why we develop robust procedures, conventions, standards, common languages of accounting and technical performance and so on. In this way, surely, the power of reason, the common sense and goodwill of people, and their acceptance of the overall need to make the organisation succeed for its own member's survival sake, will mean that sensible consensus decisions can be taken which triumph over organisational politics? Perhaps!

But let us return to the real world. How many big investment decisions, whether in IT or any other field, do we really feel are the result only of sober calculation, and how many are the result of processes which might be better represented in the way that a novelist or a playwright describes the ebb and flow of fortunes and ideas of individuals, unexpected accidents, interference of events from other spheres, and strongly held personal beliefs? Or even by what Keynes called 'animal spirits'? If we take this political view we may be called cynical and defeatist by those who see, or need to argue for, the simple truths of the formal decision-making models. Indeed, it might be thought we offer a counsel of despair which denies the possibility of any sensible way of proceeding in these matters. But this is not my view. Rather, what I wish to suggest is that we have sanitised and over-simplified organisational politics in the interests of stuffing it into the neat and tidy categories of our formal procedures for making business and technical decisions, and as a result we have deceived ourselves on some key issues.

4. STRATEGY IS POLITICAL

Conventional models of IT system development and strategy formulation advocate starting the process with a clarification of business goals and business strategy, and then proceeding to generate IT objectives, perhaps by identifying critical success factors in the business, or focusing on important links in the value chain. (We are probably all familiar with the waterfall model which is one way of capturing the spirit of this process.) Now, as a way of organising an agenda for a sensible discussion amongst people with diverse views, this is wholly admirable. The flaw comes in believing that it has a necessary and inbuilt likelihood of producing a robust conclusion which will command consent. Furthermore, it frequently assumes that if such consent is established it will then remain stable during the development of the system or the implementation of the strategy. In general, it cannot, for the very simple reason that whenever people form views of the future, and then act upon them, their actions, and their subsequent evaluations of those actions, will normally change their perception of their goals, and of what should have been their goals at the beginning of the process, and consequently they will either discredit the system or the strategy, or change it, or both.

Let me pause to take stock of the argument I have developed so far. The ways in which we use information technology are becoming more and more strategic. By this I mean that the IT systems are not used only as more efficient tools for the carrying out of simple tasks, but rather they are used in new and unfamiliar tasks, which are elements of new business activities, such as new products, a significantly modified service, or a new way of delivering a product or service to the customer. In these cases, the IT system design and implementation is part and parcel of some larger and multi-faceted change in the organisation itself, both in terms of its structure and operations, and in terms of the stance it is adopting towards its markets and competitors. The two problems I have identified which arise in this situation are:

- the failure of normal business techniques for assessing the costs and benefits of the IT investment,
- and the shortcomings of the system development processes which are supposed to produce systems which meet the eventual business requirement satisfactorily.

Lying behind both of these failures of management technique and best practice is something I have called organisational politics. We have already seen in the example of Pensco, how organisational politics and the strategic use of IT are difficult to separate. I would like to use now some further examples from the work we have done at UMIST PICT on the application of IT to hospital management. I am again indebted here to my colleagues, particularly Dr Brian Bloomfield and Dr Jenny Owen.

5. IT IN THE NHS

In recent years, a major area of IT investment in the NHS has been in 'Resource Management' systems. These are essentially Management Information Systems in the classic sense. They start with masses of data on patient diagnoses, days in hospital, and tests and treatments performed on patients; then apply standard costs for each activity, and generate management information about the patterns of care for different patient groups, and the patterns of care of different doctors. They can be used to highlight differences in practices and costs between medical staff, and between hospitals, and to raise the visibility of efficiency and effectiveness issues in the dialogues between doctors and managers.

So, typically, once you have an RM system functioning in a hospital, the Unit Manager, or a senior doctor, or perhaps both together, can call up a report on, let us say, the patients treated in the past six months with a specific diagnosis such as renal failure, and review the average cost per case, the reasons for any systematic departure from average cost, the variations between two renal consultants in treatment profiles and cost per case, and, in turn, their variation from regional or national averages. If there are significant variances within the hospital or between the hospital and its competitors, then a discussion may be triggered about whether any medical practices should be reviewed, or whether more far reaching measures are indicated such as increasing or decreasing the resources allocated to this area of treatment.

Clearly, these systems enable new levels of managerial surveillance and intervention in areas which were previously the private domain of doctors working under their received principles of 'clinical freedom'. Indeed, the express view of the NHS Executive on the purpose of these systems was that they should help to entice doctors to take on the responsibility for acting on this managerial information, by accepting budgets and working within them, using the new management information to assist that task. It therefore sought to change the position of doctors with respect to the management process.

It will not surprise you to hear that the initial reactions of many doctors to the proposal that they become involved in the teams designing and implementing such IT-based management information systems was hostile. Some of the arguments they deployed were concerned with 'wasting money on administration while services were underfunded', but at bottom their concerns were also 'political' in the sense I am using; that is, they identified the systems as a potential curtailment of the freedom of action and autonomy they were accustomed to. Of course, this was not merely cynical protectionism; for many doctors the issue was perceived as one of principle: they see their job as to give their patients the treatment they see as appropriate, and not to get directly involved in cost trade-offs between patients, or groups of patients. The fact that doctors have always done these trade-offs, but in less transparent ways, is of course a counter argument to this.

It is easy to imagine, then, the early meetings of the Resource Management teams in particular hospitals, which had the task of designing and implementing, or more recently, purchasing and implementing, these information systems. Under the guidance of principles 'received' from the IT community, the meetings would begin with organisational goals and progress to data requirements, performance measures and reporting arrangements. But quite quickly, whether dealing with goals, performance or reporting, the meetings would run up against fundamental cultural and value conflicts between those members who were doctors and those who were managers. The former emphasising the subtlety, complexity and, ultimately, judgmental character of medical work, and the latter emphasising the possibility of systematising data on groups of patients with similar conditions and analyzing it. On the surface the confrontation is about effectiveness versus efficiency; underneath, the conflict is about responsibility, visibility and control.

But the surprising thing, given the entrenched power positions of the participants, is that these situations did not typically remain deadlocked for too long. As the meetings progressed over periods of months and years, and as one hospital got to hear about what another was doing, and as doctors began to talk in their professional bodies, views began gradually to shift. Eventually, some doctors were, in a sense, 'converted' to the point of view that measures of relative efficiency were useful, and even compatible with received notions of clinical freedom (others, of course, still disagreed). Other doctors found themselves in situations where the features of the IT systems they were offered included not only 'cost accounting' type functions, but also the ability to generate interesting clinical data about treatment patterns and results which could be useful for research and for medical audit procedures. Insightful IT professionals in some hospitals designed the data and the screens in such a way as to attract the doctors precisely toward this 'clinical relevance' which could be built into the systems. At the same time, other events were taking place in parallel, beginning with the move towards clinical directorates as effectively 'departments' of hospitals, and moving on more radically to the NHS reforms and the introduction of trusts, the internal market, and fund-holding GPs. This combination of factors has resulted in an evolution over a period of nearly five years, to a position where the medical profession has now more or less accepted resource management both at the national level and in many hospitals. A change in culture, in attitudes to the balance between management and medicine, and indeed, in the self-understanding of doctors, has begun to take place amongst doctors. Many factors have contributed, but the interesting thing for us is that this change in culture has happened through an encounter with the task of designing strategic IT systems.

The organisational politics and the IT systems have marked each other; they are joint products; indeed, there are those in the NHS who would argue that it almost does not matter if the IT systems do not yet work very well; they could be said to have achieved their aim if they have contributed to this re-casting of the managerial agenda and the tighter integration of doctors into that agenda. This almost makes the IT an instrument of organisational change, rather than a neatly packaged management tool which simply 'requires' some minor organisational change to accommodate it.

The point of recounting this story is to underline my point that the strategic IT choices made in organisations depend not only on technical issues such as data integrity and system interconnections, and not only on rational evaluations of business policy to which everyone can be asked to subscribe, but on political 'readings' of the situation in the organisation (in this case, the NHS) and of the interests which people have in re-shaping the organisations' goals and structures.

Someone might want to object to this analysis on the grounds that the NHS is somehow 'unrepresentative' of organisations in general, because of its size, ambiguous federal structure and political visibility, and because of the 'most peculiar practices' of its principal employees. My response is to agree that the NHS is special, but to argue that the underlying principles of organisational politics and IT are exhibited in the same way, but to varying extents, in all organisations.

6. IT SYSTEMS DISRUPT PERCEIVED 'GOALS' AND 'INTERESTS'

What the NHS examples illustrate is an interplay between three classes of phenomena:

1. The varying understandings which different groups of employees may have of the 'central' goals and values of their organisation.
2. The understandings those same groups of employees have of their own identities, interests and positions in the organisation.

3. The extent to which IT-based systems, whether for operational or management control applications, challenge or reinforce those understandings of goals and interests.

In one sense, I am therefore simply arguing that people in organisations behave politically with respect to IT system development because they behave politically with respect to all major proposals for action and change, and IT is no exception. At a deeper level, however, I am suggesting that IT systems can often elicit a greater degree of political behaviour; partly because of its proximity to the core strategic issues, as I have already indicated, but also because of another reason. Organisations are in some senses *defined* for their members by the way they are portrayed and captured in the information systems. Therefore whenever you define a new information system you are putting 'into play', in the political sense, some very central features of the organisation itself.

All IT plans and development activities therefore reflect and reproduce, albeit imperfectly and often in unpredictable ways, the intentions and objectives of some combination of the various parties involved. These plans might then unfold for a period as though those objectives were in fact stable. But in a comparatively short period of time, and well before the plans mature, these intentions and objectives will change, as will the perceptions of the usefulness of particular IT designs and implementations, thus resulting in new sources of conflict and tension that impinge further upon the IT plans.

In essence, the assumption of a rational progression from goals to actions (the basis of waterfall models and the like) is undermined by the experience of the actions themselves. Therefore, we should see that perceived interests and goals are produced through actions (including IT planning processes and their implementation); they do not simply pre-exist those actions. There are a thousand stories and aphorisms in the IT world about unreasonable users who 'change their mind' about what they want between the requirements analysis stage and the final signing-off of the system. My point is that we are unreasonable if we expect them to do otherwise!

How do IT professionals deal with this political reality in organisations? What political strategies do they use to pursue their perceived interests of getting systems designed, built and used?

One answer to the question, of course, is that they use formal systems development procedures which directly involve users and all the appropriate constituencies. They begin with clarification of business goals and proceed to operational requirements, and so on and so on. So far so good. But those same IT professionals who construct systems and IT strategies as a framework for systems development will commonly observe (but perhaps in private and not in a professional context) that even if they use these methods they frequently fall foul of conflicts between individuals and groups. These conflicts are often seen by the IT staff as 'irrational'; 'personality clashes'; manifestations of the preservation of 'vested interests'; the consequence of ingrained habitual routines; or a reflection of political engineering on the part of certain individuals or groups. These views are, I think, based on an implicit model of human behaviour in which calculative interests and preoccupations with competence are predominant. Our research, by contrast, recognises the importance of interests and competencies, but suggests that it is necessary to complement this with a perception of the way people *understand* their own actions at a day to day level. It sets them in dynamic context.

Everyone in an organisation decides on their actions, and makes sense of those actions, through a process of replicating some practices which are already part of the organisation (deeply rooted in its past), and perhaps also through rejecting some practices and substituting others. In this way they regularly create and reinforce an idea of who they are (their identity) and what part they play both in the organisation and perhaps more broadly beyond its boundaries. Thus our self-understanding, and our understanding of our organisational position and associated interests, is 'socially constructed' within the organisation; it is a joint social achievement. We define who and what we are not according to some absolute external yardstick, but according to the complex network of understandings which others have of their positions, and of ours. These networks, and the self-understandings with which they are associated, are the lens through which people actually perceive and calculate their interests and seek to display their competence. They are also therefore the very territory which is 'in play' whenever strategic issues are under discussion.

If we agree that behaviour in organisations – the real stuff of 'organisational politics' – is like this, it is not surprising that the clear statement of goals which seems to be so necessary to any sensible IT application plan is in fact a moving target. It could not be otherwise. Nor is it therefore surprising that we see in IT strategies, as in business strategies, not only the overt content (expressed in instrumental and concrete terms: 'to launch a new pensions product', for example), but also the covert content, which is to secure new or sustain existing power relations with respect to other members of the various organisational networks. We saw this clearly in the examples from the NHS. So, when seen in this light, the 'foundering' of overly rationalistic IT strategies on the rock of organisational politics is not some technical failure, or some shortcoming in the clear-sightedness or rationality of the parties involved. On the contrary it is simply 'how the world is'.

At this point one might hope that the solution lies with outsiders, such as management consultants, who can intervene from an external reference point and not be enmeshed in the power networks of the organisation. Indeed, it is common, (but again only in informal settings) to argue that the role of consultants is not to choose the technical solution but to legitimate the one desired by a sub-set of the client organisation. Can outsiders 'handle' organisational politics for us in this way? From our research, in which we have observed management consultants in long term relationships with clients, we would argue that there is indeed genuine novelty and competence transfer between organisations brought about by the intervention of consultants, but that it should not be seen as 'technically correct' nor 'organisationally neutral' by reference to some absolute yardstick. On the contrary, the consultant/client relationship is simply a new set of networks and intersections of existing networks, in which all the parties are governed by the same principles and routines of organisational politics as those I have outlined earlier. But, in this case, the conflicts and struggles reflect the consultant's concerns to achieve a construction of 'the problem' which not only accords with that of key functionaries in the client organisation, but is also consistent with the ability of the consultant to implement a recognised solution to that problem (and thus affirm his or her competence as a consultant; as a solver of problems the client cannot overcome.) Whatever other good reasons there may be for using outsiders, and there are many, it is not the case that the fundamental circumstances are changed in this matter of shifting perceptions of objectives and organisational self-understanding. The same general types of problems associated with IT applications plans may therefore arise. It would be just as incorrect to 'blame' the consultants for the problems as it would be to expect them to solve them. Their 'outsiderness' is progressively diluted through their engagement with the client organisation and its politics and problems.

7. CONCLUSIONS

IT professionals and business users have developed an approach to IT which is profoundly coloured by a kind of 'technical rationality' with two major components; namely, use an organised sequence of steps to progress from organisational context to concrete IT system content; and secondly, conduct a conventional analysis of costs and benefits for each project.

I have argued that this rationality is no longer inspiring confidence in users, and that the more the IT application is central to the strategic agenda of the business, the less likely this rationality is to deliver a satisfactory outcome. The underlying phenomenon which causes this failure of technical rationality is its failure to cope with the 'alternative' political rationalities which are conducted through shifting patterns of meanings, interests, and power relationships.

Should we therefore abandon the technical rationality of cost-benefits and formal systems development and formal IT strategy? In part yes and in part no.

It will be clear by now that I think that the simple cost-benefit approach to strategic IT investment is dangerous, especially so if you believe the answers! Like all investment situations which are non-routine, the actual numbers are only one of the inputs to the process of judgment and bargaining which eventually makes the decisions. However, the other aspect of technical rationality is less easy to dismiss. The need to specify a design before proceeding to build a system is difficult to fully escape – even with novel techniques such as rapid prototyping, re-useable code, and modular software. The principle of involving the users from the beginning is a great advance in the IT community, it also has an honourable pedigree in technological innovation outside the IT sphere. But, perhaps where we go wrong is to involve the user a lot at the beginning and at the end, but not very much in the middle. But, as we have seen, this is where all the interesting changes in people's interests and desires take place. Perhaps we should adopt the maxim of P.D. James and seek a closer link between 'Devices and Desires', throughout the development process. Major gains could be made if all concerned with IT were to more readily accept the view that there is no such thing as a perfect IT system, and no such thing as an unchangeable IT strategy. But the changes will only be seen as justified, rather than as failures or problems, if there is shared ownership. If the IT system you are dealing with is really only important in the context of a broader cultural change that is being attempted, then get people to focus on that, and measure the benefits in those terms rather than through some proxy cost-benefit analysis of the IT system!

NOTES

This chapter is based on the Fourth Annual Charles Read Memorial Lecture, delivered by the author at BAFTA, London, on 20th May 1992. A full text of the lecture is available as PICT Policy Paper No. 20. The author acknowledges the support of the Economic and Social Research Council, through the PICT Programme, for the research on which the chapter is based, as well his colleagues in the PICT Centre at UMIST. Further details of the arguments above can also be found in

R. Coombs, D. Knights and H. Willmott (1992) 'Culture, Control and Competitiveness: Towards a framework for the study of Information Technology in organisations', *Organisation Studies*, **13**(1), 1992

B. Bloomfield and R. Coombs (1992) 'Information Technology, Control and Power: The Centralisation and De-Centralisation Debate Revisited', *Journal of Management Studies*.

4 Structured risk analysis for information systems

David G. W. Birch and Neil A. McEvoy
Hyperion, Guildford, UK

This chapter shows that assessing and managing risk in an information-driven organisation can be handled using structured techniques and made at least semi-quantitative in a valid way. Thus, decisions about information systems investment (and associated counter-measures) can be made subject to the same risk analysis discipline as other areas of corporate expenditure.

The chapter discusses information risk using examples to illustrate the range of risks, and standard structured analysis techniques to provide modelling support for risk analysis and risk management. The particular risk analysis technique used is Structured Risk Analysis (SRA), a technique originally developed at Hyperion by the authors. The chapter ends with two examples of SRA projects which illustrate the mechanisms and benefits of performing such structured risk analysis.

1. INTRODUCTION

In the particular case of Information Systems (IS), there has often been a reluctance to tackle the subject of risk – due to perceived complexity and inexactness – and therefore handle risk analysis and risk management effectively. This has led to a situation where many ISs do not retain even the simplest risk management techniques which were present in the paper systems that they are replacing. Clearly, with the growing importance of IS in all aspects of corporate operation, ISs must be made subject to appropriate risk analysis and risk management disciplines.

Being in business is a risk. However strategic an IS may be to a business, the threats to that IS – whether fire, flood or hackers – are only part of the spectrum of threats that surround the business. The purpose of risk analysis should be to assist managers in making informed decisions about investment and developing risk management policies which place IS risks in their correct position in the overall spectrum of business risks.

In the case of computers and communications, the counter-measures that can be employed to reduce risk are well-known, and an array of techniques are available, but high counter-measures expenditure on every aspect of an IS is out of the question in a commercial organisation. Therefore, this expenditure must be directed to reduce corporate exposure to IS risks in the context of overall business risks. In particular, risk analysis must be able to answer the following questions:

- how much is it appropriate to spend on counter-measures?
- where should this spending be directed?

There are insecure systems in operation which may cost businesses millions of pounds if the insecurities are exploited. There are also systems with inappropriate and over-expensive security counter-measures which are just as responsible for losing money. By way of illustration, suppose a risk loses a business £10,000 per year. It is clearly inappropriate to spend £200,000 in closing this risk, since the same investment would yield more than enough to cover the losses if invested in some other way.

Managers thus need a methodology which is geared up to cataloguing and evaluating the risks to information (rather than plant and machinery), and enabling them to make informed decisions as to computer and communications counter-measures.

2. INFORMATION SYSTEMS RISKS

2.1 Information systems

As we are constantly hearing, we are now entering the information age. We already have an economy where most people work in the service sector and where the information resource, rather than labour or capital resources, is seen as the key to corporate strategic advantage:

> "For industrial companies. . . information has been a cost and hard goods a product. Increasingly, for information age companies, information is the product and machinery merely a cost – and a relatively small one at that." (Mobley and McKeown, 1989)

Following the introduction of computing to the business community many years ago, there were a number of waves of computerisation. First, the automation of existing manual systems to improve speed, efficiency and reliability – the earliest areas for computerisation in business were accounts systems. Second, the extension of computer systems to include the core areas of business activity – especially where information is the key to the business, but also in manufacturing, retail and so on. Third, the creation of new systems which have a strategic impact on the business – more so in newer or more competitive sectors. These strategic systems are those that impact corporate strategy: whether by opening up new areas of business or allowing managers to make strategic decisions with confidence.

For many organisations, then, information has become a fundamental strategic resource. The corporate planning process has been extended to include information, and this has bypassed the associated risk management procedures, which are geared up to handling plant, equipment, markets and so on.

Information is an asset in the full sense of the word – it has a value and it earns a return. In this sense, it is little different to a piece of real estate, a milling machine or a typewriter. What is it, however, that makes information an asset? An old, and very worthwhile definition is that information is an asset because it has surprise value – information is something that you didn't know before and affects a decision that you are going to make. We can go a bit further than that and say that information has to improve the quality of decisions as well. Obviously, for information to beneficially affect decisions it has to be the right information. The right information at the right time is then a tremendous asset. Consider a store which captures the identity of all goods at the point of sale. This information can be used to instantly re-order from suppliers using Electronic Data Interchange (EDI), ensuring the availability of popular lines whilst keeping stock levels low. The information has thus been used to both increase revenue and reduce costs, i.e. it has earned a real return.

Another example. Airlines need to supply their seat availabilities to travel agents. Any failure to do so will result in bookings going elsewhere. A reservations system which is habitually less reliable than those of the competitors might well threaten the viability of an airline by decreasing its load factors. In passing, it should be noted that SABRE, the reservations system of American Airlines (the world's second largest airline) is far more profitable than the parent airline: the implication of this is clear – that information (routes, fares, schedules) is as much of an asset to American Airlines as 'planes.

2.2 Risk

A recent survey of computer 'disasters' in the UK found that they were divided into three broad categories, as shown in Figure 4.1. Deliberate human action ('hacking' and fraud) accounted for nearly half of the disasters, and natural causes (fire, flood and so on) nearly one-third. The Audit Commission carried out a major survey of 1500 organisations from 1987–1990 and found 73 (detected) cases of computer fraud and 26 (detected) cases of hacking that caused losses. Interestingly, they also found that only 23% of computer fraud and abuse had been uncovered through internal controls, and that most came to light because of tip-offs or confessions.

Not all frauds are to do with finance, banking and money. In 1989, Gayle and Irwin Schreir were convicted in Tulsa of wire fraud in a scheme using travel agency computers to manipulate the American Airline frequent flyer program (known as AAdvantage). Gayle was a former employee of a travel agent and very

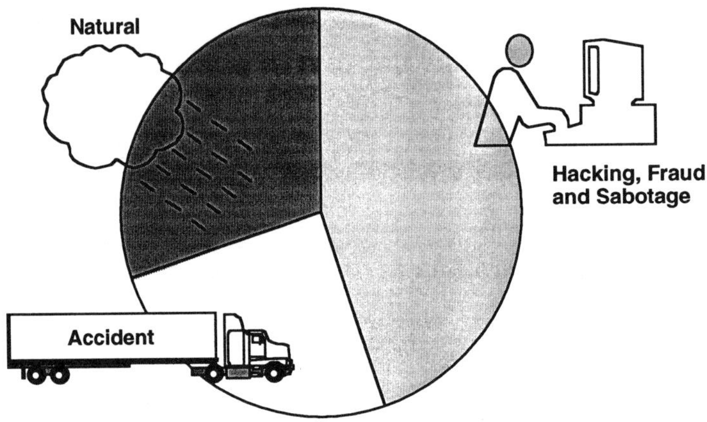

Figure 4.1 Causes of computer disasters (UK).

knowledgeable about the SABRE computerised reservation system. She used the system to find people booked on flights who were not members of AAdvantage and then credited their miles to bogus accounts. The miles accumulated in the bogus accounts and were then traded in for AA tickets which were sold on the open market. AA discovered the fraud when an auditor noticed that a large number of AAdvantage members appeared to live at the same address! AA estimated that their losses were anywhere between $0.5–2.5M.

For another example of an IT-specific risk, look at Black & Decker's experience. A software fault wiped out the data relating to their fully automated national distribution centre. An operator then unwittingly corrupted a back-up tape. In a later audit, the system's lack of controls were criticized (after all, they allowed a back-up to be overwritten with garbage!). In the end, staff working overtime had to re-key all of the warehouse data. This involved employees wearing mountaineering gear climbing the Northampton warehouse's racking and operating the computer controlled cranes by hand. A Black & Decker official said "You cannot measure the problems in cost. It was more expensive in terms of customer goodwill" (Davies, 1991).

The widespread use of information technology has introduced new vulnerabilities, and therefore new risks, into the organisation. Furthermore, IT changes some of the basic assumptions that have previously been made about risk. Some of the factors that need to be borne in mind are: the value of hardware in many organisations is insignificant compared to the value of the information that it processes (it has to be, otherwise it's not earning its keep); the interconnection of computers and communications equipment causes a huge increase in the complexity of risk evaluation; and that more and more applications today are 'on line', which means that any interruption in service provision causes business losses.

The Bank of New York (BoNY) specialises in settling transactions in Government securities. It takes securities from the selling bank, pays for them, passes them on to the buying bank and collects the money. On November 21st 1985 a small software error caused BoNY's computers to stop passing them on the purchasers and collecting the money. Securities continued to flow in, but none left. By 11.30am, BoNY's overdraft at the Federal Reserve had reached $12 billion, while the computer staff were still trying to find the fault. The fault was not rectified until 2.15am the following day, at which time the overdraft stood at $44 billion and was threatening to disrupt the financing of the US budget deficit. The error cost BoNY $4M in interest charges (Davies, 1991).

Information from administrative systems may not have the same immediate value as information from mission-critical or strategic systems, but it has value nonetheless. Imagine a competitor was able to gain access to your corporate E-mail system. Even if no sensitive information is allowed over the E-mail, a competitor could still benefit from monitoring the traffic to determine your long-term strategy or trends within your organisation or customer base. Over a period, the competitor could use this information to build a sustained competitive advantage.

If this sounds far-fetched, consider the case of WTVT in Florida (Smith, 1989). In January 1989, an employee noticed that a number of computer files were missing: an investigation revealed that over a period of weeks, the station's newsroom computer had been the subject of repeated illegal access. A subsequent police investigation led to the arrest of an ex-employee now working for a rival station. If this activity had not been noticed by an alert employee, WTVT could easily have found itself in a situation where a rival always seemed to get their best stories and was able to schedule effectively against them. Remember that even quite small changes in audience share can mean a significant change in advertising revenues.

3. RISK ANALYSIS

3.1 Concepts

Risk analysis is based on the principal concepts of threat, vulnerability, attack, risk and countermeasure. These concepts (as applied to information) (shown in Figure 4.2) exist in one form or another in all risk analysis techniques, and have wide application (Carroll, 1990). It is the precision of their specification which makes the results of risk analysis prescriptive (and therefore of value to business).

A threat pertains to information and is something which will have an adverse

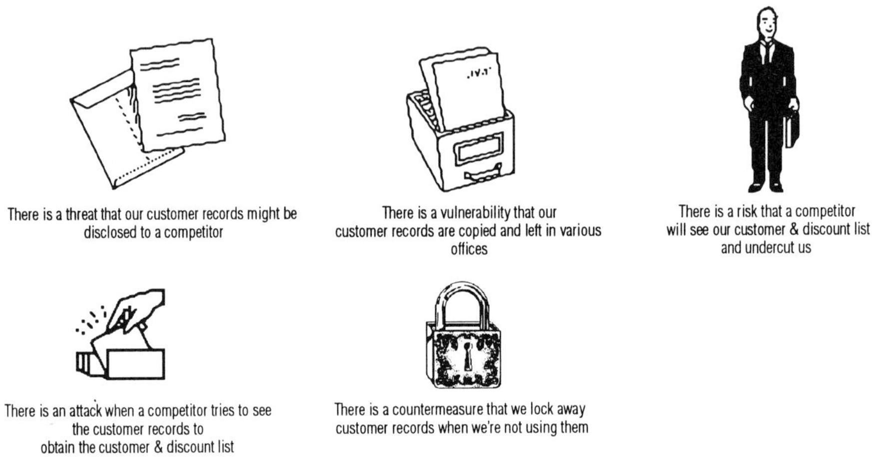

Figure 4.2 Risk analysis concepts.

effect on an organisation. A threat exists whether or not there are any practical or apparent ways in which it might ever be manifested. The threats to an IS are independent from the physical implementation of the IS. That is, whether your IS is a single PC on your desk or a network of supercomputers around the globe, the threats to your business area the same.

A vulnerability is a characteristic of a physical system which, while being independent from any specific threat, allows (in principle) a threat to be exploited. Vulnerabilities are a property of the physical implementation of the IS and are independent from any threats to the IS.

Threats and vulnerabilities are divided into three categories for the purposes of analysis: confidentiality, integrity and availability. This CIA classification, as it is called, is adequate for describing all of the various threats and vulnerabilities that can affect a business.

A risk is something which exists when a threat and a vulnerability overlap. That is, there is a threat to the business and a vulnerability which may be exploited to realise this threat. An attempt to exploit a risk – that is, to realise a threat – is called an attack and the person, agency or organisation attempting to exploit that risk is the attacker. Note that the same risk may be exploited by different attackers: in each case, this constitutes a separate attack. Note also that not all attacks are successful.

A counter-measure is something which reduces exposure, either by reducing the probability of loss (reducing vulnerability), the loss associated with a threat (reducing impact) or the loss resulting from attack (either by reducing the size of the loss or making it predictable – like house insurance).

In many cases, risk management has consisted only of counter-measures procurement outside of any strategy. Counter-measures, such as insurance cover, may be wholly inappropriate because they are based on a model of computing that dates back to the introduction of computers into the organisation (the days before PCs and networks), or because proper risk analysis techniques have never been applied in an organisation. Remember that pointless counter-measures lose money just as effectively as a hacker stealing it.

Information technology has now spread throughout organisations to the point where all aspects of business are now either computerised or heavily dependent on computers. Organisations now rely so heavily on computers and communications that they could not survive without them for more than a few days and, in increasingly many cases, a few hours. When a 'disaster' strikes, organisations can only survive with well-rehearsed contingency plans. Amazingly, surveys continue to show that only a quarter of companies have a contingency plan that they have any confidence in, and three quarters of the contingency plans that were tested didn't work!

3.2 Methodologies

Risk analysis methodologies tend to fall in to one of two categories: qualitative or quantitative. Qualitative methods look for problem areas in a system and match suitable controls to the problems. Quantitative methods attempt to estimate an overall Annual Loss Expectancy (ALE) figure for an organisation and then compare the costs of counter-measures to changes in the ALE to assess their worth. This is not straightforward: probabilities and estimates of losses can be imprecise and inaccurate leading to wildly wrong ALE estimates.

To illustrate the range of risk analysis methodologies in use, it is worth looking at a few commercial examples:

- *RiskPAC* is a simple, questionnaire-based risk analysis package for PCs. It is flexible in its approach but rather limited, so it works best with small systems that have relatively few assets. It works out the ALE for the system and recommends counter-measures.
- *CRAMM* was developed for the UK government by the CCTA. It is an impact-driven methodology which uses a questionnaire-based approach to identify hardware and software assets and the threats. It is supported by a PC package marketed by a number of commercial organisations. The package takes in the questionnaire information and suggests counter-measures (although these are limited and testify to the public sector origin of the package). CRAMM is comprehensive, but it is also time consuming (Moses,

1990). It has gained wide acceptance in the UK but is has a number of drawbacks related to the use of questionnaires.

- *MARION* is a PC package which contains an extensive database of actual computer-related insurance claims. The objective of the package is to describe a business in terms of activities/assets held in the database and then use the real insurance claims to assess the risks. Provided you are sure that the business is accurately represented, this can be a worthwhile approach. It it less useful in the area of selecting counter-measures.

These are just a sample, but they show the different approaches that can be taken. A number of them share a common questionnaire-based approach to creating risk catalogues. This is simple, but it does not give managers any assurance that the risk models created are correct or complete.

Some qualitative methods do make exposure assessments in terms of ranking values, and maximum and minimum values for financial exposure. This hybrid approach – using metrics or rankings instead of trying to calculate exact values – is certainly the one most currently in favour (Dorey, 1991).

3.3 Structured Risk Analysis

SRA (Structured Risk Analysis) is one such hybrid risk analysis methodology developed by Hyperion in the UK for the risk analysis of information systems. It is an information-driven methodology which uses structured analysis models of an organisation to provide a comprehensive and consistent means of approximating ALE (McEvoy and Harris, 1990). SRA will be used to illustrate the risk analysis process throughout the rest of this chapter. SRA, as shown in Figure 4.3, represents a synthesis of the advances made in risk analysis and structured analysis over the past few years.

Rather than use questionnaires or interviews to establish the catalogues of assets, risks and so on, SRA uses the models produced by structured analysis techniques. This ensures both completeness and correctness. Over the past few years, the use of structured analysis techniques to handle IS has become widespread, and many methodologies are current. Methodologies such as Structured Systems Analysis and Design Methodology (SSADM) (CCTA, 1990) have been around for some time, are in use in many organisations and are well supported by CASE tools, training courses and other materials. All of these methodologies share the use of structured models, easy to understand in diagram form, as the basis for collecting, verifying and disseminating information. Similarly, many of them share the same basic tools. These are some form of data flow diagram (DFD) for modelling the functionality of a system, some form of logical data model (LDM) for modelling data structure, and some form of entity life-history (ELH) for modelling the events which occur. SSADM, which is

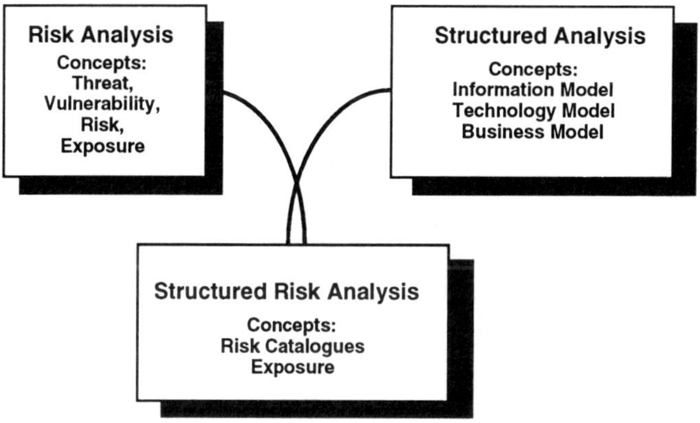

Figure 4.3 SRA origin.

widely used in the UK, will be used for the structured models throughout this chapter.

3.4 Necessary models

Three structured analysis models are required to capture all of the information necessary to support risk analysis. These are the process model (often called the logical model or the service model), the information model (often called the logical data model or entity relationship model) and the technology model (often called the physical model or system model) (McEvoy and Harris, 1990).

The information model shows the elements of information (not data) in the business and the relationships between those elements. In essence, the elements of information are business entities and the relationships between them are business rules. To carry out high-level analysis to highlight the main areas of exposure, a high-level information model is sufficient to identify the primary corporate information assets. An example of such a model is shown in Figure 4.4.

The process model shows the information flows in an organisation, the sources and sinks of information and the information processing or retention centres. Business analysis begins by creating the Level-0 Process Model (L0PM) which treats the business (or the part of a business that is under examination) as a single information processing centre and identifies all of the sources/sinks of information. Analysis then proceeds to Level-1, which identifies major information processing centres. Note that, as shown in Figure 4.5,

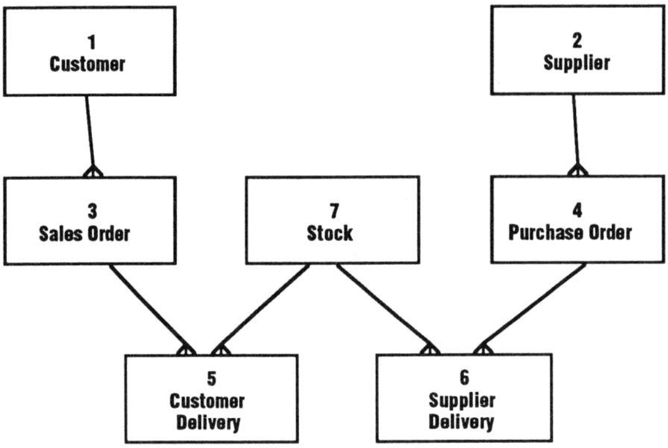

Figure 4.4 Example information model.

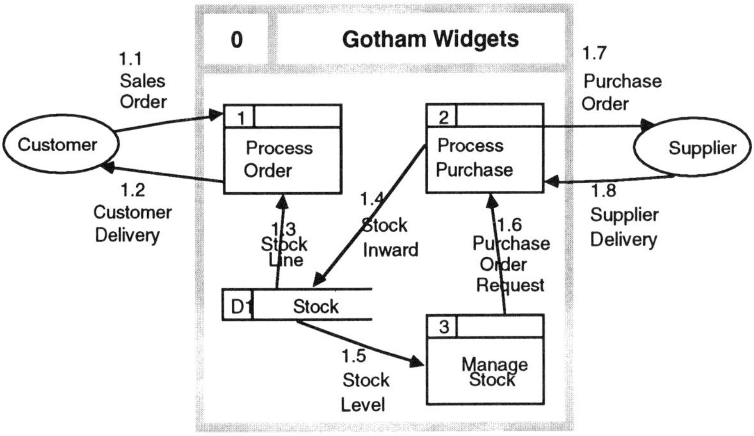

Figure 4.5 Example process model.

once the process model is in place, a unique labelling scheme now exists for all information flows.

The technology model shows the actual computer and communications systems that are in place in an organisation, with no reference as to their actual purpose or use. This separation of concerns is fundamental to the structured business analysis procedures. Each entity in the technology model is a physical asset of the IS. These physical assets may be hardware, software, communications links and so on as shown in Figure 4.6.

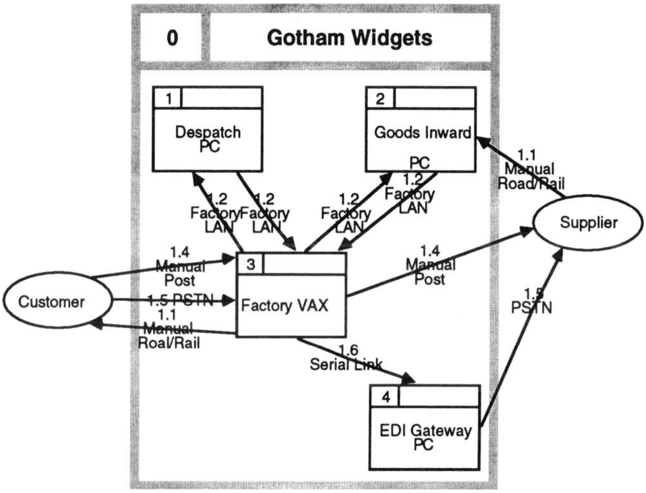

Figure 4.6 Example technology model.

3.5 Threats and vulnerabilities

For every information asset on the information model, three threats are catalogued: the integrity threat (TI), the confidentiality threat (TC) and the availability threat (TA). Each information asset is already labelled (because of structured analysis), and so each individual threat is similarly labelled for cataloguing. So, information asset 3 (say) would have three entries in the threat catalogue: TI3, TC3 and TA3.

The next step is to determine (in the event of an attacker realising a threat) the loss to the defender and the gain to an attacker. It is not possible to define a generalised impact metric because the nature of business impact varies from business to business. In the case of commercial information systems, a money-based metric is obviously useful. To avoid the difficulty of working with large numbers, a logarithmic metric can be used. As an example, a suitable impact metric (based on the FIPS metrics) might be as follows: Loss or Gain amount less than £10, Impact Metric 0; Loss or Gain amount less than £100, Impact Metric 1; and so on. Table 4.1 shows an excerpt from a threat catalogue constructed from the information model shown in Figure 4.4.

Vulnerabilities are catalogued against the networks and computers in the technology model. Each physical asset on the technology model (either a data flow or a data store) is already uniquely labelled, so each of the vulnerabilities will be

Table 4.1 Example threat catalogue

Inf. Asset	Information Asset Name	Threat ID	Description of Threat to Information Asset	Loss (L)	Gain (G)
1	Customer	I1	Customer Lost/corrupt	3	1
	Customer	C1	Customer Disclosed	3	3
	Customer	A1	Customer Not Available	2	1
2	Supplier	I2	Supplier Lost/corrupt	4	1
	Supplier	C2	Supplier Disclosed	4	1
	Supplier	A2	Supplier Not Available	3	1
3	Sales Order	I3	Sales Order Lost/corrupt	2	1
	Sales Order	C3	Sales Order Disclosed	2	3
	Sales Order	A3	Sales Order Not Available	1	1
4	Purchase Order	I4	Purchase Order Lost/corrupt	1	1
	Purchase Order	C4	Purchase Order Disclosed	1	1
	Purchase Order	A4	Purchase Order Not Available	2	1

similarly labelled. Three vulnerabilities are assigned to each physical asset: the integrity vulnerability (TI), the confidentiality vulnerability (TC) and the availability vulnerability (TA). So, physical asset 1.3 (say) would have three entries in the vulnerability catalogue: VI1.3, VC1.3 and VA1.3. To later calculate exposure, we need to capture two parameters of each vulnerability: the cost of exploiting that vulnerability (C) and the probability of exploiting the vulnerability successfully (P). Costs are described using the same metric as for threat impact whereas the probability of successful attack is indicated using a similar logarithmic metric (-3 very unlikely, -2 unlikely, -1 possible, and so on), as seen in the example in Table 4.2.

Although there may be a great many physical assets (depending on the level to which the technology model has been developed, of course) it is usually

Table 4.2 Example vulnerability catalogue

Phy. Asset	Physical Asset Name	Vul. ID	Description of Vulnerability of Physical Asset	Cost (C)	Prob (P)
1	Despatch PC	I1	Despatch PC Tampered	3	-2
1	Despatch PC	C1	Despatch PC Accessed	1	0
1	Despatch PC	A1	Despatch PC Damaged	2	-1
2	Goods In PC	I2	Goods In PC Tampered	3	-2
2	Goods In PC	C2	Goods In PC Accessed	1	0
2	Goods In PC	A2	Goods In PC Damaged	2	-1
3	Factory VAX	I3	Factory VAX Tampered	3	-3
3	Factory VAX	C3	Factory VAX Accessed	1	-1
3	Factory VAX	A3	Factory VAX Damaged	2	-2
4	EDI Gateway PC	I4	EDI Gateway PC Tampered	3	-2
4	EDI Gateway PC	C4	EDI Gateway PC Accessed	1	0
4	EDI Gateway PC	A4	EDI Gateway PC Damaged	2	-1
1.1	Road/Rail	I1.1	Road/Rail Tampered	3	-2
1.1	Road/Rail	C1.1	Road/Rail Accessed	1	0
1.1	Road/Rail	A1.1	Road/Rail Damaged	2	-1

straightforward to assign the costs and probabilities associated with the vulnerabilities because they are generic – it takes the same effort to tap a PSTN connection whether the PSTN line is being used for credit card verification or playing games over a network – and the vulnerability catalogue can be constructed without complication.

3.6 Risks and attacks

A risk exists where there are a threat and a vulnerability that coincide with a shared attacker. The Risk Catalogue is formed by examining each threat in the Threat Catalogue and matching it against the vulnerability catalogue. The best way to do this is in two stages[1]:

- First, a cross-reference between the process model and the technology model is created (this may already be present in system architecture documentation)
- Then a cross-reference between the information and business models is created.

With these in place we match threats and vulnerabilities using the following method: for each threat, select the information asset; cross-reference the information asset to the business model to determine which information flows and stores involve that asset; cross-reference the information flows and stores from the business model to physical assets in the technology model; and finally for each physical asset, select the vulnerabilities. This results in a Risk Catalogue, as shown in Table 4.3.

This step-by-step cross-referencing is not complex because of the structured nature of the underlying models. The cross-referencing is achieved using tables and models which already exist as part of the structured analysis process. The attacker catalogue identifies potential attackers: at this level we need only use the broad categorisation identified previously. That is, we only consider three classes of attacker: malicious, non-malicious and natural causes. For the sake of simplicity, we will assume that attackers within a class are homogeneous: thus, we do not need to identify every single attacker. We can now construct the Attack Catalogue. For each risk in the Risk Catalogue, we define one attack for each attacker type.

Remember that the scope of deliberate attacks can be quite wide, as they cover fraud, malicious damage–even 'electronic picketing' such as the alteration of bar codes on warehouse goods (Lack, 1989) – whereas accidents and natural dis-

---

[1]This description simplifies the method considerably, In practice, the business model used is more than a process model and information model: it may also include an event model.

Table 4.3 Example risk catalogue

Risk (R)	Threat (T)	Vuln. (V)	Description of Risk	Loss (L)	Incn (I)	Prob (P)
RI1-1	I1	I1.1	Customer Lost/corrupt—Road/Rail Tampered	3	0	-2
RI1-2	I1	I1.4	Customer Lost/corrupt—Post Tampered	3	0	-2
RI1-3	I1	I1.5	Customer Lost/corrupt—PSTN Tampered	3	0	-2
RI1-4	I1	I3	Customer Lost/corrupt—Factory VAX Tampered	3	0	-3
RC1-1	C1	C1.1	Customer Disclosed—Road/Rail Accessed	3	3	0
RC1-2	C1	C1.4	Customer Disclosed—Post Accessed	3	3	0
RC1-3	C1	C1.5	Customer Disclosed—PSTN Accessed	3	3	0
RC1-4	C1	C3	Customer Disclosed—Factory VAX Accessed	3	3	-1
RA1-1	A1	A1.1	Customer Not Available—Road/Rail Damaged	2	0	-1
RA1-2	A1	A1.4	Customer Not Available—Post Damaged	2	0	-1
RA1-3	A1	A1.5	Customer Not Available—PSTN Damaged	2	0	-1
RA1-4	A1	A3	Customer Not Available—Factory VAX Damaged	2	0	-2
RI5-1	I5	I1.1	Customer Delivery Lost/corrupt—Road/Rail Tampered	2	0	-2
RI5-2	I5	I3	Customer Delivery Lost/corrupt—Factory VAX Tampered	2	0	-3
RC5-1	.C5	C1.1	Customer Delivery Disclosed—Road/Rail Accessed	2	2	0
RC5-2	C5	C3	Customer Delivery Disclosed—Factory VAX Accessed	2	2	-1

asters are much easier to enumerate. To reflect this, the class of deliberate attacker can be subdivided into a number of different attackers where the potential of attack varies greatly (because of very different gains and so forth). A simple Attacker Catalogue is shown in Table 4.4.

Next, a frequency of occurrence (O) must be assigned to each attack. As in the case of threat impacts, we will use a general purpose logarithmic metric for O. In the example, we have chosen some simple rules, so we calculate O as follows:

- for Natural attackers, O is -1 (that is, we assume a natural disaster once every ten years)
- for Accidental attackers, O is 0 (that is, we assume that accidents happen once per year)
- for Deliberate attackers[2]
  - for Competitors, O is P+I (that is, the greater the incentive the greater the frequency of attack)
  - for Vandals, O is P-C (Vandals are assumed to have no gain, only costs).

Table 4.4 Example attacker catalogue

Class	Attacker	ID
Natural	Fire/Flood	N1
Accident	Anyone	A1
Deliberate	Competitor	D1
	Vandal	D2

[2]Again, this is a very simplified exposition: in practice, the assessment of O is one of the most complex areas of risk analysis.

These simple metrics allows us to make a useful estimate of O. Now, since for each of the attacks in the Attack Catalogue we know the frequency of occurrence O (from our calculations) and the impact (from the threat catalogue), we can define the exposure (E). Once again, the metric varies depending on the system but will we continue with the general case and measure exposure using a logarithmic money per time period metric. The simple metrics we are using mean that we can calculate the annual exposure to a risk as the sum of the impact (of the associated threat) and the frequency (of the associated attack), so that E = L + O. Given the logarithmic nature of the exposure so calculated, we can define the ALE for each risk as the highest exposure of any of the attacks associated with the risk, as shown in the example Attack Catalogue in Table 4.5.

This leads us to the final catalogue of interest. We take the risks and ALEs as shown in Table 5, extract them and sort them by ALE. This gives us the Exposure Catalogue, as shown in Table 4.6.

In this example, this highest exposures relate to the disclosure of customer

Table 4.5 Example attack catalogue

Risk ID	Incn (I)	Attack N1	Exp (E)	Attack A1	Exp (E)	Attack D1	Freq (O)	Exp (E)	Attack D2	Freq (O)	Exp (E)	ALE
RI1-1	0	RI1-1/N1	2	RI1-1/A1	3	RI1-1/D1	-2	1	RI1-1/D2	-5	3	3
RI1-2	0	RI1-2/N1	2	RI1-2/A1	1	RI1-2/D1	-2	1	RI1-2/D2	-5	3	3
RI1-3	0	RI1-3/N1	2	RI1-3/A1	1	RI1-3/D1	-2	1	RI1-3/D2	-5	3	3
RI1-4	0	RI1-4/N1	2	RI1-4/A1	0	RI1-4/D1	-3	0	RI1-4/D2	-6	3	3
RC1-1	3	RC1-1/N1	2	RC1-1/A1	3	RC1-1/D1	3	6	RC1-1/D2	-3	3	6
RC1-2	3	RC1-2/N1	2	RC1-2/A1	3	RC1-2/D1	3	6	RC1-2/D2	-3	3	6
RC1-3	3	RC1-3/N1	2	RC1-3/A1	3	RC1-3/D1	3	6	RC1-3/D2	-3	3	6
RC1-4	3	RC1-4/N1	2	RC1-4/A1	3	RC1-4/D1	2	5	RC1-4/D2	-4	3	5
RA1-1	0	RA1-1/N1	1	RA1-1/A1	2	RA1-1/D1	-1	1	RA1-1/D2	-4	3	3
RA1-2	0	RA1-2/N1	1	RA1-2/A1	2	RA1-2/D1	-1	1	RA1-2/D2	-4	3	3
RA1-3	0	RA1-3/N1	1	RA1-3/A1	2	RA1-3/D1	-1	1	RA1-3/D2	-4	3	3
RA1-4	0	RA1-4/N1	1	RA1-4/A1	2	RA1-4/D1	-2	0	RA1-4/D2	-5	3	3
RI5-1	0	RI5-1/N1	1	RI5-1/A1	2	RI5-1/D1	-2	0	RI5-1/D2	-5	3	3
RI5-2	0	RI5-2/N1	1	RI5-2/A1	2	RI5-2/D1	-3	-1	RI5-2/D2	-6	3	3
RC5-1	2	RC5-1/N1	1	RC5-1/A1	2	RC5-1/D1	2	4	RC5-1/D2	-3	3	4
RC5-2	2	RC5-2/N1	1	RC5-2/A1	2	RC5-2/D1	1	3	RC5-2/D2	-4	3	3

Table 4.6 Example exposure catalogue

Risk ID	Risk Description	E
RC1-1	Customer Disclosed—Road/Rail Accessed	6
RC1-2	Customer Disclosed—Post Accessed	6
RC1-3	Customer Disclosed—PSTN Accessed	6
RC1-4	Customer Disclosed—Factory VAX Accessed	5
RC5-1	Customer Delivery Disclosed—Road/Rail Accessed	4
RI2-1	Supplier Lost/corrupt—Road/Rail Tampered	4
RI2-2	Supplier Lost/corrupt—Factory LAN Tampered	4
RI2-3	Supplier Lost/corrupt—Post Tampered	4
RI2-4	Supplier Lost/corrupt—PSTN Tampered	4
RI2-5	Supplier Lost/corrupt—Serial Link Tampered	4
RI2-6	Supplier Lost/corrupt—Goods In PC Tampered	4
RI2-7	Supplier Lost/corrupt—Factory VAX Tampered	4

records (i.e. a competitor reading customers' orders). This is as would be expected, since for our example company it is competitors stealing business (by undercutting, targeting, incentives and so on) that is the biggest problem. The value of the highest exposure, 6, indicates that Widgets Inc. has a current exposure of around £1M per year.

4. RISK MANAGEMENT

4.1 Risk management discipline

We can now see that when structured risk analysis techniques are used, risk management becomes a discipline rather than an art (Condon, 1991). The Risk Manager uses risk analysis to determine exposure and uses this information to formulate security counter-measures policies.

Risk analysis is a continuous process for the security manager. Naturally, when starting with a 'blank sheet' a comprehensive risk analysis will have to be performed. This initial risk analysis must be maintained to reflect:

- reduction in vulnerabilities by procurement of counter-measures
- changes in the information or business models as the business changes
- changes in the physical model (new computers or networks, etc.) supporting the same information (hence changes to the vulnerabilities).

The well-defined relationships between the underlying structured models and the SRA process, as shown in Figure 4.7, makes the maintenance of the risk models straightforward.

Once the risk analysis has been performed, a plan should be constructed to procure the counter-measures required to mitigate the most important threats.

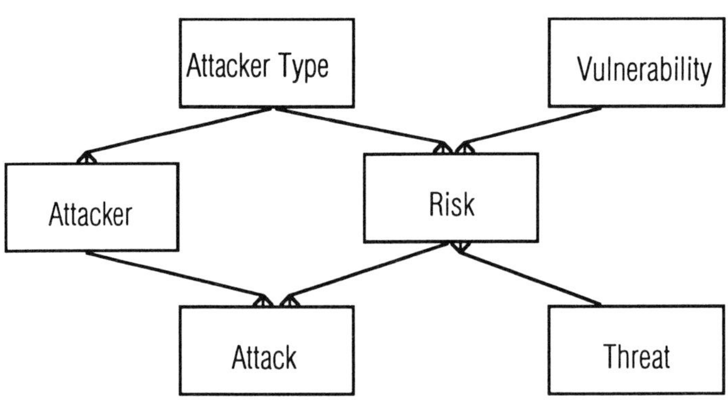

Figure 4.7 SRA relationships.

Obviously, this will be subject to budgetary constraints. The appropriate size of this budget can be determined by the relative magnitude of the information risks compared to the business's other risks.

Finally, the security manager needs a high level of confidence that the security measures are actually working. This is achieved by security audits.

4.2 Counter-measures

Once exposures have been determined, the structured catalogues all the Risk Manager to work back to the Vulnerability Catalogue to determine where counter-measures expenditure would be best directed. The Risk Manager has three basic options with regard to each exposure: acceptance, insurance or avoidance (by counter-measure procurement.) The choice depends on the size of the exposure and the likely frequency of successful attacks, as shown in Figure 4.8.

The procurement of counter-measures depends upon the scale of the risks and the size of the organisation's counter-measures budget (which will depend upon its overall priorities), but will be procured to counter the risks with the highest exposure first.

As with any other purchase, value for money should be sought. In this case, this implies that the ratio between the reduction in exposure implied by use of the countermeasure and the cost of the countermeasure should be large.

As well as the capital outlay required, the effect of the use of the counter-measure on ordinary work should be assessed as part of the cost. All counter-measures cause some degree of inconvenience, for example: slower database access,

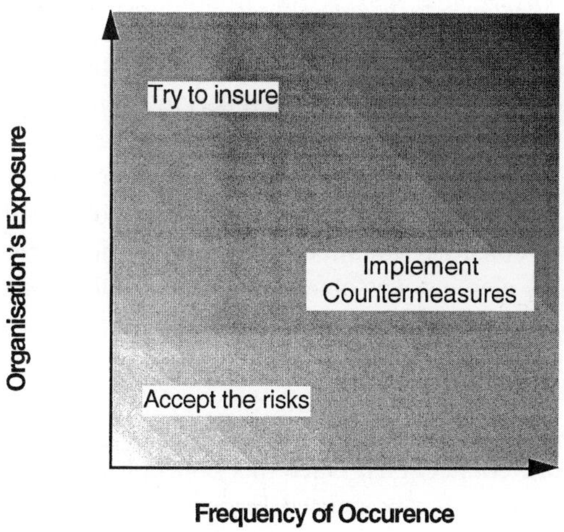

Figure 4.8 Exposure options.

when complicated access control is required, or slower communications when encryption keys have to be transferred before message transmission can take place.

In addition, staff may have to be employed (usually on a part-time basis) to manage a particular countermeasure – for example someone to set up and manage access control lists or key distribution facilities. Such factors can often outweigh the capital outlay required for a counter-measure in the long run.

5. RISK ANALYSIS EXAMPLES

5.1 Purpose

The two examples used in the chapter demonstrate the risk analysis process and its results in real organisations. One shows how a risk analysis exercise can reveal an exposure catalogue very different from the one assumed within an organisations (and thus significantly redirect counter-measures expenditure without increasing it.) The other shows how risk analysis can help to quantify and support decisions which managers within an organisations suspect need to be made, but cannot make without corroborating analysis support.

5.2 International ticker engine

This first example shows how different the calculated exposure of a system can be from the assumptions about exposure that are made in the absence of proper risk analysis. A major financial institution was planning an upgrade to one of their mission-critical systems. This system – let's call it the International Ticker Engine, or ITE – was for gathering financial information from a number of sources around the world, processing this information into a 'user friendly' form and then sending the information (via satellite and terrestrial links) to a number of subscribers who pay a substantial subscription fee to receive this information. The information model for the ITE showed a number of basic elements of information (assets, traded instruments, trades, prices, and so on) that were obtained from a number of sources and used to construct a number of services which were delivered to users. In general, the same element was obtained from more than one source and a primary source superseded the others. Figure 4.9 shows the associated process model.

The institution developed a basic technology concept which implement the link between the Service Provision function and the User over both satellite broadcast links and terrestrial network connections. Once this concept had been defined, it was determined that a substantial risk existed because unauthorised users could potentially 'listen in' to the satellite broadcast channel (from the

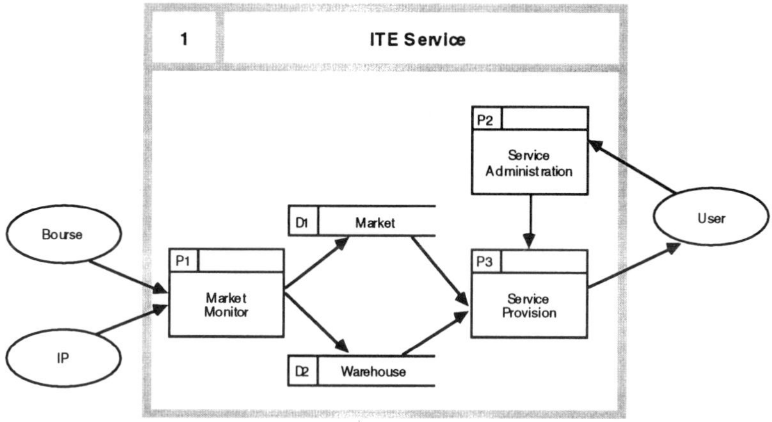

Figure 4.9 ITE process model.

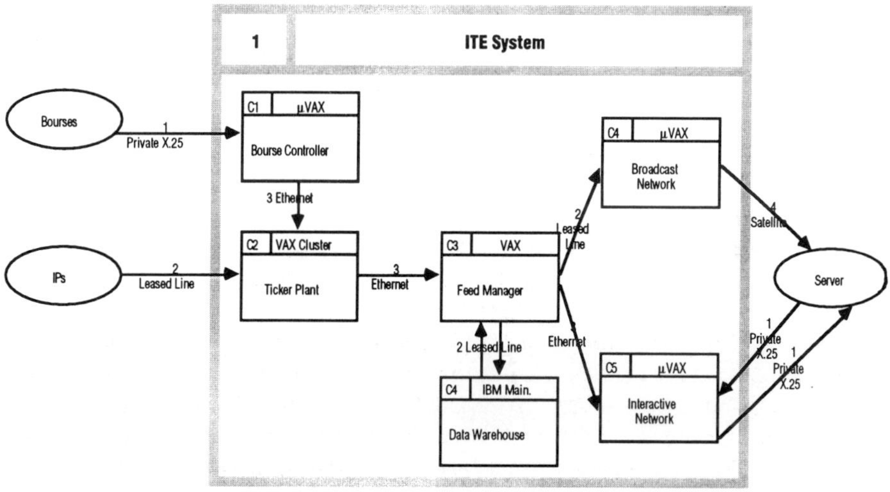

Figure 4.10 ITE technology model.

Broadcast Network to the Server) and thus avoid paying subscriptions. Hyperion were then engaged to carry out a risk analysis study and recommend the level of countermeasure to be applied to the broadcast channel (i.e. DES, RSA or other encryption), which had been determined to be the greatest risk. The developed technology model is shown in Figure 4.10.

This was a very interesting case, because the direct losses to the organisation were in most circumstances very low even though the gain to attackers could be very high. The main danger was that the organisation could be subject to legal action to recover losses to third-parties if the integrity of the service was compromised. Even in Europe, organisations are vulnerable to lawsuits by subscribers or users if mission-critical (to them) services are disrupted. Therefore, the loss to be considered in relation to many threats was the loss to third-parties for which the organisation would be liable.

The primary result of the study was that the organisation's exposure to unauthorised receipt of satellite data was relatively low and could easily be solved by simple encryption of the broadcast link. The major exposure, insufficiently studied in the System Architecture Phase, was to unauthorised input of information to the central system. Two main recommendations followed: encryption to reduce the probability of unauthorised reception and authentication of input to preserve the integrity of the services.

5.3 Manned space mission

Hyperion were selected by an international agency to use the SRA methodology to carry out a risk analysis study for a manned space mission. Figure 4.11 shows a

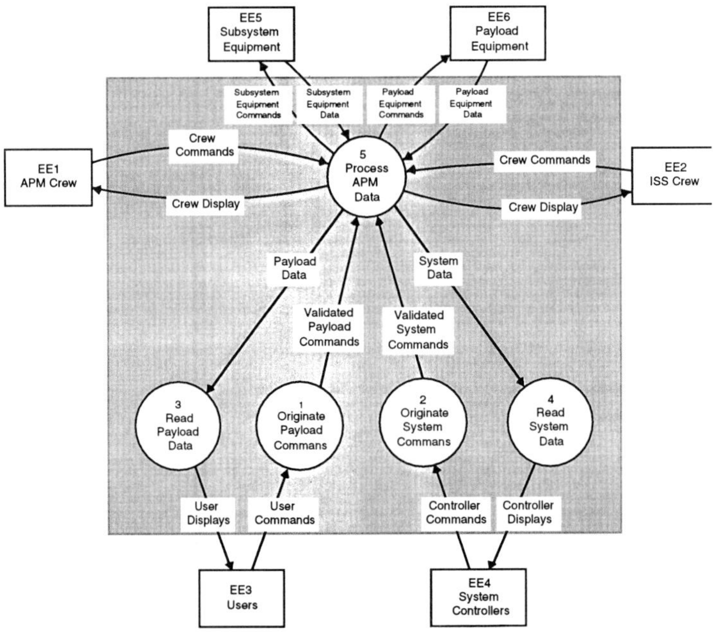

Figure 4.11 MSM logical model.

simplified level-1 DFD from a logical model of the spacecraft:

Most users (University departments: not the most secure computing environments!) are connected via a LAN to user site systems and from there via public X.25 networks to mission control. Controllers access the mission control computers directly over a LAN. A μwave link provides communication between mission control and the spacecraft master computer. Status and results are sent to mission control and user sites respectively, via the μwave link. Controllers can control the systems directly, schedule system activities and update systems software. Users can only schedule payload activity, which has to be checked in advance by mission control.

In this case, because of the difficulty of assigning values to safety-related issues, the client chose a 3-point measurement scale (low, medium, high) for 'costs' and a 5-point scale (slight..extreme) for exposures.

The confidentiality risk with the greatest exposure is for interception of results on the downlink. The most likely attacker is a research institution, whose budget is 'high', whilst the cost of intercepting the downlink is 'low'. The next most serious risk is interception of payload commands at mission control. The integrity risk with the greatest exposure is for a false onboard program to be created at mission control (this is the greatest risk overall). The most likely attacker is a disaffected employee, whose budget is 'medium', whilst the cost of exploiting mission control's vulnerability is 'low'.

The integrity of the mission control computers can be improved by implementing a rigorous security policy. The software used to enforce this security policy should be trustworthy. Orange Book (or ITSEC) type evaluation should be used to provide a high level of assurance of the software's trustworthiness. The availability of the mission control computers can be improved by using 'hot standby' fault tolerant machines. Preferably these should use a separate power supply, and be split across two or more sites. In this way, if a disgruntled employee takes a pick-axe to a computer, he cannot cause the service to stop. The integrity of the agency LAN can be improved by applying DES-based MACs to onboard programs which are transmitted across it. The confidentiality of the downlink could be similarly improved by using DES. RSA is not required since the mission supports a closed community of users.

6. SUMMARY

The purpose of risk analysis should be to assist managers in making informed decisions about investment and developing risk management policies which place IS risks in their correct position in the overall spectrum of business risks. High counter-measures expenditure on every aspect of an IS is out of the question in a commercial organisation so this expenditure must be directed to reduce corporate exposure to IS risks in the context of overall business risks.

In today's world of business and public administration, information is a critical asset, from which a profit can and should be derived. To do this, the right information has to be in the hands of the right people at the right time. Failure to achieve this will result in loss of potential profit for a commercial organisation or an increase in costs for a public body. In all cases, the quality of service delivered to the organisation's customers/clients/users will suffer.

To do this, information security risks must be quantified (so far as possible) on the same scale as other risks. In this way, the relative importance of these risks to an organisation can be properly assessed. Obviously, an organisation will wish to invest to mitigate the risks to which it is most exposed. These may or may not include information security risks. Furthermore, the scale of such investment should be commensurate with the likely benefit. In other words, investment in IT security should show the same rate of return as any other investment.

Successful businesses take risks, but only calculated ones. Information security risks should be treated in exactly the same way as any other risk. Thus, we can see that information risks cannot be properly assessed unless the information itself can be valued.

This chapter has shown that the subject of measuring and managing information systems risk is not a 'black art' but a discipline with tools and methodologies that allow managers to make rational decisions about existing or planned information systems, corporate exposure to those systems and the counter-measures expenditure that would be appropriate.

As the examples here have shown, even the highest level risk analysis yields worthwhile, and is some cases surprising, results enabling managers to reduce corporate exposure to manageable levels.

ACKNOWLEDGEMENTS

Many thanks are due to John White of KPMG for his many helpful comments on the draft of this chapter.

REFERENCES

Carroll, J M, 1990 Coding Ethics and Law into Risk Analysis, *Proc. of Compsec 90*, Elsevier, London.

CCTA, 1990 *SSADM Version 4 Reference Manual*, NCC Blackwell, Oxford.

Condon, R A, 1991 Scientific Approach to the Risk Business, *ICL Today*, p18, April.

Davies, D, 1991 The Nature of Computer Dependency Risks *Computer Law & Security Report*, **7**(4): pp161-164.

Dorey, P G, 1991 Risk Assessment–Current Methodologies and Software Products, *Information*

Security Monitor, **7**(1): pp5-7.

Lack, K, 1989 Electronic Picketing and the Consequences for EDI, *Information Security Monitor*, **4**(2): pp6-8.

McEvoy, N A. and Harris, R, 1990 Structured Security Analysis using SSADM, *Proc. SSADM Users Group Conference*, SSADM UG, Keele.

Mobley, L and McKeown, K, 1989 *Build on IBM*,Penguin, London.

Smith, J, 1989 TV Newsman Charged With Hacking, *Information Security Monitor*, **4**(3): p2.

Moses, R, 1990 The Current Status of CRAMM: The CCTA Risk Analysis and Management Methodology, *Proc. of Information Security: Confidentiality, Integrity and Availability*, Unicom, London.

5 Accounting for IS investment

Tim Connolly
Partner, Partners for Change

1. INTRODUCTION

Much management attention has been devoted in the past few years to understanding and better managing the overhead cost base, which had hitherto been denied much more than a cursory glance in many organisations, due not least to the absence of any meaningful analysis of the composition of the costs that were collectively and somewhat arbitrarily grouped together in the management accounts. Approaches such as Activity Based Management have opened the eyes of many to the factors which cause overhead cost to be incurred, and to the linkages between costs, with significant consequences for the way that not only the cost base, but indeed the whole business, is managed.

The ubiquity of Information Technology guarantees its position as both one of the largest areas of non-direct spend and one of the most critical to understand if cost and business management is to be effectively applied. At the same time, however, it is one of the most difficult to submit to traditional cost management techniques because, for many businesses, the expenditure and the benefits gained from that expenditure cannot be directly linked to outputs. For every instance of a business that has derived a clearly identifiable benefit by, for example, accelerating cash flows through the introduction of a new invoicing system, there are perhaps ten or twenty struggling to evaluate the bottom line impact of enhanced communications networks or a revamped accounting system.

Given this situation, IT investment decisions in many organisations have had all the characteristics of a corporate act of faith. Whilst it may be possible – if not always easy – to cost specific projects, the measurement of the effectiveness of this expenditure is notoriously difficult and, in many cases, is scarcely attempted, let alone achieved.

Three issues therefore need to be considered:

- how to establish the appropriate level of IT spend for an organisation or some part of it;
- what to pay for; and
- how to measure the effectiveness of that spend by reference to the benefits derived.

This chapter will suggest that all three issues should be addressed by considering the following questions:

- what drives cost in the IT environment? What factors and events determine the level of expenditure on IT?
- how can IT effectiveness be defined?
- how can such effectiveness be measured and controls implemented?

2. COST DRIVERS

It would be easy to set into motion a discussion of the factors and events that determine the level and extent of IT spend. They can, however, be broadly considered under four headings.

The first heading is *user demand.* Any IT function is, to some extent, responding to the requirements, whether specified or not, of those people who consume the outputs of the function. The problem is that this relationship may have become confused over time to the extent that it is no longer recognisable, even to the suppliers and users themselves. It is common, when helping organisations to map out the services performed by the IT function, to have to help suppliers to stand back and think not only about what they are doing, but who they are doing it for.

As more and more companies, especially large ones, question the value of vertical organisation structures, the critical importance of understanding the supplier–user interfaces at work becomes more apparent. Management, responsible for resource deployment decisions, must be able to see how resources are being consumed in pursuit of corporate objectives, either the short-term delivery of a product or service to a customer or the longer-term achievement of a strategic goal. The ultimate users of internal resource should be able to influence, although not necessarily control, the way in which services are delivered to them so that they can ensure that this is done in a way that maximises their ability to deliver, in turn, to the market. The whole issue of management by business process depends upon the organisation's ability to link expenditure decisions, wherever taken, to the impact those decisions have on an ultimate deliverable.

This issue is clearly linked to a second main heading, that of *supplier perceptions.* The poorly-defined internal relationships referred to above leave the providers of services such as IT in an extremely difficult position when it comes to setting expenditure targets. Without a clear understanding of both policy and operational requirements, many spending decisions are taken in the dark. I came across a good example when working with a large service company, one of whose problems was the high level of IT support, in terms of both expenditure and head-count. As part of the evaluation process, we asked IT departmental managers to define not only the services they provided and who for, but also their overall objectives. The illuminating answer to the latter point was that they saw their objective to be to keep the company at the leading edge of technology. This was completely at odds with the view of the management team, who, whilst they were able to contest the supplier's stated objective as 'gold-plated', were, equally revealingly, unable to easily define precisely what they did require of the IT service. The solution to this sort of problem can be obtained, as it was in this case, by the supplier defining in some detail the services provided and the cost of those services. It is then up to the management team, with extensive input from the supplier and from direct users of the service, to prioritise the services and to decide which, if any, should be changed, enhanced or eliminated so that the supplier delivers a service which is consistent not with its own perception of user requirements, but with those of the business as a whole.

The third driver of cost in the IT function is the *complexity* of the organisation and of the relationships between different parts of it. This has already been referred to above, and is clearly integral to the questions of user demands and supplier perceptions. It is pertinent to add, however, that there will generally be a strong positive correlation between the complexity of the organisation and the cost of operating within it.

Similarly, the final main heading for identifying cost drivers is also one that pervades the whole supplier–user interface. This is the *organisational structure and culture* itself, meaning both the segregation of the business into departments and, more importantly, the question of how those departments communicate with and feed back to each other. In many businesses one has the powerful impression of a number of silo tanks, each fairly self-contained, operating in more or less total ignorance of how what is going on within a particular silo is influencing, or influenced by, other links in the chain.

All of the above drivers are relevant to the evaluation of IT expenditure, and must be understood before progress can be made towards the development of a meaningful approach to accounting for IT investment.

3. DEFINING IT EFFECTIVENESS

The definition of IT effectiveness follows on fairly logically from the above analysis of cost drivers. A structured supplier–user dialogue, based around the supplier-prepared definition of services provided, can be used as a basis for defining *which outputs are required.* Clearly, this question must be answered by reference not only to immediate operational needs but to longer-term strategic requirements as well. This definition of outputs must determine *the level and nature of resources required.* Unnecessary services can be cut and the delivery of inefficient ones redesigned, with cost-saving potential. Through this process, supplier and user are taken to a stage where agreement is reached as to what the user is entitled to expect from the relationship, in terms of level of service, timeliness, flexibility and cost. Often this agreement will be formalised in an internal contract which will be used to evaluate supplier performance periodically. It may therefore also incorporate *agreed performance standards.*

It is essential to define IT effectiveness not only to develop a meaningful approach to accounting for the investment in IT; it is also specific to every organisation, to the extent that every business has different objectives. Therefore the process of defining IT effectiveness should not be skimped, and indeed it offers a valuable opportunity to revisit corporate objectives and to examine and review their impact on investment decisions.

4. MEASURING EFFECTIVENESS AND IMPLEMENTING CONTROLS

The key aspects of measuring effectiveness are fourfold and all emerge from the discussion of cost drivers and the definition of effectiveness. Firstly, *user evaluation* continues to be critical. The principle that the level and quality of service should be determined by agreement between supplier and user must be continued into the ongoing measurement process. Periodic reviews of internal services should be incorporated into normal practice. User evaluation can be supplemented more broadly by the development of *key performance indicators* which reflect the priorities and objectives for IT services. User evaluation will also drive the measurement of *value for money*, which may require the establishment of external benchmarks to place the service offered in context. Finally, the measurement process must incorporate *actions to correct shortcomings*, which may range from short-term corrective measures to deep-rooted business process redesign, cost reduction or outsourcing.

5. WHAT ABOUT ACCOUNTING?

It will be noticed that this chapter has made only passing reference to the specific issue of how businesses should account for their expenditure on IT expenditure which can justifiably be regarded as an investment. This is because accounting for IT is only useful and meaningful to the extent that it reflects what is actually represented by IT spend. This means that it should be based not simply on the cost of the resources provided, but rather on the cost of services delivered and on the relationship between the cost of these services and the benefit obtained by the organisation, which can only be valued by reference to the end user of the service. The conclusions emerging from this analysis as far as accounting for IT investment is concerned are:

- costs should be built up by activity, rather than resource; activities comprise the building blocks from which both services and costs are defined,

- activity costs should reflect what drives the expenditure and, in particular, at what level the activity is incurred; for example, IT processing costs are highly volume specific and will move broadly with activity level which are, in turn, directly determined by the number of items being processed. On the other hand, IT development costs are determined by the number and size of IT projects under way and have little or nothing to do with volume throughput. The difference between these two types of cost, and indeed between various volume-related costs that have different volume drivers, should be reflected in the accounting system,
- in conclusion, the costs of IT should not be considered in isolation from either the benefits towards which they contribute or the various influences which determine expenditure levels. Accounting for IT needs to reflect the dynamics of the behaviour of all the different types of cost that are incurred in the function. This requires that accounting information is placed carefully in the context of the strategic and operational influences to which IT expenditure is subjected.

6 IT value for money: going beyond financial analysis

Tom Coleman
Principal Consultant, Ochre Management Services

1. INTRODUCTION

This chapter describes a set of techniques which provide an appraisal of the *total value of Information Technology expenditure*. The methodology is based on research into how over 100 of *The Times* top 200 companies evaluated the soft benefits of IT. It has been used in a wide variety of organisations, particularly within the financial services sector (e.g. insurance, reinsurance and building societies).

Whether a company is getting full value from it's IT systems is often a point of contention. A number of surveys have found that the majority of projects are perceived as providing no significant value. Systems are often introduced as an 'act of faith' without formally planning how the benefits are going to be realised. Then when, almost inevitably, the blurred goals are only partially achieved, the IT group comes under pressure from the board, and CIO can mean 'Career Is Over' rather than 'Chief Information Officer'.

However, I believe that there is a growing acceptance that investment in IT is critical for achieving business strategies into the 1990s. It is key to the reengineering programmes being adopted by many companies and, although cost containment is still the key issue for most organisations, IT budgets have not been hit as hard as many other functions.

The problem is in understanding what exactly the business is gaining. To paraphrase a well known advertising truism 'I know that I am wasting 50% of the money I spend on IT, I just don't know which 50%'. The failing is not in the use of technology itself, but in understanding what benefits it brings.

Our research showed that where formal investment appraisal techniques were being used, they were overwhelmingly based on Return on Investment. Financial CBAs (Cost Benefit Analyses) are the only measure used by most companies and the softer, intangible benefits are either ignored or treated as 'a nice bonus if they happen'.

Our survey found that on average, half the value of IS (Information Systems) projects is contained in intangible benefits. And if these benefits are not identified in the first place, it is hardly surprising that the feeling remains that nothing of great importance has been achieved.

2. THE LIMITATIONS OF FINANCIAL APPRAISAL

Financial appraisals are based on an 'investment' view of decision making. Managers have a certain amount of money under their control and they decide to 'invest' in the projects that will bring the largest return. Often there are 'hurdle rates' or similar criteria which specify a minimum level of return (although you find that manipulating the figures to meet the cut-off is very common). However, increasingly IT decisions simply do not fit in with this investment view of the world. For example:

- A Building Society is trying to make an investment decision as to whether to join a nationwide network of cash dispensing machines, to provide a type of service that they believe some of their customers will demand. The return on investment in this situation is almost certainly negative. Apart from the equipment and set-up costs, there are also the on-going service charges. In addition, administration costs are likely to increase because of a larger number of smaller value transactions.

  However, the building society decides to go ahead with the investment, because not to do so would almost certainly result in their losing customers to other societies that provide a fuller range of services.

Another example:

- An insurance company sets up a telephone-based claims handling system to process claims more quickly. However, the key motivation is keeping up with the competition and the investment decision is based on something more powerful than additional revenue, that is the price of staying in business.

3. THE USES OF INVESTMENT APPRAISAL?

Although many organisations rely on informal investment appraisal, or CBA techniques that only tell part of the story, decisions do need to be taken and some form of assessment is inevitable. There are two main uses of appraised information:

- *Project Selection.* There are always more potential projects than resources to complete them and every organisation must have *some* process for winnowing and prioritising projects. Companies use a multitude of techniques, for example project selection may be informal or formal, controlled by the developers or Group Finance, tightly or loosely aligned to the business strategies, etc.

  Project selection should ideally continue throughout the life of the project, although in practice projects can develop a sizeable momentum and there is a strong reluctance to disinvest even when the project is clearly going to fail to pay off.

- *To initiate benefit management planning.* Many developers believe that if the system meets the specification, and is delivered on time and to budget, then it is a success. However, success is really only achieved by the business using the system to generate additional profits. Benefit management plans force the business to focus on exactly how it will make the system pay off and contribute to the company objectives. As briefly discussed earlier, intangible benefits are becoming an increasingly important part of this.

4. OUR DEVELOPMENT METHODOLOGY

Introducing an approach to estimate, measure and manage intangible benefits is far from easy. It often requires changing the relationship between the business units and the IT developers and the way that ideas are converted into actual projects. The people issues are paramount and success is very dependent upon high quality change management.

The business managers need to be convinced that they will benefit directly and that the process will not be used as a club for their backs. On the other hand, system developers need to be convinced that they will be supplied with clearer user priorities and that implementing projects will become less risky and easier. We have used the methodology described in Figure 6.1 to develop total value appraisal systems in a number of companies.

The key component of the approach is the benefit profile to measure intangible benefits. The benefit profile (see Appendix A) provides a quick view of the total benefits that is complete and easy to interpret. Alongside it are textual bullets explaining exactly where the scores have come from, and how success is going to be measured.

Information in this form improves the decision making process rather than automating it. It provides an IT steering group with a consistent picture of the projects in their portfolio, and lets them prioritise projects more rationally. An element of subjectivity is still inevitable but a small group of appraisers administer the underlying questionnaire will help to 'keep the scoring honest'.

The phases are not carried out one after another and will almost certainly overlap. Effective change management, which is the key element of Programme Management, is essential throughout the whole of development of the investment appraisal system. Although initiatives in this area are often started by the IS group, business users need to be brought in as quickly as feasible. Ideally senior business management should drive the initiative, with most of the members of the development team and steering group coming from the business functions.

1) **Investment Appraisal Audit and Business Objective Review**
Aim: *To understand the existing senior management level, business priorities and IT investment strategies.*
Review the existing mission statements, goals, objectives, KPIs (Key Performance Indicators), CSFs (Critical Success Factors) etc. Identifying where the top level management are trying to move the business, and what are the supporting IT strategies

2) **Define Change Initiation and Investment Appraisal Processes and Structures**
Aim: *To establish common terms, processes and measures for managing the value of IT with the business and IS managers.*
Determine the consensus views on how the total system delivery process is structured. Highlight any disagreements, rather than attempting to force a common set of definitions on reluctant business or IS groups.

3) **Investment Analysis Tool Selection/Development**
Aim: *To develop and validate a tool set which matches the organisational culture and the business objectives.*
An iterative approach is used, working with senior, line and project managers. The primary deliverable is a project summary sheet (see Appendix A) which includes a 'benefit profile' measuring the strategic and intangible benefits.

4) **Integration of Investment Appraisal into the IS development life cycle**
Aim: *To make sure the Information Systems development process is focused on achieving the desired benefits.*
Physically integrating the tools, although very important, is only part of the task. Obtaining support and acceptance from both business and systems developers is vital, and unlikely to be achieved if the approach is perceived as an additional layer of bureaucracy and work.

5) **Training and Roll Out**
Aim: *To ensure that the approach is universally adopted.*
Using awareness seminars, training material, one to one walk-throughs, cascade training etc. This should not be only for those directly involved in putting together business cases, one hour briefing sessions for all business managers involved in IT can be very rewarding.

6) **Support and Maintenance**
Aim: *To accommodate changing business and user requirements.*
The business objectives and priorities inevitably change. The tools also require maintenance and possibly further development, although in our experience thorough initial design will keep this to a minimum.

7) **Programme Management**
Aim: *To focus both IS and business management on benefit management and value for money.*
Portfolio management can be defined as the aggregation of all of the planned and current work. We believe that organisations need to move on further to Programme Management, where you appraise and manage benefits that would not happen unless the projects are considered as an integrated whole.

Figure 6.1 IT investment appraisal methodology.

Most companies will need to develop a new investment appraisal approach in phases, with the total implementation taking between four to six months. However, there are normally some 'quick wins' to be gained early on in the process, e.g. clarifying the process for raising changes or pulling together standard cost information for the CBAs.

5. IT INVESTMENT APPRAISAL SYSTEMS

There are three areas that you need to consider when appraising projects:

- Financial appraisal.
- Risk appraisal.
- Strategic or intangible benefit appraisal.

5.1 Financial appraisal

Putting together the CBA should be the easiest part of the appraisal. Almost all companies have standards for financial appraisal and there is usually a lot of experience and knowledge within the finance and audit groups. However, in practice, the quality of the CBAs is often poor and systems developers ignorant of the basic principles of management costing.

Education can provide major benefits, e.g. in getting the project managers to perform simple sensitivity analysis or to provide the assumptions along with the figures.

5.2 Risk appraisal

The one stable fact over the last few years is that change is continuous and increasing in pace. The nature of most businesses has become more complex and difficult to predict, and many markets have become much more volatile. Technology change has speeded up, dramatically increasing the risks involved in IT development, and the newspapers are full of organisations who have aimed too high.

Risk Management should be an essential part of any project. The key phases in initial risk assessment are:

1. Risk Identification – what are the key risks ?
2. Probability – How likely are they to occur ?
3. Impact – What will be the result if they occur ?

   (Probability X Impact provides a measure of the Hazard)
4. Manageability – What can we do to reduce or eliminate the risk ?

Common sense management principles should then be applied to manage the risks, e.g. make sure there is ownership of the problem, define and implement actions to deal with it, monitor the progress, etc. However, some risks just have to be accepted, i.e. they are fundamentally unmanageable, and the risk management process should bring these to the attention of the decision makers so that contingency plans can be drawn up.

Risks can be divided into two classes; (1) project implementation risks, and (2) post-implementation benefit delivery risks. The former covers factors such as delivery on time, to budget and meeting user requirements. These types of risks are relatively well understood and there are a number of tools available to assist you.

The second area deals with the risks that can stop benefits being realised even though the project is deemed a success on implementation. It has had much less attention paid to it and there are few guidelines or tools to help you. We use simple checklists to assess the benefit delivery risks which fall into the categories shown in Figure 6.2.

5.3 Strategic and intangible benefit appraisal

The third area of investment appraisal deals with soft, intangible benefits. Within our approach the main deliverable is a benefit profile and accompanying textual bullets, showing the projects total contribution to the Company goals.

The profile has to be customised to the individual corporation, company or division using a combined top-down and bottom-up approach. To drive the process we recommend setting up a working party that includes all of the major functional groups and/or divisions.

The members of the working party should be sufficiently senior to understand the strategic issues involved. One of their first tasks is to clarify the company's mission and the high level objectives to develop the profile. The desired outcome is a clear, unambiguous set of critical performance indicators and goals that are shared by all of the high level stakeholders.

An initial questionnaire is developed covering all of the key factors. This is then tested on a representative sample of past and planned projects.

Organisational / Cultural
Legal / Political
Business Volatility and Competition
Technical
Social and Customer

Figure 6.2 Benefit delivery risk areas.

The process is an iterative one requiring significant testing and refinement. At the beginning the questions, metrics and scores can be very tentative, but understanding rapidly improves as you evaluate projects.

The eventual result is a set of key goals and objectives covering all of the key ambitions of the organisation (e.g. Figure 6.3).

In the example shown there are nine separate classes of benefit in the profile divided into five categories. The weights refer to the relative importance of each category as defined by the senior management decision group. In the profile the weights are represented by the size of each segment.

The weighting system provides the tool with a high degree of flexibility. Changes in company or divisional emphasis can easily be introduced without having to revisit or rescore each project.

To create the profile an appraisal specialist fills in a short questionnaire with the business sponsor and/or project manager. Typically there are between 15 and 25 questions which are used to give quantitative information about the softer, intangible benefits of projects. These values are then aggregated to produce a score for the benefit categories. Finally, the benefit profile can be automatically drawn up using micro-computer software.

On average the interview takes approximately 30–40 minutes. The duration primarily depends upon the phase of the project and the extent of the information already known to the sponsor/managers.

The use of an investment appraisal specialist to facilitate the answers and scores is crucial if there is to be a reasonable base for comparison across projects and divisions. Good results are obtained by using a small team of business analysts and managers who have a reasonable knowledge of IT. These specialists have the final say on what scores are entered, which balances both the natural optimism of most systems project managers and the occasional desire of the business champions to see his or her baby thrive above all others.

Key Goal	*Business Objective*	*Example Weights*
Customer	1) Customer base	60
	2) Customer service	80
Profit	3) Sales Effectiveness	80
	4) Unit Cost	70
Culture	5) Staff Attitude / Morale	100
Decisions	6) Exploitation of business opportunities	70
	7) Management Information	75
Product	8) Brand	90
	9) Product design	75

Figure 6.3 High level business objectives.

Most of the questions are scored along two dimensions:

- Impact – will the project have a major or minor effect upon the benefit category?
- Range – how many policy holders, policies, transactions, staff etc., will be affected.

To give an example from the insurance sector, a project might reduce transaction turn-around by 25%, providing a major impact on customer service. If, however, it only affects a small number of policies, the overall score could well be below that of a project which speeds up the processing by a small amount but for a large number of policy types.

Figure 6.4 shows sample questions for one of the areas plus brief definitions.

This process also provides an analysis of the total benefits of the project, confirming exactly what is expected to be achieved as well as the key issues and assumptions.

One use of the tool is to clarify suggestions for projects *before* incurring any significant IT developers costs. You can use the questionnaire for a structured investigation of what benefits the business expects to gain before incurring the costs of feasibility investigations.

With this use of the tool at the 'bright idea' phase some of the answers are inevitably imprecise. This does not affect the overall value of the tool which is designed to appraise the project, in so far as it is understood, at any point of its life cycle.

6. CONCLUSIONS

The primary conclusion from our work is that financial measures on their own simply do not work as an appraisal mechanism for information systems. This holds true for even the most sophisticated discounted cash flow measures. There

Business Objective	*Contributing Factor*	*Question Definition*
1) Product optimisation	1) Brand	Extent to which key brand values are maintained. Quantify effect on values X,Y,Z & give metrics.
	2) Product Design	Risk and risk exposure of new or changed product. Compliance with design standards. Potential revenue to expense.
	3) Efficiency	Turn-round times for all processes

Figure 6.4 High level goals + related metrics.

are no effective techniques for converting all of the benefits of IT into hard, bottom line returns and CBAs inevitably only tell part of the story.

This is causing increasing problems for many firms as they move from using IT for 'back office' or clerical automation developments to 'front office' or strategic systems. With these newer generation of systems many of the benefits are soft and their delivery is becoming an increasingly critical issue.

What is needed is a extension to appraisal techniques which predicts and measures the total contribution to the business objectives and goals. Specifically the intangible benefits need to be dealt with in a consistent, valid and reliable manner. Appraisal techniques should accurately deal with all types of IS project. Mandatory projects are relatively few, most IT work can be foregone if the organisation is prepared to bear the cost, and in any case the benefits from 'must do' or infrastructure projects should be analysed along with the discretionary work.

Persuading IT practitioners to consider business value for money is just one aspect of getting people to accept and buy-into to the new approach. Getting the roles, responsibilities and accountabilities clarified and fully accepted by both business users and system developers is crucial. The difficulties arise not only from differences in language and culture between business and IS, but also because the business is reluctant to accept responsibility where they feel they have no real authority over the development.

Another point is that all parts of the organisation need to focus on quality throughout the systems life. An IT project does not finish with the successful delivery of a working system, it continues as long as benefits are being accrued to the business. Achieving maximum value for money means not only picking the right 'goods' to buy, but also using them productively for as long as makes economic and organisational sense.

You need to continually remember the shareholders perspective – invest in success and disinvest when the total return is insufficient, but without adopting a 'policeman's' role. Benefit reviews need to be forward looking, i.e. 'what can we do to maximise the benefits in the future?' rather than 'what went wrong and who's to blame?'.

One final point is that IT investment appraisal is not a special case. The techniques described here are, to a large extent, applicable to any business expenditure. Information system requests should be compared to other calls on the organisations resources. In doing this you must have an appraisal system that is fair, consistent, unbiased, and which takes account of all of the organisational goals, if you are to obtain maximum value for money.

APPENDIX A: EXAMPLE PROJECT APPRAISAL SUMMARY SHEET

Project name	**ADDACS**	**Date**	22/9/92
Project manager	XXXXXXXXXX	**Sponsor**	XXXXXXXXX
Signature		**Signature**	

Project Description And Objectives

Automate update and cancellation of General Insurance DDs via data from BACS system. Currently X people handle XXXX cases per day + XXX @ the RSCs. All cancellations are dealt with by XXXX due to lack of resources to process manually (500-600). we then let the batch run produce a DD for the cancelled mandate and process by XXX.

Tapes will be generated automatically from BACS data to amend XXXXX, reducing the delay to 1-2 days.

Status

Mandatory		Initiation	√	Implementation		PAM Version
Discretionary	√	Feasibility		Post-implementation		1.0

Time scale

Start Date		Finish Date		Critical Date	XXXXXXXXX

Financial Details

Manpower costs	£XXk[1]	Other costs	£XXk (H/W)
Cost Savings	£XXk[2]	Increase in Premium or Revenue	
Net Present Value	£XXk[3]	Payback	X.X years
Internal Rate of Return	XX%		

Risk Measures

Total System / Project Risk Score

H	M	L
	√	

High Level Commercial Risks

H	M	L	N
	√		

Cost case based on 'guesstimates' - further work is needed to harden up development and running costs + the benefits (particularly their life span).

Medium project risk is primarily due to pioneering aspects of the development, eg minimal experience of X400 within XXX, plus newness of BACS design (see key issues).

Project XXXX replacement (Elephant) will probably cancel direct benefits but we may be able to incorporate some of the design/code.

Single suppliers for PC and Mainframe options. Their financial soundness will require thorough investigation.

Other Key Issues

The newness of the BACS design has two major implications.

1) Overall design and implementation uncertainty/instability, eg the specifications have still to be signed off.
2) Immaturity from a technical viewpoint. The initial implementation will provide 2 ways of interfacing. Others may well be added later on in 1993 & may provide a better solution which could require starting again.

---

1 £XXk POLISY development + £XXk communications link

2 £XXX in year 1 thereafter £XXk (Staff Savings = £XXk)

3 Assumes whole cost borne by GIS IF H/W & Comms costs shared by life (Other costs - £Xk, cost savings + £XXX) NPV = £XXk, payback = X.X years, IRR XX%.

Investment appraisal: the key issue for IT?

7 Investment appraisal: the key issue for IT?

Richard C Leyton
Digital Equipment Co. Ltd

1. INTRODUCTION

In recent years, numerous surveys as well as more formal research have shown that both business and IT management have become increasingly uneasy about the basis on which IT investment decisions are made (or aren't made). The coincidence of this uncertainty and the most prolonged recession in modern times make it imperative that better approaches are employed and articulated.

Because many past IT investments were made as 'acts of faith', there is now no objective basis for assessing the benefits which were obtained from them. The cost and time overruns have been all too evident and have contributed to, even created, the perception that IT does not deliver.

It is argued by many on all sides of the political spectrum that training investment should be maintained throughout recessionary times. It could equally be argued that continued IT investment is essential if organisations (private and public) are to emerge 'lean and mean' ready to meet the challenges and opportunities of the new world order.

At the time of writing the economic scenario continues to look bleak. There is little chance of returning to the relatively casual ways of the past quarter century of IT investment, yet more than ever business needs enhanced IT capabilities. This chapter explores the issue and postulates partial solutions.

2. A REAL ISSUE, OR A NIGHTMARE SCENARIO?

The author contends that there is no doubt that in the minds of business management this is a real and live issue. Yet whenever the subject is discussed at conferences and seminars, IT professionals seek to debate the reality, therefore the starting point for this chapter must be an examination of the substance of that reality.

Perhaps nowhere is the issue more real than in the health sector. District and regional health authorities constantly face unpalatable choices – given funding constraints (and most admit that the populace has such an insatiable appetite for health care that some form of capping is inevitable) how do they trade off direct care provision (keeping wards open, additional staff or even hospitals) against new or improved IT systems? Because of the public and emotive nature of these organisations their difficulties have been well reported, but there is no reason to believe that they are unique.

According to Price Waterhouse (1992), only 34% of IT investments result in bottom line improvement. It is hard to conceive of any other venture that would be allowed to proceed with such odds against it. The same survey reveals that almost 50% of organisations had no system of benefits management, and an amazing 30% admitted a belief that measurement of benefits is impossible. All this in an annual survey where the top issue of concern to senior IT managers is shown to be *cost containment.*

These Price Waterhouse findings are of particular interest because they contrast strongly with Kearney (1990), who found that with the growing maturity of IT the management emphasis was moving from cost reduction and productivity improvements towards using IT as a strategic tool and to improve overall management and market performance. It may be that the difference is merely one of linguistics, but many will suspect that IT is perhaps only entering adolescence, and that at the first signs of real pressure juvenile behaviour has re-surfaced.

In the United States data quoted by the Sloan School of Management at MIT shows a minuscule (0.7%) improvement in private sector productivity (based on macro economic data) despite ever higher spending on IT. Nolan Norton & Co. (Thurow, 1988) analyse this further, and show that the 0.7% comprises a 2.8% increase for blue-collar workers, but 0.9% *decrease* in the white-collar sector. Given that these figures are for years when the objectives of IT systems were heavily biased towards productivity gains, the problem certainly has an appearance of reality.

Keen (1991) asserts that only 20% of the costs of IT investments are visible, and hence accounted for, at the time the cost justification or investment proposal is prepared. Writing of the mushrooming of PCs in most organisations, Strassmann (1990) describes the PC on the desk as 'merely the down-payment'.

With almost religious fervour Strassmann seeks to destroy all the most favoured indicators beloved of IT Managers, Directors and Chief Information Officers (CIOs). He demonstrates that, in the extensive range of organisations for which he has data, there is no direct correlation between IT spending and business success. Strassmann has few disciples following his alternative way (Return on Management), but he has performed a considerable service in massacring many of the sacred cows that were a shield for many an IT boss on the defensive.

In this matter there are no simple answers. Reality is specific to particular situations, but there can be no doubt that the issue is of major concern and is an obstacle to further exploitation of IT for the benefit of business. The issue is as real whether it's perceived as a vertical cliff impossible to climb or shifting desert sand which soon swallows up anything trying to cross. Judging by the limited tenure of CIOs (about three years in the USA), it must be seen as a nightmare scenario. Everyone whose future is in any way linked to IT should be concerned to address the problem – and quickly.

For many organisations the problem is exacerbated by a rush to Business Process Re-design (BPR) as a means of re-asserting control of the major business processes. Enhanced IT capabilities are practically implicit, yet the management techniques are much the same as those that gave rise to the concerns over returns on previous investments. If BPR is to be seen to succeed its practitioners *must* treat investment appraisal as a key issue.

3. A BRIEF HISTORY OF INVESTMENT APPRAISAL

We must look to the past to understand today's problems.

The evolution of the role and use of IT has been well documented and needs little comment here. Historians will doubtless analyse the amazing pace of change in the latter part of the twentieth century: the wholesale adoption of silicon technology has been unparalleled. Just as the consumer society, not only in the West, has an insatiable appetite for new and faster gadgets, so business seems to be crying out for more and more technology. From the 'point' solutions of thirty years ago the strategy focus has moved to 'enterprise integration'. From seeking easily measurable simple productivity gains, expectations have moved to more elusive *effectiveness* and even ethereal *competitive advantage*.

During the same period there has been little significant development of fundamental investment analysis techniques. In the immediately preceding period (say 1930–1960) progress was made in appreciating the time value of money, moving investment appraisal from simple payback to ROA (Return on Assets) and IRR and NPV (Internal Rate of Return and Net Present Value respectively). As potential uses of IT have become ever more sophisticated and fundamental to organisations, a chasm has opened between the impact of technology and the standard methods by which we evaluate that impact.

In the early days of IT its use was frequently confined to or heavily influenced by the Finance Department: more often than not the embryonic data processing section reported to the Finance Director. So the justification for IT investments was done by accountants for accountants in accounting terms, if it was done at all. In difficult cases formal justification would be by-passed either stating that the benefits were 'self-evident', or that 'there is no choice', or even 'this requires an act of faith'.

As IT became all pervasive and the scale of the total expenditure more visible the rules subtly shifted (some would argue that the game changed) and much expenditure fled the CIO's cost centre as the boardroom conversations turned to *value for money*. As Tom DeMarco observed as long ago as 1982 writing in a project management context "Costs will migrate out of any activity that is measured more carefully than its neighbouring activities" (DeMarco, 1982).

So far this may appear an inditement of the IT profession with finance as co-defendants. That would be a false perception because the problems extend to other business areas attempting a paradigm shift. If anything the problems have been more extreme for those trying to introduce high-tech methods into the manufacturing process. In the US CAM-I established a series of projects with a consortium of industrial, accounting and academic members, with the objective of defining more appropriate cost management techniques (concisely described in Brimson, 1988).

Bela Gold takes the problem one stage further (Gold, 1988), arguing that a competitive dimension must be superimposed on even the newest forms of investment evaluation. This should be little surprise to those who have been exposed to discussions about competitive edge systems – however the impact of Gold's hypothesis is not limited to such systems, but recognises the dynamics of the marketplace and the effect of competitors investment decisions on each other.

The cause of better investment evaluation was significantly advanced by the development of the Comprehensive Cost of Ownership model (CCOO) by Dr Michael Treacy and the Index Group (1989) (Figure 7.1). Perhaps surprisingly, many organisations hadn't previously looked outside the four top left boxes of the model when considering new investments. Even more surprising, indeed alarming, is the difficulty that they have in identifying their actual current costs for inclusion in a baseline model against which to evaluate alternative strategies.

4. THE BUSINESS NEED

Based on long experience working with customers, as well as academia and collaborators in research consortia, we see a need for an integrated approach to

	ACQUISITION	OPERATION	CHANGE
HARDWARE			
SOFTWARE			
PEOPLE			
NETWORK			
FACILITIES			

Limits of traditional cost of ownership evaluations

Figure 7.1 Comprehensive cost of ownership model.

investment appraisal which goes well beyond current practice. The approach needs to include, at least, the following:

- consideration of total life-cycle costs
- full evaluation of direct and indirect benefits (tangible and so-called intangible)
- strong linkage to business objectives and critical success factors
- full evaluation of the uncertainties and risks inherent in most projects.

If this could be achieved (and the chapter goes on to outline an approach) it would make a worthwhile contribution to improving the reputation of IS projects for (non-)delivery of the expected value for money. However worthwhile the contribution, it will still be much less than is needed. The perception will persist that planned benefits are not obtained, and/or are delayed, and/or that costs overran the estimates, etc.

All the available research highlights one inescapable fact: *Benefits of IT do not manage themselves, they have to be actively managed.* Thus a further vital missing link is a method for pro-actively managing the achievement of the benefits: for ensuring that what was promised is achieved at the right time and cost, and that variances are tracked and managed throughout the life of the investment.

Given the heritage of broken promises and user distrust, these seemingly modest proposals would transform business managements' perceptions of the IS contribution. There is one important corollary regarding benefits achievement – the business must accept that the responsibility for obtaining the benefits from IT investments is theirs, and theirs alone: IS can assist but they do not own the processes, people and other resources which are impacted.

5. PROPOSED APPROACH

The concepts described in this section have not been packaged into a formal methodology definition for this chapter. Such formality would obscure the key concepts and force the inclusion of information redundant to the current purpose. The emphasis, therefore, is put on WHAT is suggested, rather than trying to address the more detailed HOW questions.

For ease of understanding, the overall benefits management framework is described first, followed by some specific investment appraisal details.

5.1 Managing the benefits

The typical approach that organisations adopt to benefits management is depicted in Figure 7.2. In essence they conceive of IT systems to support some business

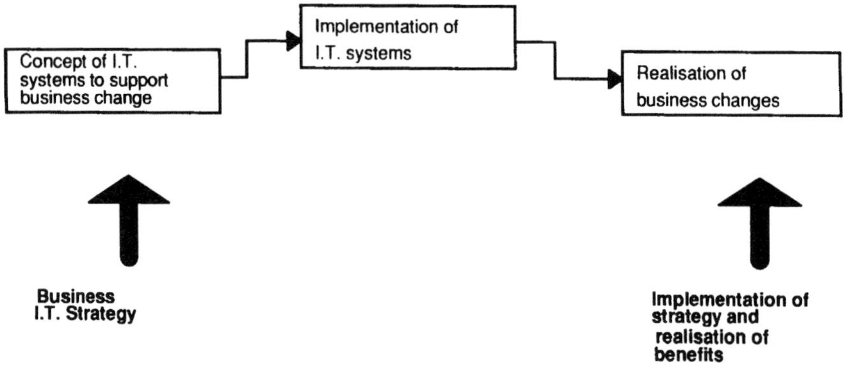

Figure 7.2 Traditional benefits management.

change; the IT systems are implemented and benefits are expected to accrue (automatically). Bitter experience shows that it just does not happen like that: that is a salutary lesson for a technology company to learn. The problem is that the expected benefits are only very tenuously linked to the needs of the business. If the business pressures are elsewhere no great effort will be expended to implement any business or process changes, and no management procedures exist to monitor whether or not planned benefits are realised. Furthermore, if the absence of benefits is noticed, IS will probably be castigated for the failures of the business to take advantage of the new system.

Rational consideration suggests that a broader and more integrated view is needed. Figure 7.3 depicts a revised model that expresses what is required. Note that the first step is to define required business changes, in accordance with the business objectives, quite independently of implementation considerations (e.g. what will be automated and what will be processed clerically). The IT design and implementation steps are then mirrored by organisation and business process design and implementation steps. The other vital additional component is that required to manage the achievement of the planned benefits (embedded in a feedback loop to the business planning process).

These concepts can then be taken an incorporated into an overall framework which embraces all the key factors, as shown in Figure 7.4.

This framework is not intended to imply a single consecutive process; that would be far too limiting. Organisations seeking to improve their benefits management will need to assess their current situation and priorities and choose an appropriate entry point. Similarly, this very simple diagram omits any concept of iteration, feedback and monitoring (except the outside loop indicating a continuum). The four 'activity groups' are:

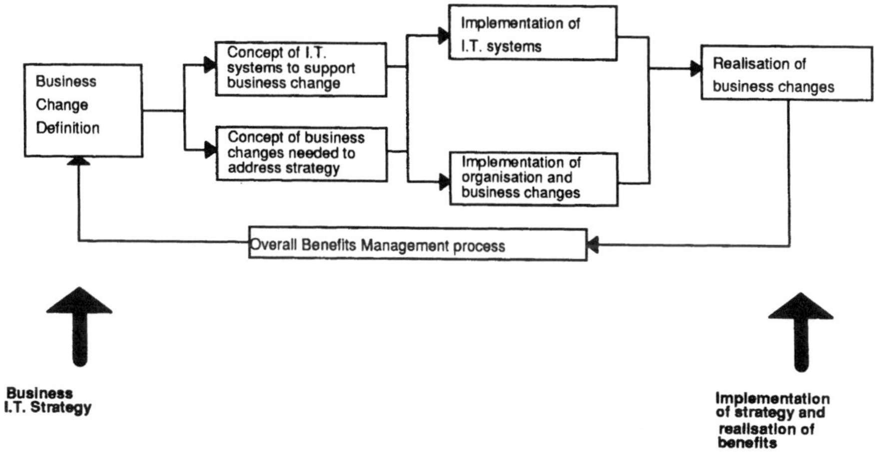

Figure 7.3 Active benefits management.

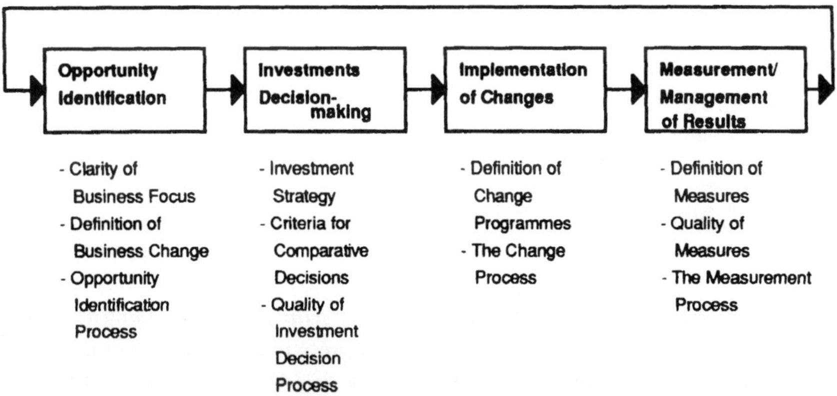

Figure 7.4 Benefits management methodology framework.

- *Opportunity Identification* – which includes all the activities and techniques associated with understanding the objectives of the business; its critical success factors (key results areas); its performance metrics; the business plans; the opportunities for change; the need for change.
- *Investment Decision-making* – as well as specific investment evaluation techniques this group includes activities related to setting investment strategy for projects within the organisation, and assessing the effectiveness of the investment strategy.

- *Implementation of Change* – experience shows that effective change only occurs consistently when a properly planned and integrated change management programme is implemented. Formal methods and disciplines *must* be adopted, and strongly supported by senior management.
- *Measurement and Management of Results* – is concerned with defining the methods of measurement; monitoring; reporting and managing variances; tracking the effectiveness of the whole process. This will be a completely new activity for many organisations and implies acceptance of some additional investment prior to commencement of a growing benefits stream.

Managing the Benefits (MTB) requires the development of relatively few original techniques, but a completely new management framework. (The new techniques that are required are concentrated in the investment analysis and results management areas.) Within the framework a good deal of flexibility may be permitted to allow selection of techniques and methods from a menu of approved options. The menu being constructed to suit the needs, culture and financial regulations of the organisation, and the size of its IT investment programme. Some organisations will have most of the individual pieces in place and will have to expend minimum effort to take real control of achieving the benefits potential of their investments: others will face a larger and longer task. All will find it helpful to adopt a structured diagnostic study to objectively determine the priorities and starting point for a benefits management programme.

5.2 Investment evaluation methodology

It is quite possible to use a methodology such as IEM (Investment Evaluation Methodology) as a free-standing investment analysis process (and indeed, the one described has been so used in the USA, and has acquired an excellent reputation). In Europe, we believe that the business climate requires that more comprehensive investment appraisal should be matched by a determined effort to manage the attainment of the forecast benefits; hence the positioning of IEM within the MTB framework.

Before describing the characteristics of the methodology, it is necessary to re-emphasise the extent of the impacts of IT systems on even large and diverse organisations. Fully determining and evaluating those impacts are very significant tasks which should not be lightly undertaken. Past methods are perceived to have failed, so will IEM if it is undertaken superficially or merely to obtain a favourable investment decision.

The formal description of IEM is in the classic methodological style, but that is not the most helpful way to describe its concepts and key features. Therefore, this description should not be used to critique the method itself, or the consultancy process supporting its implementation.

5.2.1 *Environment*

A thorough understanding must be gained of the environment in which the proposed system will exist. This may seem obvious, but all too often little more than lip service is paid to this requirement.

The business objectives and critical success factors of the enterprise or division should be readily available and should, naturally, influence all that is done within the environment or domain. (Theory and practice diverge even at this early stage, often because business realities are not reflected in restatements of business objectives.)

Current performance measures will provide an understanding of the real criteria used to judge business success, and which should be expected to influence acceptance or otherwise of an investment proposal. Specific performance measures are particularly necessary for the areas most likely to be affected by the proposed investment.

5.2.2 *Activity modelling*

This is to investment appraisal what tool-based project planning is to project management: it forces rigorous analysis in place of generality and ambiguity. Documented activity models also provide a baseline for the assessment of the impact of changes occurring later in the investment life-cycle (after approval has been given).

In the USA it is common for this activity modelling to be performed using techniques borrowed from Activity Based Costing (ABC). In Europe ABC is less established, indeed the very mention of it provokes intense debate among professional accountants, and alternative activity modelling techniques may be more appropriate. The specific method is relatively unimportant provided it is rigorous, provides maintainable documentation, and is understandable by staff from a variety of disciplines.

5.2.3 *Proposed investment*

Much information about the proposed investment will be available from well understood conventional methods. Much cost information should be provided by a life-cycle analysis using the Comprehensive Cost of Ownership concepts described earlier.

Traditional investment or cost-benefit analysis may mention in passing uncertainty of estimates, dependence on other projects, cultural barriers to change etc., but little use is made of such information. IEM makes effective use of such data as can be gleaned from investment project documentation, the experts involved and relevant management.

5.2.4 *Impact analysis*

A second set of activity models depict the processes that will exist following implementation of the proposed investment. Direct impacts are readily identified as the differences between the *before* and *after* sets of activity models.

Indirect, second and third order, impacts are frequently as important as some of the direct impacts and also need to be identified and quantified. Establishing these indirect impacts often requires innovative facilitation techniques which encourage multi-dimensional thinking.

Quantification of those impacts (positive and negative – benefits and costs) will often be a complex task requiring the identification of cost drivers (formally or informally, depending on the circumstances) and the questioning and testing of every assumption. The existence of the activity models greatly enhances the quantification process, but inevitably some impacts defy objective assessment. In these cases, it may be appropriate to seek expert estimates which can be built into the models (as a range of expected outcomes).

5.2.5 Modelling

May be regarded as a largely technical task, although experience shows that skillfully architected spreadsheets greatly help the latter stages of the process and the subsequent management reporting.

An additional element incorporated into IEM models is the concept of *learning curves*, used to represent the fact that benefits are gained over time (at varying rates). These learning curves can be incorporated at any appropriate level, thus eliminating the gross generalities of many traditional methods.

5.2.6 Risk and sensitivity

Before any conclusions are drawn the models are examined for undue sensitivity to changes in the values of any particular variables. Any that are discovered may be totally genuine, but need to be carefully re-examined and estimates re-evaluated. (These will also indicate priorities for management of the investment implementation project – assuming that the investment is approved.)

Consideration of many risk (or uncertainty) factors is integral to the process. At the final stage the model is flexed using simulation techniques to determine the risk profile of the investment, so that the eventual outcome can be forecast with a confidence factor attached.

6. SUMMARY AND CONCLUSION

This chapter has demonstrated the serious mismatches which exist between the high-profile, strategic use of IT and the techniques by which IT investments are evaluated, and also between the expected and perceived outcomes of those investments. It has demonstrated that techniques exist to overcome some of the perceived problems with traditional investment analysis, and that these must be placed in the context of an overall benefits management programme to maximise the chance of achieving the expected benefits.

Appraisal and management of IT investments is indeed a key issue for IS and business management, but success requires joint commitment and action throughout the investment life-cycle.

ACKNOWLEDGEMENTS

The concepts and the practical experience described in this paper owe much to the pioneering work of Patty Pollard (from Digital US Manufacturing) and Sally-Ann Moore (from Digital, European Headquarters). None of this would have been possible without the enthusiastic co-operation of customers and partners across the world.

REFERENCES

A T Kearney Limited, 1990 *Breaking the Barriers – IT Effectiveness in Great Britain and Ireland*, A T Kearney, London.

Brimson, J A, 1988 Bringing Cost Management Up to Date, *Manufacturing Engineering*, June.

DeMarco, T, 1982 *Controlling Software Projects – Management, Measurement, Estimation*, Yourdon Press, New York.

Gold, B, 1988 Charting a Course to Superior Technology Evaluation, *Sloan Management Review*, Fall.

Keen, P G W, 1991 Shaping Future Business Success, *Management Centre Europe Seminar*, Brussels.

Price Waterhouse, 1992/93 *Information Technology Review 1992/93*, Price Waterhouse, London.

Strassmann, P A, 1990 *The Business Value of Computers*, The Information Economics Press, New Canaan, CT.

Thurow, L C, 1988 Sloan School of Management, *Nolan, Norton & Company Symposium.*

Treacy, M E *et al.*, 1989 *The Cost of Network Ownership*, Index Group.

8 Evaluating and managing the IT investment

Andrew C Rowsell-Jones
EIS Ltd

1. INTRODUCTION

The objective of this chapter is to discuss methods used to evaluate and manage IT investment. It also suggests how the use of personal accountability for benefits delivery increases the chance of an IT investment providing quantifiable, business improvement.

Before discussing evaluation and management methods, the terminology used throughout the chapter is clarified. 'IT' is used to mean not only information technology in the sense of technical infrastructure, but also to include the information systems which manipulate, communicate and present information.

The following assumptions have also been made about IT investment:

1. IT investments do not deliver business benefit on their own, it is the business change which they facilitate that delivers the benefit. Business Process Re-design, the Learning Organisation, Empowerment and Management Process Re-design are all manifestations of organisational change, enabled by IT investment.
2. Organisational change programmes are much more successful when the people who are charged with their delivery are involved in deciding what needs to be done. Commitment stems from a shared perspective of key issues, a common sense of purpose and a candid acceptance of the trade-offs. (Barclay, 1987)
3. Results focused programmes, with clear personal targets and accountabilites, are more likely to succeed than those centred around activities. For example, ensuring that sales staff attend customer service training and tracking internal documentation standards, is less effective at delivering bottom line improvement than providing appropriate incentives on the basis of actual customer performance delivered. (Scaffer and Thomson, 1992)

In essence, the underlying logic of our approach is intuitive; to realise benefits from an IT investment, it is essential to plan implementation management right from the beginning of the evaluation cycle. This planning must include the business changes anticipated as well as provision of technical resources. Despite being intuitively obvious, this approach is not often applied.

If this is common sense, why don't people apply it universally? The answer varies. In some organisations a coercive management style precludes the necessary consultation between the scheme originator and those who will ultimately deliver it. In others it is the existence of strict, functional hierarchy which prevent cross communication. In others there may be 'class' issues which prevent discourse. In most it is the lack of priority attached to the project which prevents business management putting in the time.

IT related business benefit is derived from people changing the way they operate and interact. The probability of success in bringing about this change is increased by fostering a sense of ownership of the need for change. By involving those people, who in the end will actually deliver the change, as early as possible in the process of deciding what that change should be, this can be eased.

IT related business benefit cases are the accepted way of representing a proposed investment to the decision maker. These benefits cases predict the future. They seek to evaluate 'benefit' by calculating the difference between today's value of some appropriate measures and their future, projected values. Sophistication of this approach comes from the choice of measures and targets and from applying discounting due to risk. The benefits case for a particular investment proposal is therefore very open to manipulation by its supporters.

To address this, there must be no doubt that a proposal's supporters will be measured on their delivery performance. Every item of a benefits case should have an owner, and an incentive programme that encourages its owner to deliver to the expectation. Adding clearly defined time scales and resolving interdependencies, provides a clear set of personal accountabilites for management.

In summary the benefits case must be written so that, should the investment proposal go through, managers are clearly aware that their personal targets will reflect its expected benefit.

2. BACKGROUND TO RESEARCH

This chapter is the product of research carried out by the author and others at Nolan, Norton & Co European Institute, London Business School and EIS Ltd, and separately by KPMG. The author is grateful to KPMG for making the findings of the IMPACT (1992) study available for inclusion in this chapter.

3 UNDERSTANDING THE BUSINESS NEED FOR IT INVESTMENT

3.1 Why do companies invest in IT?

There are four generic approaches to justifying investment in IT (Nolan, Norton & Co, 1986), namely:

1. It will change the organisation's cost base for the better. This can mean cost reduction, where cost (in terms of people, assets or resources) is taken out. It can mean cost avoidance; where costs may stay the same but the organisation achieves a greater through put or capability. Cost replacement is sometimes given as a third category of cost benefit. It is a particular form of cost avoidance where overall cost is increased, but not as much as it would have done had a particular programme not been implemented.
2. It will bring about some increase in revenue. IT investments have been justified on the basis of their ability to improve customer service, give marketing departments better insight into markets and add features to products, sales or field service functions, etc.
3. It will improve management efficiency. IT investments have been justified by their impact on management span of control, speed of decision making, quality of decision making, 'comfort' and other factors.
4. It will deliver some strategic advantage. The strategic impact of IT investment has been the centre of some debate. Approaches include mapping potential investments to the organisation's Critical Success Factors (Rockart and Delong, 1988). Other approaches consider the likely impact of the proposed investment on a corporate business process model (Heduan, 1992). Another useful approach is to consider the impact of the investment on Core Competencies (Hundson, 1992).

There is also a fifth class of need which may be partially explained by all of the above. Fundamentally, human work is organised around flows of goods and services and increasingly, information. All organisations therefore have a fundamental need for storage, retrieval, processing and communication of information.

Readers will see that there is a clear distinction between benefits which are financial, or at least numeric in nature, and those which are 'less tangible'. It is the opinion of the author that, whilst 'less tangible' benefits have an important role to play in explaining and selecting amongst investment options, once selected delivery requires very clear quantified targets, bounded with definite timescale and clear, individual accountablilities.

3.2 Why do organisations question their investment in IT?

There are two reasons why an organisation may be questioning its investment in IT. On the one hand, it may consider that it does not have a need for IT, or, on the other, it may recognise its need, but the lack of any track record in gaining benefit makes it reluctant to sanction further investment. In other words, past experience with IT investment is 'it does not deliver'.

Since information is fundamental to the control and coordination of all human enterprise, reluctance dominates over ignorance of need. Indeed, when the press report that "Throughout industry, top executives are asking what returns they are getting from their investments in information technology" (*Sunday Times*, 21 June 1992), "The answer too often, is little or nothing", they are reinforcing the non-delivery message.

The task therefore is to define an investment appraisal and management approach which will make a clear, beneficial impact on the organisation. It is just such an approach which is described below.

4. TECHNIQUES FOR FOCUSING AND PRIORITISING IT INVESTMENT

The author uses a three phase process to focus and prioritise IT investment. The phases are: Surfacing of Issues, Generation of Opportunities; and Selection of Options. Each phase is outlined below.

4.1 Surfacing of issues

The purpose of the first phase is to decide what the objective of the IT investment should be. There is a need to identify, and to get agreement throughout the whole community of interest (senior management and middle managers responsible for a business unit), with what the business need is that must be addressed. This business need may be usefully thought of as the gap between where a company is now and where it needs to be.

This gap analysis can be approached in a number of ways, e.g. by considering what actions are necessary to deliver the 'Business Vision' and where IT may support this process. A similar approach can be used, but instead of starting with the vision, which can be esoteric, vague or simply impractical, the start point can be the documented business strategy. The third form of gap analysis is be based on some strategic opportunity for the organisation. In this third type of gap analysis, IT planning and business planning are closely linked. However, for all of these analyses, the community of interest must share a view of where the organisation is now, so that they can form an opinion of what needs to be done.

4.2 Generation of opportunities

The purpose of the second phase is to identify and document a reasonable number of investment opportunities. Decisions on strategic investments are more effective when an informed choice is made amongst a number of alternatives, rather than whether to adopt a single proposal or not. (See later for 'single option fallacy'.)

The documentation of these opportunities must include a benefits case for each. Since the decision of which investment opportunity to invest in will be based on trade-off between cost, risk and reward all these elements must be included. However, equally important is the fact that the benefits cases should make explicit linkage between the proposed IT investment and the business changes that will actually deliver the proposed benefit. They should also clearly identify sponsors and success measures, expressed as personal targets with mile stones and time scales.

In presenting the benefits case for evaluation, Thomas Davenport of Index (Pollard and Tapscott, 1989) believes that companies should categorise their investment opportunities in order to see which style of cost benefit analysis is appropriate because, he argues, it does not make sense to cost justify all types of systems in the same way.

Davenport categorises investment opportunities into four types depending on cost and certainty of success. If the cost of the investment opportunity is expected to be low, and the likely benefit certain, the investment belongs in the 'comfort' category. Investments in PCs are usually of this type. The main concern with these systems is aggregate cost rather than unitary investment cost.

Investments which are more expensive, but of known value, are be placed in the 'confidence' category. Thus, for example building a new G/L, or upgrading a mainframe, would be assessed on a return on investment basis. Little specific risk discounting is needed.

Low cost investment opportunities, that offer uncertain benefits are placed in the 'comfort' category. These systems should be viewed as small scale prototypes. They are a proving ground for the benefits case before too much resource is committed to their implementation. Again, aggregate cost and their impact on management time is the main concern.

On the other hand, high cost investments with uncertain benefits, which include most strategic investments, belong in the 'confusion' category. The main concern with this type of proposed investment is risk management and contingency planning.

The final choice of factors to include in the benefits case depends very much upon local management and accounting requirements. The author uses a combination of seven measures to describe an investment in benefit terms. The scale and certainty of investment is taken into account by the use of weighting.

The measures include a quantification of financial returns expected from the investment. However, they also include improvements in operational performance, fit to strategy, replacement need (i.e. an assessment of how badly performing is the existing process) and risk. Risk is expressed as 'chance of success' since all the benefits are additive. This approach has the advantage of using a number of factors to describe the potential investment which add to a single measure. However, by maintaining the individual identity of these factors, final selection can be made by the community of interest making trade-offs between each factor, from amongst their available investment options.

4.3 Option selection

The purpose of the third stage is selection of the investment opportunity. The final selection process is critical to effecting whether the benefits will be realised or not. The whole community of interest must decide its own approach to delivering. Helping a group reach consensus on a decision can be very difficult. Fortunately, a technique known as Decision Conferencing (or to be more correct, group multi-variant utility analysis) has been developed by the London School of Economics to facilitate group decision making (Barclay, 1987).

Decision analysis allows both hard (quantitative) and soft (qualitative) factors to be bought together in the decision for group discussion. The author has used this technique to great effect with groups engaged in strategic planning and IT investment option selection. The main advantage of this technique is that it builds a shared understanding of the trade-offs that have been made to reach a decision, and has provided a forum for everyone to feel 'consulted about the decision'.

Formally, there are six steps which must be carried out to gaining consensus for the decision (Barclay, 1987):

1. Generate a shared perspective of the key issues concerning the company. In any group, each individual may well have a different view of the problems and their situation.
2. Generate a common sense of purpose. Unless all members of the group are able to pull together, when implementation starts, the likelihood of success is dramatically reduced.
3. Align business measures with business goals. Inevitably when choosing a benefits case based upon some forecast of the future shape of the company. To be successful, an investment must put forward a benefits case that can be fitted into line manager's (and director's) targets. If the benefits case assumes certain changes to business measures, it is essentially that this is understood and agreed.
4. Manage strategically. Be prepared to abandon plans, measures and structures before they become obsolete.
5. Balance the conflicting objectives of the stake holders.
6. Face up to the trade-offs that have to be made between areas of responsibility.

The decision conference uses the benefits case from each proposed investment to allow comparison amongst them. If there really is only one option to evaluate, avoid the pitfall of evaluating it in isolation. To do so would be to fall for the 'single option fallacy (Barclay, 1987).

The single option fallacy assumes that to do something has costs and risks, but to do nothing is cost free and risk free. This is rarely the case. The do nothing option may represent an opportunity foregone, and may actually be a high risk scenario if there is some pressing need to take action of some sort.

5. MANAGING BENEFITS REALISATION

The 'soft' side of goal alignment is achieved by early involvement in the planning process. A shared understanding of corporate objectives and predicament acts as the trigger for change. However, the most important factor that governs successful delivery of the benefits plan is the degree to which it is aligned to the goals of the individuals who can deliver it. The higher the degree of goal congruence between personal and corporate goals, the greater will be the chance of their organisation getting the benefits it expects.

EIS Ltd have developed a consulting approach which helps its clients plan and implement business improvement. The consultancy uses an executive information systems (EIS) to facilitate easy monitoring and to provide feed back on organisational performance. The advantage of EIS technology is its rapid development and implementation.

Using an EIS it is possible to evolve management processes and represent them in 'real-time'. EIS development is fast enough to keep pace with organisational change as it occurs, allowing management to evolve to keep pace. 'GoalFocus', EIS Ltd's management tool, developed as a consequence of work carried out with British Steel and ICI, is being used to ensure the delivery of business benefit.

6. SUMMARY

The following is a simple set of recommendations which, if followed, will increase the likelihood of IT investment delivering business benefit.

6.1 Benefits case

1. Potential investments in IT must be seen in the context of their impact on the rest of the business. IS investment alone does not deliver business benefit.
2. Business cases should be produced by a cross functional team who will be delivering those benefits.
3. Benefits cases must be expressed in terms that the decision makers understand.

6.2 Choosing and focusing

1. Decision makers must choose amongst a number of options. There is no such

thing as a single option.
2. Choice should be made by the group who will be responsible for overseeing the business changes associated with the IS investment.

6.3 Delivering the benefits

1. The benefits case must contain quantified benefits, linked to individual responsibilities.
2. Some form of monitoring device (we suggest an EIS tool) should be used to provide immediate feedback on goal performance.
3. Business goals and individuals goals must link. The benefits case must be part of managers' targets or it will not get delivered.
4. Corporate incentives/sanctions scheme should be implemented/modified to encourage delivery of the plan, monitor and reassure people on how they are doing against their business objectives.

REFERENCES

Barclay, S (1987) *A users' guide to HIVIEW*, Decision Analysis Unit, London School of Economics and Political Science.

Heduan, M (1992) *Managing IT investment as a business process*, UNICOM conferences Ltd, Uxbridge, UK.

Hundson, D (1992) *Bridging the gap between IT and the business*, Business Intelligence Ltd.

IMPACT (1992) *Investment appraisal – a guide towards best practice*, KPMG Peat Marwick.

Nolan, Norton & Co.(1986) *IT Fundamentals*

Pollard, P L and Tapscott, R L (1989) *Investment Evaluation Methodology*, Digital Equipment Corporation.

Rockart, J F and Delong, D W (1988) *Executive Support Systems*, Dow Jones Irwin.

Scaffer, R H and Thomson, H A (1992) Successful change programmes begin with results, *Harvard Business Review*.

9 Managing IT investments as a business process

Mick Heduan
British Telecommunications plc

1. INTRODUCTION

Information is the 'Super Resource' (Yates, 1990) available to managers in today's business environment. Information can become the tool which differentiates organisations in competitive markets. Information is the key to competitive survival and more importantly, a key to competitive advantage.

The modern delivery vehicle for this super resource is Information Technology (IT). IT should ensure that the right information is delivered to the right person at the right time in the right form. Investments in IT should be given special consideration by organisations. All investments in IT should be managed effectively, and the management of IT investments should be a key business process. Only then will organisation have a super resource at their disposal that can enhance business performance, customer satisfaction and increase shareholder value.

This chapter outlines some of the many activities carried out by British Telecommunications (BT) between 1988 and 1992 in the area of Process Management, focusing particularly on BT''s ability to manage IT investments.

All these activities have provided a significant contribution to increasing shareholder value, customer service and the quality of products and services BT provide to its customers and stakeholders alike.

2. HISTORY AND BACKGROUND

Between 1988 and 1990 BT conducted a *Strategic Systems Plan* (SSP) study (Brown *et al.*, 1990). The study covered the following main steps:

- Creating a logical business model of the Present Operations (PO)
- Confirming business direction
- Establishing a logical business model for Future Operations (FO).

The strategic modelling aspects of this study were carried out using Information Engineering (IE) techniques. At the time, the SSP study was considered one of the largest applications of computer-aided software engineering (CASE). The

CASE tool Information Engineering Workbench (IEW) was used to support the modelling activities of the study.

2.1 Creating the Future Operations (FO) business model

In the first phase, BT's top level objectives were analysed to determine what major functions the business should carry out. These functions were then progressively broken down to a suitable level where the activities could be expressed as processes with a definable start and end point. This decomposition of processes continued down to the fourth level from the top, which was considered to provide a sufficient level of detail.

At the same time, data flow diagrams were produced capturing the interfaces between processes and the information flows between them. Subsequently, other stages of information engineering methodology were used to scope the logical process model into business areas, producing a comprehensive record and model of the Future Operations.

The production of this business model, which concentrated on UK operations only, was a major step forward on the path towards having a top-down structured approach for the specification of business processes and IT support systems.

The model was then divided into blocks of closely related functions and processes forming strategic systems areas. These areas subsequently provided the proposals for the realisations of systems, that is the IT and IT-related investments necessary to support the process objective.

In addition to the work of the SSP study, policies were developed to assist the smooth migration from the existing applications, technical and data architecture, to those needed to support the Future Operations model. Applications, technical and data architectures and standards reflecting these policies were produced for company-wide guidance.

Two of the key Business Processes contained within the FO model are the Manage Information Resource and Plan Business processes. The work detailed in the remainder of this chapter was dedicated to improving these processes with the over-arching objective of improving the management of IT investments in BT.

3. IT ECONOMICS IN BT

BT is a huge organisation which depends fundamentally on IT to survive. After all, the telephone network itself is a huge example of IT and network technology.

Within such an organisation it is always difficult to separate out IT spend from spend on the network infrastructure. However, an indication of the size of BT's IT spend can be drawn from figures available for mid-1989–90. Pay cost was approximately £141m, non-pay cost was approximately £120m and capital spend reached £128m out of a total capital budget of £210m[1].

These figures demonstrate the scale of spend associated with large support, infrastructure, integrated and strategic systems development investments. The following example illustrates the scale of some of the business problems being addressed by the effective use of IT within BT.

3.1 A typical project – circa 1990

BT runs its own Motor Transport Organisation. We are all familiar with the BT van, now with its grey livery and reflective BT logo on the side. Behind the vans is a large organisation in its own right, the Motor Transport Organisation.

To illustrate the size of Motor Transport as an internal service organisation, the following data was applicable during the first half of 1990. One IT project, DRIVE (Heduan, 1990a), an integrated IT type investment, was being developed to transform Motor Transport into a professional, customer responsive, efficient and effective fleet management organisation, to be run on commercial principles.

The BT fleet at the time was colossal, consisting of 36,000 light vans, 31,000 heavy goods vehicles and 12,000 cars. Maintenance and repair cost alone were exceeding £2.5m per annum. Motor Transport staff costs were running at £45m and fuel costs were averaging £35m. BT were also running over 200 fully equipped transport workshops capable of meeting all types of servicing and repair work.

The challenge behind DRIVE was to transform the existing separate systems base, which suffered from poor support, capacity problems, outdated hardware, duplication of process and no single database into a single integrated system, giving increased management control, reduced support costs and increased visibility. This was to be achieved technically using a single IDMS/X database running on the BT INTERNET (ONA) secure managed network.

However, the transformation of the Motor Transport organisation was not attributable only to DRIVE. Several enablers were in place to effect this transformation. These included the introduction of a Quality Management System (QMS), local financial control, using industry standard costing techniques and the implementation of a Just In Time materials strategy. In this respect, DRIVE represented a typical project in BT where the impact of IT was just one of a number of factors affecting change.

4. MAKING BUSINESS PROCESSES WORK

Business processes do not exist and work in isolation. Processes must interact

---

[1]For the purpose of this chapter, IT investments that form part of the main telephone network infrastructure, such as digital exchanges, are excluded from the discussion.

smoothly with each other to contribute to fulfiling common business goals and objectives. This implies that business processes must be dynamic.

In BT the task of translating a business need or requirement supporting strategy and business objectives into an IT based solution satisfying that need was a function of the relationships between the business processes Plan Business and Manage the Information Resource.

However, the simple existence of such well documented and structured business processes is not enough to ensure that IT investments are managed effectively and business requirements are met. The processes need ownership, commitment and need to be supported by tools, techniques and training that facilitate best practice throughout the end-to-end performance of the process.

In the case of BT it was necessary to overhaul the organisation's traditional approach towards IT investments. This required a radical and innovative move towards changing many of the well established processes used for producing business cases. The critical factor, however, in BT – as with most large organisations – is getting senior managers to accept IT as being a primary vehicle for change. Only then will the commitment, support and enthusiasm towards introducing IT exist to the degree required to successfully manage IT investments.

Some of the tools and techniques which have been developed to support and improve the above processes are discussed in detail in the following sections.

5. IMPROVING PROCESS PERFORMANCE

5.1 Developing new tools and techniques

In December 1989, a study of the available processes used for IT benefits analysis and investment appraisal techniques was undertaken. During the study a comparison of some eight different processes took place. This comparison was against what BT considered to be an optimum process at the time.

Some of the more well known processes evaluated in the comparison were, SESAME (Lincoln, 1990) and Return On Management (Strassmann). The comparison included a mix of BT oriented processes and external methodologies and, using decision analysis, critically evaluated each process against a set criteria. These criteria contained the desirable attributes of a process BT would like to have in place for the future.

The decision analysis output produced a league table of the original eight processes ranked in order of their ability to achieve BT's desired process requirements.

The next stage was to take the best attributes of the top three scoring processes and develop these into BT's optimum process. This was done by adding functionality and making the result more BT specific. The outcome of this exercise was the development of the 'Benefits Evaluation of Systems and Technology' process (BEST) (Heduan, 1990b).

The BEST process was unique within BT in that it's key features involved identifying, evaluating and quantifying intangible benefits and linking both tangible and intangibles to the key Business Processes, either existing processes or those still under development in the SSP project.

At the macro level BEST offered the business an opportunity to rank IT investment proposals by their worth, both to the business strategy and key business processes, using intangible benefits along side tangible benefits.

This enabled a trade-off to take place ensuring the best overall business impact from any given set of IT investments. At the micro level BEST gave visibility to the benefits that would be potentially available to a single business process. This information could be used to set objectives and targets for managers who were responsible for managing the IT project or the business process supported by the project.

The major drawback, however, with the BEST process was that the quantification of intangible benefits, although nevertheless rigorous in detail, was subjective. This subjective evaluation was viewed with considerable scepticism by the accountants and bodies who approved business cases before committing capital to the project. As a result a more robust and scientific methodology was sought which would reduce the risk surrounding subjective quantification.

5.2 The information economics approach

With the assistance of Professor P K M'Pherson (City University and M'Pherson Systems Ltd), BT introduced the Information Economics approach for IT investment appraisal. Software tools were employed to facilitate assessment, weighting and combinatorial rules in 'utility space', in terms of an IT investment's monetary value and strategic worth.

This work was directly linked with the BEST process helping define areas of potential benefit and linking them to existing processes from the SSP process model.

The approach to Information Accounting (INFACC) (MacPherson, 1990) assessed monetary value using Return On Investment (ROI) with an emphasis on locating and measuring 'trickle through' effects by following work strings beyond the immediate systems domain. It followed a model developed in manufacturing automation which views the information impact of 'islands' of IT on the entire business process.

The strategic value within (INFACC) is assessed in a combinatorial matrix of basic attributes. These are assigned subjective values (between 0 and unity) and weights corresponding to their relative importance within the company. Senior managers would be directly involved in weighting the attributes according to their contribution to the company's overall strategic objectives. These attributes were expressed as follows.

- *Strategic Alignment* – the relative support for one or more business strategies.
- *Competitive Advantage* – the improved posture the investment will foster with regard to market and conditions.
- *Organisational Risk* – the effect the change has on the organisation.
- *Technological Risk* – the skills currently available for the project and whether the technology is mature enough.
- *Core Information Requirements* – the relative satisfaction of the information and decision making needs of the business.
- *System Structure* – how the system aligns with the technological, information and infrastructure strategies.
- *Personal Quality* – the perceived improvements in job satisfaction, environment, human–computer interaction, personal or group facilities.
- *Managerial Quality* – the impact on managerial capability through communications, information access and quality and decision support.

5.3 Investment expert system tool kit (InVEST) (Heduan and Bonner, 1990)

During the spring of 1990 BT joined a European Working Party formed to address the issues and concerns arising out of managing the benefits of IT investments. The working party was organised by the Nolan Norton European Institute who were part of the KPMG group. The working party was also supported by the London Business School.

The working party consisted of three key bodies, the 'Gurus and Academics', 'Consultants' and 'Users'. The convergence of these experts presented an ideal opportunity to address in detail ways of overcoming the main concerns of senior managers regarding IT investments.

Over a period of several months the main issues were extracted from the users by the consultants, objectively addressed by the gurus and the results packaged in the form of a self-assessment diagnostic health check, to be used by senior managers in the participating organisations.

The check list constituted current best practice in the process of managing IT investments. A four stage process model was constructed addressing opportunity identification, decision making, management of change and measurement of results, surrounding IT investment proposals.

In BT the checklist itself was transformed through the use of IT. The original diagnostic checklist was expanded to include an additional stage, an action plan for improvements. This action plan was based on the response the IT decision maker/investor made to each stage of the original four stage process model, and was geared to improving any weaknesses in their approach.

The entire model, now consisting of a five stage process, and more BT oriented was encapsulated within the concept of an Expert System. Market research was conducted within BT to establish the reaction of senior managers to each of the five stages, and a prototype expert system, InVEST, was built around the second stage, the decision making process.

InVEST linked an investment proposal to key businesses processes and suggested potential benefit areas within that process domain. InVEST could guide the user through the maze of problems associated with producing business cases and managing IT investments. InVEST was informative, introducing the user to the world of investment appraisal and, using hypertext, explained the meaning behind accounting terminology that often confused managers.

Expert systems are often perceived as a threat and a form of de-skilling requiring a sensitive approach towards their use. These factors, coupled with a major change to the organisation, placed many barriers along the path to the full use of an expert system for IT investment appraisal within BT. However, as a prototype, developed to explore the concept and principles of using an expert system for IT investment appraisals, InVEST was greeted with enthusiasm and support.

It must be recognised, though, that there are some products, tools or techniques that, despite being of sound origin and unquestionable value, are too innovative for organisations to accept and handle. In certain cases, the organisation may not be ready to accept the use of expert systems or new benefits analysis techniques for reasons of culture, politics and tradition.

6. CHANGE

6.1 Factors affecting and influencing change

The one thing that remains constant in organisations today is change. But why does change happen at all? There are many internal and external factors that drive change at a rapid pace. These should be understood and managed effectively if successful change is to result with minimum long-term negative effects.

Moss Kanter (1991) suggests there are up to five forces that affect change. These are seen as:

(a) departure from tradition,
(b) a crisis,
(c) a new strategic direction,
(d) prime motivators, and

(e) action vehicles.

The change resulting from IT projects usually behave like the forces at (a) and (b).

It is essential that change, as mentioned above, is managed in addition to the effects IT projects can bring. An effective change process requires leadership, infrastructure, education and visibility of all the change factors affecting an organisation. This process must work in harmony with the process of managing IT investments.

6.2 Accepting IT as a vehicle for change

A fundamental requirement for effective management of IT investments is that organisations accept that IT is a key vehicle for change. It is widely acknowledged that cost justification of IT is more complex than for many other investment decisions. It is nevertheless essential that it be undertaken and that it be conducted giving special consideration to IT as being the vehicle for change. However, not all change through IT can easily be expressed in neat, tangible, positive cash flows supporting a traditional cost benefit model of investment appraisal.

Like BT, most large service organisations have been through the phase where the impact of IT investments could be clearly seen in terms of reductions in staffing levels and increased productivity. Many of today's IT investments bring about changes that differentiate and transform organisations and give a competitive edge. This often involves increasing staffing levels in the early days to realise benefits in the longer term.

IT investments must be appraised and managed with this in mind, otherwise the most organisations can expect is competitive survival.

Accepting the impact of IT in this way requires a new approach to IT investment appraisal. This in turn requires new tools and techniques that focus on the intangible soft benefits and allows expression of these against business and marketing objectives. Areas such as profit contribution, revenue protection, revenue generation, staff morale, customer loyalty and corporate image, to mention but a few, should be included in the analysis.

Traditional methods of investment appraisal are inappropriate as they tend to focus on the capital cost of the technology, and not on the value of the information and its contribution to business and marketing objectives.

Organisations must therefore be prepared to experiment with alternative methods of evaluating IT investments. An investment portfolio will have a radically different impact on the performance of the business if projects are ranked when the focus of prioritisation is on intangible benefits that support marketing and business objectives, rather than the capital cost of the project.

6.3 Organisational change – Project Sovereign

In a world of turbulent change BT's aim remains constant, to become the most successful world-wide telecommunications group.

The days of being a monopoly supplier, serving subscribers in an unregulated market with no competition are long gone. The new BT is slimmer, more responsive, efficient, committed to continuous improvement and strives to meet the expectations of it's customers and stake holders alike.

Since the late 1980s a number of change programmes have been instituted in BT. Many of these programmes have long time scales involving major cultural and organisational change. They include the company-wide roll out of TQM principles, the introduction of Quality Management Systems (QMSs), registration to BS5750 and ISO9001 standards, and the restructuring of BT's operations. The 'Putting The Customer First' campaign was at the heart of all these programmes.

During the spring of 1990, Project Sovereign introduced change of major proportions. The entire company was again re-focused to put the customer first. New BT values were introduced, quality imperatives were set, a customer commitment was made and the culture of the organisation began the slow process of change.

Experience with these changes has demonstrated that in the absence of an effective process to manage change, large-scale change can stifle innovation and creativity and take years to recover from. A change process is required that can harness the innovation and creativity developed in the old organisation, and migrate ideas, concepts, motivation and opportunities to the new organisation. Without such a mechanism, process improvement initiatives, that increase shareholder value and customer service, may be lost for ever or reinvented at a considerable cost.

7. THE CURRENT SITUATION

7.1 Process management improvements

BT is a complex company. The complexities arise in providing a large number of products and services to varying types of customer in many locations in the UK and across the globe using a common network and common infrastructure of supporting processes and systems.

Providing and improving BT's products and services requires a detailed knowledge of what activities need to be carried out to deliver them and how these activities interact with each other. This knowledge enables change to be assessed in any part of the company to determine the impact on customer requirements and how they can be met in the optimum way.

The objective behind process management is therefore to improve service to customers by developing and rolling out an integrated set of streamlined processes with supporting systems and data.

The processes, which should be flexible and resilient to change, should be designed to be executed to a consistent standard across the company. The design of business processes should be recorded at a single reference point. The point used for establishing and improving processes in BT is known as the BT Business Model (BTBM) (BT, 1992). The BTBM forms the formal repository for the company of it's analysis of business activities. The model defines BT in terms of its processes, their inter-dependencies and the information that these processes need to operate.

The original work on the SSP Future Operations Model, as described above, has been used as the foundation for today's business model and has undergone many improvements. However, in September 1991 the Process Management Programme Control Board established Process Improvement projects to address the support processes for the planning and provision of information systems and planning and controlling the business.

The critical importance of these processes as an enabler for change and their fundamental role in the achievement of business goals is now well recognised by senior managers in the company.

The perceived performance of the existing processes was that they could not meet the demands placed on them by the changing business environment. A project team have therefore charged with identifying radical improvements to these processes.

Some of these process improvements will be achieved through introducing new tools and techniques such as those discussed earlier in this chapter.

In addition to the above, a new support process is being developed called 'Manage The Process For Change'. This process will be designed to assist the organisation in handling rapid and constant change. It's focus will be the non-system changes, e.g. people, skills and organisation. Within this process change requirements will be defined and the control of change will take place through authorising and managing change programmes and projects. A 'Validate and Verify Change' stage is also being proposed which will act as the end-to-end quality assurance process for all aspects of change.

8. CONCLUSIONS

1. Organisations must accept there is no magic solution, no 'off-the-shelf' answer to the problems surrounding the management of IT investments. There will always be a wealth of potential solutions on offer with consultants offering a helping hand and an important objective view of the situation. However, organisations must work hard to integrate off-the-shelf solutions within their company's culture, tradition, rate of change, accounting practices and political regime.

2. Senior managers must be committed to accepting the power of IT and its ability to change organisations and improve business performance. Information delivered through IT must be seen as and treated as a 'Super Resource' to the company. Information must be seen as an asset having real value.
3. Organisations must experiment with new innovative investment appraisal processes, and they must be given a chance to demonstrate their efficacy. These processes, once proven, should form the tools and techniques that support the key process of managing IT investments.
4. Realisation of IT benefits should be clearly linked to the company's Management By Objectives (MBO) system. Benefit plans should be in place along with the appropriate target setting and measurement processes. Managers must accept they are responsible for the delivery of benefits .
5. Business Processes and Process management must be the key driver behind managing IT investments. The processes for 'Planning and Providing Information Systems', 'Planning and Controlling the Business' and 'Managing Change', in BT, are key to successful management of IT investments and should work in harmony.
6. The use of Knowledge Based Systems (KBSs) or expert systems to assist in the management of IT investments should be considered seriously, whether for use in pro-active mode, as a learning aid, or in reactive mode, as a macro tool for analysing IT proposals. The principles behind the InVEST prototype expert system are still applicable in BT today.

REFERENCES

British Telecom Business Model – BTBM Handbook, BT Process Management Unit, 1992.

Brown, D W, Bell, R C and Mountford, J A (1990) Strategic Planning Of Business Operations & Information Systems, *British Telecommunications Engineering*, 9, April.

Heduan, M J (1990a) *A Study of the DRIVE IT Investment for the NNEI Working Party*, June.

Heduan, M J (1990b) *Benefits Evaluation Of Systems & Technology – BEST – Process Documentation and Guidelines*, January.

Heduan, M J and Bonner, C J (1990) *InVEST – A Prototype Expert System on Managing the Benefits of IT Investments*, Delivery Report September.

Lincoln, T (1990) SESAME – *Managing Information Systems For Profit*, John Wiley & Sons.

M'Pherson, P K(1990) *INFACC Information Accounting Project For British Telecommunications*, M'Pherson Systems Ltd.

Moss-Kanter, R (1983) *The Change Masters*, Unwin Paperbacks, London

Strassmann, P *Return On Management – Measuring ITs Contribution To The Business*, Strassmann Inc.

Yates, H J (1990) Information Resource Management, *British Telecommunications Engineering*, **9**, April.

10 Evaluating risk in major IT projects

Catherine Griffiths
IC-Parc, Imperial College, London
Leslie Willcocks
Oxford Institute of Information Management

1. INTRODUCTION

Some major IT projects succeed in delivering outstanding paybacks – most do not. Contrary to the hype and raised expectations that usually accompany announcements predicting immense gains to be made, most fail to deliver the promised benefits. Managers find that once a major IT project commences, complexity and scale introduce a whole realm of new problems not originally anticipated. In these circumstances, a fire fighting approach to management often develops, the focus is lost and the IT project quickly runs out of control. Consequently, it is found that most major IT projects collapse after a considerable waste of resources, effort and mis-directed funding.

The main body of analysis (Collingridge, 1992; Davidson and Huot, 1991; Morris and Hough, 1987) about why major projects fail has tended to concentrate on explanations of individual project circumstances for the purposes of allocating blame. Evaluation of any outcomes is rare because investigation of failures usually re-inforces the picture that in most cases the projects should never have been started. Evaluation of successful projects is even rarer because it is often considered unnecessary. When the management, control, direction and focus are effective the payoffs become obvious. Either way, this has left the impression amongst many that the management of major IT projects is ultimately a question of luck.

While analysis of individual cases is always helpful, this approach alone has not led to a significant improvement in the number of major IT project successes. Rather, it has tended to emphasise the difficulty of managing these projects and to highlight their individuality. The evidence suggests that systematic breakdown of procedures and analysis does not provide a sufficiently robust method for introducing success in future projects. It was this fact that prompted the current investigation, and has led to some reappraisal of major IT projects of national significance. The aim is to establish a better understanding of the interplay of factors that influence the outcome of these projects, and to investigate the extent to which the evaluation of risk forms part of any process.

Research shows that little analysis has been undertaken to assist with the definition, understanding and control of risk within major IT projects. The issues surrounding the organisation, resources and management of these projects have frequently been considered so great that scale and complexity have provided an umbrella of excuses for poor or partial delivery of objectives. Overall, it appears that risk factors are not considered as a main variable in projects, and consequently they are massively underplayed and under-assessed. This approach stems from a lack of understanding of what risk is and how it operates in major IT projects. From these studies it can be seen that in successful cases risk may not have been managed better as a separate component but rather that over-riding imperatives may have forced control of risk in a way that has delivered a successful outcome. In other projects, the lack of any over-riding imperatives may be one of the causes of failure and therefore a contributor to higher risk levels (Griffiths and Willcocks, 1994). By making the risks more explicit, it is hoped to set the parameters for what is realistically possible, what risks need to be reduced, and how their management can be pursued to increase the likelihood of successful major IT projects in the future.

Four major IT projects have been selected for investigation. Only one of these cases has been regarded as a truly successful implementation: the TradeNet system of Singapore. This is an electronic data interchange (EDI) system introduced to facilitate the handling of all documentation for trade passing through the country's ports. Another case study used here is the French Minitel videotex system because it demonstrates a partially successful implementation of a major IT project. The introduction of Minitel was an attempt to deliver a national form of electronic communications which would attract a large domestic usage. The last two cases investigated are the Computerised Rural Information Systems Project (CRISP) of India, which aimed to improve the allocation of resources to the rural poor; and the Transfer and Automated Registration of Uncertified Stock (TAURUS), the system proposed for Stock Exchange dealings in the City of London. It was supposed to automate the back office paperwork processes which confirmed share deals that had been executed. All four case studies have been considered of national importance to their initiators, to have been unique in their objectives, and to have required specialist combinations of abilities that are unlikely to have existed on any previous projects.

It will be argued in this chapter that risk, far from being an uncontrollable variable outside the scope of project planning, is an integral part of an approach which can be evaluated and managed. This will be done by starting with a review of the main problems experienced in managing major projects in general, before progressing to an analysis of the problems of managing IT projects in particular. A review of risk issues and the frameworks that have been proposed for dealing with them will be carried out before discussing four case studies to demonstrate the practical issues involved in evaluating risk. The significant risks experienced in major IT projects will be investigated and a framework will be put forward for assisting in the prediction and management of risk in future projects.

2. PROBLEMS IN MAJOR PROJECTS

An analysis of case studies and a review of existing literature about major projects in general shows that most experience overruns, are often over budget, do not perform in the way expected, involve severe strain on participating institutions, or are cancelled prior to their completion after the expenditure of considerable sums of money (Appleton, 1991; Currie, 1994; Davidson and Huot, 1991; De Greene, 1991; Donovan, 1993; OTR Group, 1992; Willcocks and Margetts, 1994). A summary of the evidence suggests that these problems relate essentially to issues of size, complexity, long time span, uncertainty, governance and management peculiar to larger scale projects. While all major projects are notoriously difficult to define in detail or to predict accurately, it is found that with major IT projects the IT component adds a different dimension of risk which tips the balance towards project failure rather than towards project success (Collingridge, 1992). As a result, most major IT projects fall short of their original objectives, are aborted before full implementation or require massive amounts of additional funding to deliver what was originally envisaged. IT therefore appears to add a component of complexity and uncertainty not usually present in major projects that do not involve technology.

3. PROBLEMS IN MAJOR IT PROJECTS

Moving from major projects to the problems experienced from managing IT in general, it is found that a range of cultural, technological, educational, communication and business implications flow from decisions to introduce new technology (Keen, 1991; Scott Morton, 1991). Many of these problems are definable and can be incorporated within an effective management framework (Earl, 1989). However, in a majority of projects these issues are not addressed as part of the process of management but are handled as unexpected outcomes. As a result, many technology projects are characterised by crisis management and fire-fighting rather than by adherence to a well structured plan (Charette, 1991; Hochstrasser and Griffiths, 1991). Recent studies (Bessant, 1991; Earl, 1989; Willcocks and Margetts, 1993) show the following shortcomings in IT-based projects:

- lack of a unified strategic framework;
- lack of organisational adaptation to complement technological change;
- IT supplier problems with hype preceding delivery;

- poor management of change leading to inappropriate organisational and project structures, processes and culture;
- over emphasis on the 'technical fix';
- a misguided belief in technology leading to unwanted products or services;
- lack of skills to support implementation;
- lack of exploration of a wide range of options, resulting in the exclusion of lower technology alternatives.

Current research (Willcocks and Griffiths, 1994) has also shown that the lack of relevant quality assessment measures has contributed to problems in IT projects. The definitions of quality vary with each project, according to circumstances and specific objectives. Compromises have to be made to take account of resources, timescales and costs; however, it is found that quality assessment is often omitted from this process altogether. The quality assessment approach that needs to be considered can be at three distinct stages: the planning, control and improvement levels. Each of these parts of the project definition and management can be structured specifically to ensure they contribute to overall effectiveness. Slippage in projects can often be related back to a breakdown in this quality assessment process. The positive benefits of quality control can be seen in the TradeNet case study, particularly when contrasted with the approaches adopted in the TAURUS implementation or with CRISP.

Many technology projects eventually become successful implementations despite experiencing some or all of these problems. Post mortems and evaluation show, however, that for the majority projects costs could have been controlled better and delivery dates maintained if these areas of management had been addressed more effectively at the outset (Iliff, 1994; Strassmann, 1985).

4. RISK IN MAJOR IT PROJECTS

Risks in computer-based IS projects are surprisingly under-managed. The surprise comes when the large size of Information Technology (IT) expenditure and the history of disappointed expectations is considered (Hochstrasser and Griffiths, 1991; Keen, 1991). Surveys regularly report IT introduction and usage as a high risk, hidden cost process. As one example, a recent OTR Group survey, in reviewing IT projects over the previous 10 years in 200 organisations, found that for projects over £660,000, 90% were over budget, 98% had changed specification, 60% were over time, and 20% were inappropriate (OTR Group, 1992). Despite this, significant omissions occurred at investment appraisal stage, with only 30% of the companies surveyed applying any risk analysis. Indeed, there is a lack of managerial use of risk analysis in capital budgeting decisions generally, with one study finding managers lacking the required understanding to apply formal approaches and/or unable to find an approach that is systematic, easy to apply and cost-effective (Pike and Ho, 1991). Such under-analysis of risk is also common in major IT projects, despite the higher risks involved. Three neglected areas, where particular risks have been identified, are (Griffiths and Willcocks, 1994): when new technology is introduced; where stakeholders interests have not been incorporated; and where risk/reward benefits have not been assessed.

4.1 New technology

Working with new technology always introduces heightened levels of risk, (Hochstrasser and Griffiths, 1991; Willcocks and Margetts, 1993), which in turn affect the timing, costs and delivery deadlines. Delays due to research and development, as well as experimentation, may also result in unexpected or unwanted results. These factors can cause original projects to be sidetracked and initial objectives to be changed, with insufficient appreciation of the wider implications. More often, time pressure results in experimentation passing into fully-fledged implementation before a sufficient testing phase, with sub-optimal consequences when the technology is operationalised, and large on-going 'maintenance' costs. As Collingridge (1992) has shown, when the dimension of scale is added, all too many technology-based projects fail, or at least sub-optimise, because the technology has been too experimental for the scope of what is being undertaken. This may particularly be the case where governments sponsor major projects and where there are national aspirations inherent in equating technological innovation with economic progress (Madon, 1992).

In all four case studies below, governments saw new technology projects as embodying some aspect of national pride, and consequently exerted influence on them to different degrees. In Singapore, the government took the lead and ensured a strong control throughout the project. In India, the government's initial interest was superseded by political elections and so waned for a time, while in France Minitel has only succeeded because of the high profile the government continued to take to ensure the allocation of financial resources. With the TAURUS project the government was involved but not as a facilitator, rather as an observer, who could interfere when necessary.

4.2 Stakeholder risks

Risk is involved in all IT projects, but here it is understood to be the negative outcome that has a known or estimated probability of occurrence based on experience or some theory (Charette, 1991). Risk of a negative outcome only becomes a salient problem when the outcome is relevant to stakeholder concerns and interests. Different settings and stakeholders will see different outcomes as salient.

Examples of these different stakeholder interests will vary in a project depending on the impact the project will have on such key issues as whether jobs are to be lost, financial gain to be increased, or spheres of influence and control to be altered. In TAURUS the groups who were to suffer from any technical implementation of business processes were the Registrars. This stakeholder interest was neglected and so the registrars could see no benefit in working to achieve a successful project outcome. In contrast, with the TradeNet case the stakeholders who lost out over discussions on detail were able to benefit from a more effective system which generated greater profitability. With CRISP stakeholders could see centralisation of information as a threat to their local autonomy and therefore participants subverted the systems being applied.

4.3 Risk and reward

A fundamental part of risk assessment is to identify the risk in terms of its probability and impact, then evaluate what might be the acceptable tradeoffs between risk and reward. One problem with many of the financial and statistical techniques often applied to assess risk is that decisions on the risk-reward tradeoff are invariably arrived at through what has been called a 'formal-rational analysis'. This assumes a high degree of objectivity in the calculations; moreover the appearance of objectivity can be enhanced by expressing the calculations and results in numerical form. Business managers often favour this form of risk control because the potential advantages of IT investments can be balanced against the chances that predicted outcomes may not materialise. It has been found, however, that managers may scale down the size of expected project benefits to try and minimise the risks that are inherent in a project proposal. By doing this they frequently can claim the projects to be 'safe' (Strassmann, 1990). Objective analysis under these circumstances becomes difficult, and can often decline into a process of completing paperwork without undertaking sufficiently rigorous investigation.

The problem with a dependence on formal-rational risk analysis is that it omits the influence and impact of such crucial factors as perceptions, politics, culture and attitude to risk which cut across all such analysis and decision-making in fundamental ways. As all four case studies discussed below show, it is these factors which either work towards or against creating ultimate success or failure in the projects.

Risk analysis is a process in itself, and should not be regarded as a single event (Hay and Williamson, 1991). All the evidence suggests that risks will change over time. One-off assessments are not sufficient for effective control because this cannot take account of the dynamic aspects of risk management. This difficulty explains why risk evaluation is often neglected in practice. An illustration of this changing risk is, for example, where an experimental prototyping operation has been successful but fails to provide the same benefits when introduced on a company-wide or country-wide level, as is demonstrated by the CRISP project in India. The risk profile of a major project needs to set the parameters of what is realistically possible, what risks need to be reduced and how their management can be pursued.

5. RISK FRAMEWORKS FOR MAJOR IT PROJECTS

A number of frameworks have been generated from research and experience to assist risk assessment at the feasibility stage of IT projects. The Cash, McFarlan and McKenney (1992) framework suggests that there are at least three important project dimensions that influence the inherent implementation risk. These are: project size (staffing levels, elapsed time, cost, number of departments affected), experience with the technology, and project structure (a highly structured project with fixed, certain outputs not subject to change during the lifetime of the project experiences less risk). A version of how these factors relate to one another, and engender different levels of risk, is shown in Figure 10.1. This provides a simple

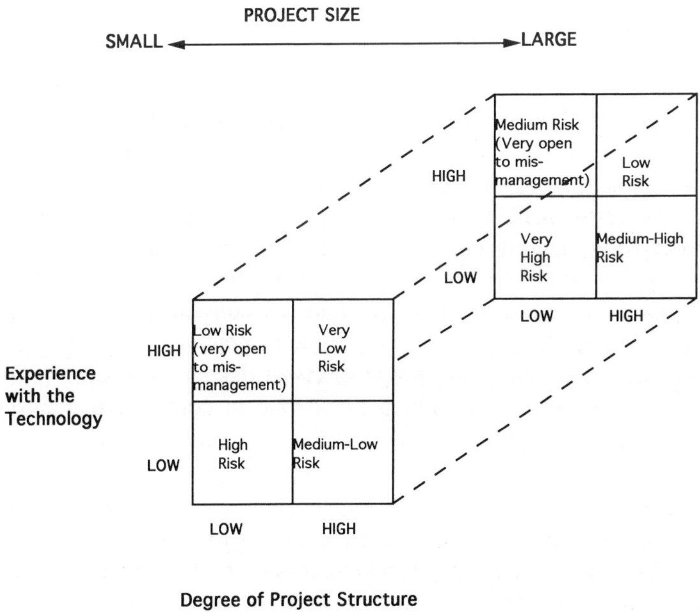

Figure 10.1 Introducing risk frameworks (adapted from Cash *et al.*, 1992)

and useful starting point for analysing risk, and serves to highlight why large-scale IT projects are inherently risky.

The framework developed by Parker, Benson and Trainor (1988), has defined five major risk areas that need to be assessed:

- Organisational risk – looking at how equipped an organisation is to implement the project in terms of personnel, skills and experience;
- IS infrastructure risk – assessing how far the entire IS organisation needs and is prepared to support the project;
- Definitional uncertainty – assessing the degree to which the requirements and/or the specifications of the project are known. Also assessed are the complexity of the area and the probability of non-routine changes;
- Competitive response – assessing the degree of corporate risk associated with not undertaking the project; (for major projects the risk may be to many organisations or even perceived as a national one);
- Technical uncertainty – evaluating a project's dependence on new or untried technologies.

Clearly attitudinal, cultural and political issues greatly influence risk perception and the way it is handled (Douglas and Wildavsky, 1983). In every project different settings and stakeholders will see different outcomes as salient or relevant to them. Unless these interest groups are convinced of the rewards, their own involvement will be minimal and will almost certainly be counter-productive to the eventual project outcome (Das Gupta, 1989; Madon, 1991; Patel, 1987).

Two components for the control of risk are defined more strongly by Dougherty and Fragola (1988). These are the necessity of separating out what constitutes risk assessment from what is simply risk management. According to their definitions, risk assessment is about the process and procedures used for identifying, characterising, quantifying and evaluting risks and their significance. Risk management, on the other hand, refers to any techniques used either to minimise the probability of an accident or to mitigate its consequences with, for instance, good engineering, design, improved operating practices or continuous maintenance procedures. Separating out these aspects of risk and how they apply provides a more realistic structure in which to operate to control the relevant forces which often combine to cause projects to fail.

Further work on the cognitive perspectives of risk taking by Kahneman and Lovallo (1993) illustrates that decision makers regard most projects as unique and fall into the trap of disregarding the statistics of the past as well as the opportunities of the future. As a result, it is found that forecasts of future outcomes are often anchored on plans of success rather than on past results. If this is combined with the lack of appreciation of the aggregate effects of looking at single risks it is found that predictions of success are commonly over-estimated at the commencement of a project. This approach characterised the pre-implementation of both Minitel and TAURUS although the determination on the part of the French government has sustained the former implementation. With TAURUS, the initial project has collapsed.

In the following case studies very different management approaches will be compared to show how risk issues have been addressed. Although it is over-simplistic to split these studies into successes and failures, two cases, TradeNet and Minitel, have provided some positive payback to their stakeholders. CRISP and TAURUS have not done so directly. They have, however, now both been re-defined drastically and re-focussed since the original investments were made.

6. SINGAPORE TRADENET: TOWARD AN INFORMATION ECONOMY

6.1 Background

The application of IT in the Singapore TradeNet system has been portrayed as a major success story (Collingridge, 1992; Donovan, 1993; King and Konsynski, 1990; Sisodia, 1992). What made the project so effective? One major aspect was that by 1985 Singapore's pre-eminent trading position was being threatened by the prospect of severe recession combined with an escalation of Far East competition, notably from Hong Kong. The scale of the threat concentrated the minds of a high level committee that subsequently defined two areas for achieving competitive advantage through expanding external trade. The quality of trade could be improved through streamlining all pertinent legal, financial and documentation processes. Secondly, cost containment could provide an attractive fee and port charge pricing structure. The project began with the critical acceptance that investment in IT was an integral part of achieving these objectives (King and Konsynski, 1990). The absence of such an acceptance, and the lack of high level support and finance so obviously present in the Singapore example, have been contributory factors to failure in many other major IT projects. However, their presence provides a platform for, not the delivery of, success (Kahneman and Lovallo, 1993).

6.2 Detail

In the TradeNet case a further contributory factor was the groundwork set in place in the 1970s. The Government had established a Committee on National Computerisation (CNC) to define how Singapore could harness the power of IT.

The CNC reported that, as a first step, a massive education process was needed because at least 10,000 IT professionals would be required by 1990. The education programme and the introduction of computers into government departments was well underway by the time of the 1985 economic crisis.

It was also appreciated at an early stage that commitment and agreement would be needed from a number of important interest groups, in order to change any aspect of the process of trade. A series of discussions between the Economic Development Board, National Computer Board and Trade Development Board (TDB) ensued, the main focus being the simplifications and streamlining of documentation integral to the trading process. The TDB was given the task of mobilising key organizations such as the Civil Aviation, Port of Singapore Authority and Customs and Excise to gain their commitment to create a trade-oriented EDI system. This system was to be called 'TradeNet'.

A major risk in IT projects relates to definitional uncertainty about information requirements (Iliff, 1994). In the TradeNet case this was first tackled by developing a detailed understanding of what existing trade procedures were being followed. To cope with the detail, and also the sensitivity of commercial and political issues, a sophisticated structure of committees was established so that every interest could be represented. The TradeNet Steering Committee (TNSC), set up to oversee and verify all procedures, was split into three sub-committees representing maritime, air and government agencies/statutory institutions. Figure 10.2 illustrates the reporting structure implemented to ensure effective communication between interested parties. The three sub-committees met regularly and produced a series of reports on current procedures, resulting in a final definitive report on trade activities and related documentation (Sisodia, 1992). This revealed that replication of the existing complex, multi-form procedures into electronic form would not achieve quality improvement and cost containment. Only a massive simplification process could achieve this. The TNSC therefore decided to have designed a single form for use in trade agreements as a basis for a computer specification.

In parallel, the TDB began testing a prototype on-line system called Trade-Dial-Up which allowed traders to complete forms on-line. The fact that this worked in controlled circumstances introduced the idea of developing this system into the EDI system being sought by Singapore. However, moving from concept to build, and ensuring that IT in the diverse range of companies and agencies that needed to be part of a successful trade networking system were integrated – this presented a massive technological problem, typical of many major IT projects. It was realised that the existing skills base and experience within Singapore were not sufficient. Management and coordination of the project were necessary, and the TNSC made the decision to seek outside assistance.

The process of selecting from an invited shortlist of companies was assisted

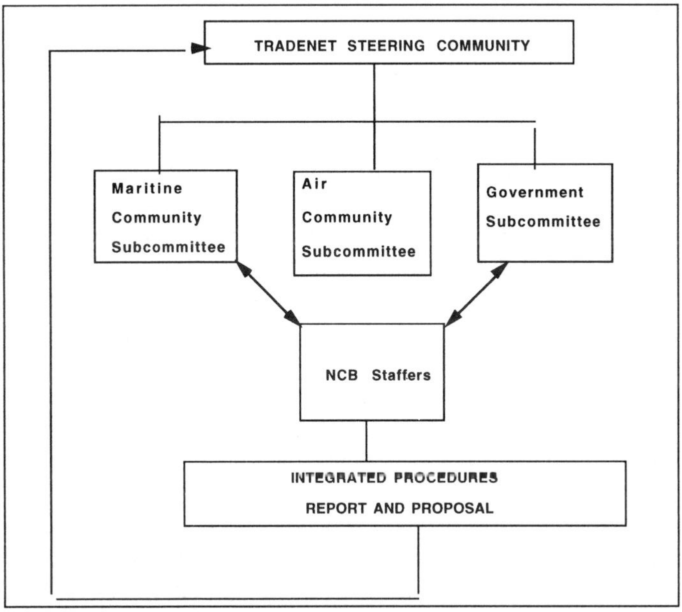

Figure 10.2 Organisational structure for TradeNet

by the clear terms of reference and information requirements already generated through the committee process. Tendering companies all had experience in dealing with large-scale IT projects. Feasibility studies were undertaken and similar systems investigated in other countries. A new management structure that established clear ownership was created for the next project stage. The TDB, Port of Singapore, Civil Aviation Authority and Singapore Telecoms established a separate company whose aim was to operate the TradeNet system for profit. This company awarded IBM the contract to establish systems integration and have responsibility for all systems aspects except software. The latter contract was awarded to Computer Systems Advisers, Pte. Ltd. of Singapore. Many of the problems engendered on multi-supplier IT projects were minimised by clear delineation of responsibility for every aspect of implementation. Parameters were set out for a comprehensive implementation of the project according to well defined and detailed specifications. In practice, especially over long time scales, it is well known that user needs change as expectations and knowledge develop (Hochstrasser and Griffiths, 1991; Iliff, 1994; Strassmann, 1985). To counter the problem of user requests side-tracking the project the main project manager directed that a rigorous assessment procedure should operate. No changes to the agreed implementation could be made until requests were analysed according to the time, impact and cost that would be incurred by undertaking them. By this means a thorough justification process had to be introduced to force a change from an earlier agreement. As a result, objectives were essentially maintained, and implementation held very firmly on track.

In January 1989 TradeNet was officially declared operational. Direct capital cost were S$20 million, the project stuck to agreed timescales, and the two overriding objectives were achieved. The quality of interaction with outside customers had improved. As one example turnaround time for trade documentation had been reduced from a maximum of four days to 10–15 minutes. As another, some freight forwarders were reporting cost savings of between 25–30%. TradeNet also opened up further business possibilities as more and more companies came to want to subscribe. The system also represented a core system as pressure came to take electronic communications further into providing funds transfer, banking and even healthcare through EDI systems, with the possibility of linking into TradeNet (Sisodia, 1992).

There were solid reasons for these outcomes, not least the effective management of risks in such a large-scale project. Objectives for undertaking TradeNet were focused, explicit, and understood and accepted by all interest groups involved in project preparation and implementation. The objectives were not changed; the price of failing to achieve them was high enough for the objectives not to be re-examined and argued over continuously. Fundamental control procedures did not change and were not disrupted. The drive to achieve objectives was maintained at the most senior levels. Communication both vertically and horizontally was facilitated by a willingness to include all interested parties and to compromise on certain aspects to achieve the end results. A skills infrastructure was in place to ensure take-up of new systems. The objectives fitted into the long term objectives of the Government (Konsynski, 1990), and it was realistic to expect companies to adapt to the new systems and processes that were inevitably part of the introduction of IT. The implementation of such a major project was not hampered by a lack of knowledge and familiarity of the relevant technologies.

There was a remarkable willingness to bring in outside expertise once project scale and complexity were fully realised. This undoubtedly saved time and ensured that Singapore personnel could be introduced to a major project implementation through working alongside more experienced IT staff. Innovative technology was not introduced into the main project until it had been fully tested in controlled circumstances. The evaluation of the prototyping experiment was not used as the main reason to give the go ahead for a full technical implementation. This is interesting, because generally successful prototyping has led immediately to the introduction of technology on a larger scale. Yet, evidence is beginning to come through to show that software systems in particular, which work well in small-scale demonstrations can throw up new problems when developed on a larger scale (Fisher, 1994). In TradeNet, only when specific conditions could be replicated on the main project were decisions made to include new technologies in the overall project.

The caution and strict management approach adopted undoubtedly prevented the TradeNet project collapsing due to technological weaknesses or limitations. Moreover human and cultural factors were addressed. The project developed in such a way that all parties, including users, traders, government, suppliers and customers could see benefits from taking part. Through this strong focus, the objective of securing Singapore as a preferred trading centre was achieved. An important element in this success, was the wider and long term development of a knowledge and skills culture supportive of IT developments. This has resulted in the institutionalisation, as opposed to the mere installation of the Tradenet system into the administrative, commercial, and social life of the country.

7. THE CRISP PROJECT IN INDIA: A CULTURAL SHOCK

7.1 Background

In the 1970s it was recognised that significant sections of the Indian population were not sharing in the benefits of the expanding economy. The biggest losers were the rural poor who often had no saleable product or service to market, and no income generating skill to provide them with employment. They were entirely dependent on aid or government grants. Under these circumstances the process of alleviating poverty was self defeating because most grant recipients were left as helpless after funding had finished as they were beforehand. To provide a more consistent policy of aid which raised living standards, and facilitated employment, the government set up the Integrated Rural Development Programme (IRDP) in 1978. This programme established a process of grants and subsidies to selected poor families to purchase their first assets. A heavy IT investment programme at national level was seen as necessary to support this initiative. It could facilitate the coordination of data from the regions and provide local representatives with a helpful decision support tool. The end result would be more effective targetting of the most vulnerable, and the alleviation of endemic poverty.

7.2 Detail

The IRDP was established as a national programme for the alleviation of poverty in rural areas. The large scope of the project meant that a massive amount of detailed information about rural communities was collected locally, but because most of the processes were manually based this information could not be integrated or coordinated nationally. Computers were seen as the most effective means of supporting the IRDP nationally allowing the effective resource allocation to the most needy, and providing local areas with a decision support tool to asist in programme administration. The Computerised Rural Information Systems Project (CRISP) received the full backing of the Indian government, and finance was made available for its installation nationally.

The CRISP system consisted of microcomputers running a range of standard report generating packages. Its specific objectives were:

- to facilitate the generation of reports required by local and national government
- to create records of beneficiaries
- to collect village information for planning.

Once relevant information about rural families was generated, this was passed from the blocks (the lowest administative unit) to the districts and to central government. The aim was to evolve an integrated series of reports for villages, that could be developed into block, district and state level reports and eventually into an All-India IRDP plan.

The decision to invest in the CRISP system was based upon a successful implementation of this technology in the Karwar district of Karnataka, in Southern India (Banerji and Ghosh, 1989). In Karwar, an effective management approach had ensured that systems design and development for the IRDP application had the active participation of users. Specific skills training was given and clerks were shown how the system could help them to work more productively. As a result, the district was able to make better planning decisions, to access data more quickly, coordinate local efforts more effectively, and to arrange more field visits. All of these benefits were seen as critical to ensuring IRDP success nationally (Patel, 1987).

Once the decision had been taken to establish CRISP nationally there was little further direction or support from the centre about how to manage the technology locally. It was left to individual state governments to allocate funding, purchase equipment, and agree contracts. Some states floated their own tenders, and so kept the contracts within their own political influence. Many contracts were given to unqualified individuals or agencies. Power failures, technical problems and poor maintenance support characterised implementation in all districts. These problems often encountered at the implementation and use stages of the initiative resulted in lowered expectations and negative attitudes amongst staff.

In practice CRISP has not resulted in the massive alleviation of poverty in India, or even in the effective coordination of information for better central planning (Madon, 1991). In many states CRISP was never fully utilised, and is now a redundant system. Four main barriers have been identified as accounting for

CRISP's lack of success. Firstly, computerisation was imposed in a top-down manner, which did not take account of local requirements, practices or processes. Local administrators were not consulted about the approach or included in the decisions about speed and scope of implementation. The policy of making technology available to even the poorest in the communitiy could not on its own ensure a successful project.

Secondly, and ironically, the aim of decentralising rural development by allocating computers to the local level was interpreted as a threatening form of centralisation of information. Local officials perceived computerisation as undermining their influence; consequently they were not eager to make it effective. In many instances, it was also found that informal covert systems were at work subverting the original objectives of the formal IRDP initiative. Thirdly, education and training were not provided throughout the country. There was no formalised approach to covering specific skills training linked to broader education on the implications of IT. Many unskilled people were expected to operate computers for the first time without adequate support. Finally, installation and maintenance support were sporadic, and often insufficient to keep CRISP to the operational level that was technically achievable.

In the original implementation of CRISP in the Kanwar district these four barriers were not encountered because a close involvement by users and beneficiaries was an essential part of the whole process. When CRISP was expanded to become a country-wide implementation new technical problems were introduced as a result of increased size and complexity, but many of the neglected risk factors related to human, cultural, political and managerial issues rather than technical ones (Madon, 1992). Additionally many short-cuts were taken. The result was that a previous small-scale success developed into a large-scale failure of a major IT project.

8. VIDEOTEX: KEY TO THE FUTURE?

8.1 Background

In the 1970s and 1980s several European governments were particularly interested in technologies that offered the possibility of creating the 'information society' (Rocc, 1985). Major breakthroughs in microelectronics research made new forms of communication possible, with considerable implications for national broadcasting and communication standards. Furthermore, instead of being limited to telephone, telegraph and telex, information could suddenly be exchanged through facsimile, electronic mail and other data transmission systems. Links between users meant that systems could be interactive, and include the conveyance of graphics and text as well as voice. Videotex grew out of a combination of these developments. It used familiar business technology such as computers, and it offered potential mass market appeal because the systems could be linked through existing telephone networks. Three countires in particular, France, the United Kingdom and Germany, saw videotex as a worthwhile technology to promote and support nationally. In all three countries it was perceived as offering the most immediate means of introducing a national 'nervous system' of communication. See Figure 10.3 for an explanation and illustration of videotex.

In the United Kingdom and Germany, the governments relied on publicity and market forces to determine the eventual level of usage of the videotex systems. As a result, the levels of uptake were weak. Control of the technology was left to the marketplace as it was expected that television companies would provide the necessary terminals to subscribers of the systems. However, the 1979 launch of Prestel in the UK proved premature, and was based on false fears about overseas competitors utilising the technology successfully to gain a stranglehold on information provision. In reality the technology was not ready for the market, and user uptake was very limited despite widespread awareness of the services being offered. Germany suffered from a similar lack of interest from the market and like the UK's system it failed to gain the commercial threshold that was necessary to make it either operationally or financially viable. Consequently both versions lapsed into providing small specialist groups with limited information of particular importance to individual industries. In contrast the French government adopted a very different approach to facilitating the uptake of this new technology.

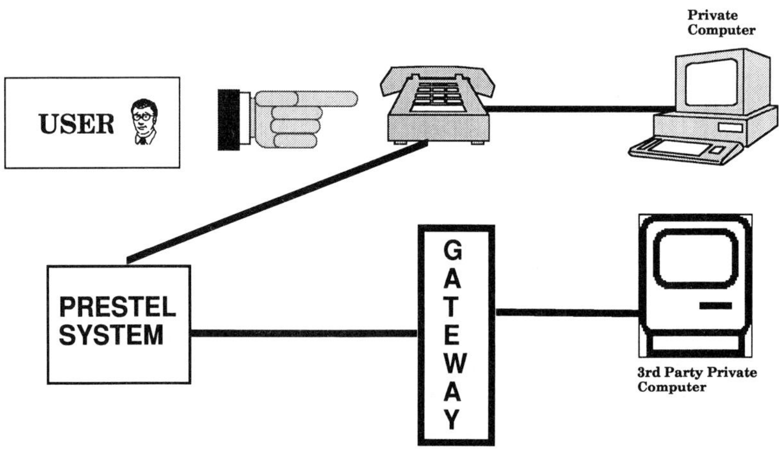

Figure 10.3 The principles of videotex. Videotex allows an exchange of information between a user and a computer via a telephone line. Information is displayed on a terminal

8.2 The French Minitel System – A Prestige Project

The French government was very attracted to a major national prestige technology project and proved willing to provide major technological and financial support to the videotex initiative known as Minitel (Rapaport, 1992). In 1978 the French government expressed its intention to replace paper based and operator dependent telephone directories with an electronic one. To ensure the day to day management of the initiative from design to implementation, control was handed to DGT, the state ownded telecommunications company. Two test sites were established at Rennes and Velizy to explore how the videotex technology would work and cope with demand. After successful initial results from the uptake of the telephone directory service, the system was made available throughout France.

To persuade potential subscribers to acquire the system, standard terminals called Minitels were distributed free by DGT together with a copy of the directory. The expectation was that savings would still eventually come through as a result of not printing the conventional paper directories. In addition it was found that specialist information services were also interested in linking into the system once potential accessibility could be verified. Effectively costs could be further recouped by charging information providers. The system evolved as a collection of information providers and subscribers linked through the public packet-switching network accessed through the telephone system. The charging of customers was coordinated through DGT who passed a proportion of the funds collected to the service providers. Importantly, Minitel did not seek to become a centralised database system that aimed to control all its information.

By 1990 Minitel had more than 4 million terminals in use. Through the network it was possible to access over 15,000 services; customers were from both domestic and business sectors. The system has been upgraded and is expandable to meet any rise in demand from services and customers. Minitel's long-term future, however, is not guaranteed and will depend on its ability to maintain its attraction particularly when confronted by newer multi-media technologies.

8.3 Outcomes

In all three countries videotex technology failed to become the centrepiece of a national IT infrastructure along the lines originally envisaged. Videotex did not provide a sufficient impetus to transform these countries into strategically networked nations along the lines of, for example, Singapore. In France alone videotex implementation acquired a significant role. There are a number of distinct reasons for this, accounted for by the different approach that France took to its management of the project.

Firstly, the French government had already established a broad framework for planning to encourage the uptake of new technology. The concerns the French had about their ability to handle new technological developments had been publicly voiced. Consequently the French government was actively seeking a likely project for official endorsement and support. Videotex fitted in well with this longer term policy because it held out the possibility of being a truly national project. Secondly, the backing of the government and its commitment to provide resources reduced the risks attached to marketing the technology. As a result no single company was disproportionately burdened at very early experimental stages of the project. Thirdly, the distance-independent cost structure encouraged a geographic diffusion of information providers. This meant that it was possible to provide a market that was not limited to one or two regions. The system could therefore have national appeal. Fourthly the monopolistic control exercised by the French DGT ensured that management, design and implementation were firmly coordinated by one organisation. Every aspect of the project design and implementation was monitored carefully, and particular standards were rigidly enforced. DGT had control of all aspects of the technology from the decisions about the specification for the terminals to the communication standards to be enforced. Fifthly, the government's focus on a tangible requirement, that is the electronic telephone directory, provided the necessary impetus at an early stage. The deliverables were clearly defined, understood and tested in a controlled study. This built up consensus, and some experience for handling the new IT.

The British and German approaches, by contrast, were too generalist and broadly based. Although both governments were actively encouraging the use of new IT, often this was promotional effort rather than linked to developing particular applications. The poor control that was provided over the design of equipment, and lack of standards to enforce delivery, budgets and performance caused critical delays in implementation. Additionally videotex became perceived by many to be a solution looking for a problem to solve; and no single organisation was prepared to risk becoming a main stakeholder in such an ill-defined implementation, with so few perceived real returns.

However, the costs of introducing videotex have been high in all three cases. None of the systems produced have repaid the initial outlays. The German and British governments have lost massive amounts of money due to the projects having to contract at an early stage. The French government has continued to subsidise its system heavily, partly because of the prestige it draws from implementing a nationally networked system. It is still exploring how it might be possible to incorporate other more strategic requirements into the videotex system in order to be able to convert it into the originally sought, national communications system. In practice, even Minitel has failed to become consumer led, and if the French government subsidy were withdrawn it is expected that system use would contract severely. This indicates that one of the major problems with introducing national videotex systems has been lack of demand for the technology, as much as problems with how it has been managed and introduced.

9. TAURUS IN THE UNITED KINGDOM: A RUNAWAY PROJECT

9.1 Background

The London Stock Exchange's first experience of a large-scale IT project had been the comprehensive implementation of electronic dealings known euphemistically as the 'Big Bang' of 1986. Effectively this had removed the need for face to face meetings between what were called jobbers and stockbrokers, as the whole process of share dealing became automated. The TAURUS (Transfer and Automated Registration of Uncertified Stock) project was conceived in the early 1980s as the next phase of automation ultimately leading to a paperless dealing and contractual system for shares. The aim was that all share certificates would be scrapped, and share transfers would be handled by book entry on a computer. The main impetus for TAURUS came in 1987 with a crisis in settlements stemming from back office, mainly paper-based, support systems failing to keep track of the massive number of share dealings and related transactions. Many of the international banks that had become owners of the main stockbroking firms exerted pressure to develop better systems. As an industry familiar with mass processing of routine financial data, the banks were keen to automate as much as possible as quickly as possible. There was, however, widespread, strong resistance to extending automation. Vested interests, such as registrars who would be put out of business if share certificates were abandoned, fought against further use of technology. This presented a major dilemma for the Stock Exchange. On the one hand it could not allow its international reputation to suffer through inefficient dealing; on the other it was aware of the need to maintain the support and confidence of all City interests.

9.2 Detail

The Bank of England appointed the Siscott Committee with terms of reference to provide a compromise that would leave no group in the securities industry worse off than before. The idea of developing a computer system remained at the heart of the solution the City was seeking. The focus of the Committee, therefore, turned to what this system should provide. Inevitably with each compromise expectations, and systems design, grew exponentially, as did the complexity of what was being sought. Although the Siscott Committee spearheaded the investigation, it did not enjoy the support of the main interst groups (Waters and Cane, 1993). Additionally, the Department of Trade and Industry began to add restrictions – such as technological, financial and legal constraints to protect investors. The main focus was lost and decisions regularly swung from developing a massively centralised computer system to the provision of an integrated network of computer databases, with the Stock Exchange acting as the 'hub'.

A complex series of committees were formed, disbanded and reformed to include major stakeholders in the City, including the banks. There were at various times the Exchange's Settlements Board Committee, The TAURUS Monitoring Group, The TAURUS Review Committee, as well as a range of different external consultants involved in the management of the project (see Figure 10.4). Due to the in-fighting and lack of clear feasible objectives, the project developed a momentum of its own. Meetings often failed to decide central issues, and communication between committees or project managers was inconsistent or non-existent. Many business aspects concerning the data to be input were not satisfactorily resolved, so further delays and legal worries developed. Despite these drawbacks, however, a decision was made to start implementation of TAURUS in 1990/91.

A project team was appointed and given the go-ahead to buy a £1 million software package from Vista Concepts of New Jersey for the core system. Work commenced on adapting the package to the London securities market, but in fact so much customisation was needed that a further estimated £14 million was spent on rewriting the software. This process was never finished. All of these decisions were made despite there being no central design for the full system, and no planned operating architecture. Subsequently it was found that large parts of critical processes, such as overnight reconciliation, had been omitted or labelled non-urgent. Due to the complex range of committees and reporting structures in existance it appears that few people had sufficient understanding of the entire project. As a result quality control was weak with many changes and much experimentation being undertaken without rigorous procedures for evaluation and

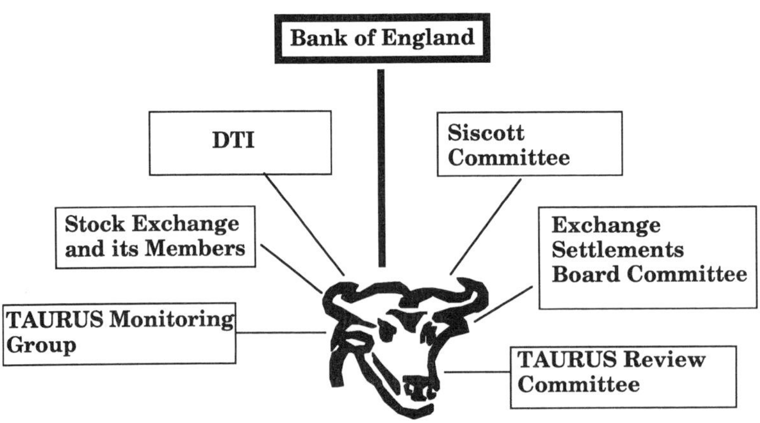

Figure 10.4 Interest groups involved in the TAURUS project

feedback being enforced. Changes to requirements were introduced regularly on an *ad hoc* basis. Delays became a familiar characteristic of the project. Five years after starting, with direct project costs probably exceeding £50 million, TAURUS was finally abandoned in 1993.

TAURUS was a project that quickly grew out of control, and its history can be usefully compared to those of other major projects that have not succeeded. The initial decision to design the system was flawed (Currie, 1994). There were no clear objectives. A crisis situation had brought together a wide, diverse group of interests which were, under the circumstances, unlikely to be conciliatory or looking for a wider, best solution for the City as a whole. Little clear thinking or vision emerged from a series of committee structures, all of which failed to realise the extent of the scope and complexity of the project (Waters, 1993; Warner *et al.*, 1992). Communication between these groups was inconsistent and intermittent. As a result the number of individuals who were involved but not able or willing to act grew as the timescales became more protracted. Communication at all levels appears to have been poor, but particularly true of the channels established between the supervisory committees and project managers. Control was not linked sufficiently to a project-wide process of evaluation and accountability operating on a regular basis at several levels.

The lack of consensus about what the computer system was to provide ensured that the implementation process would be very slow. Without a design blueprint for the system it was difficult to know at the outset what problems were likely to arise, and how the system could be designed to maximise user friendliness. The lack of design also left open the option of changing aspects of the project at short notice, perhaps often without understanding the possible consequences and implications. Although in principle standards were issued, in practice they appear not to have been followed. TAURUS was being developed broadly using the guidelines set out in the SSADM methodology specified by the UK Government for the implementation of large computer projects. In fact many of the central guidelines were not adhered to; for example testing of the system was being undertaken before the operational requirements had been specified. This meant that individuals were attempting to address the technical requirements before the overall project definitions had been elicited. The lack of adherence to stated procedures was a further cause of delays in systems delivery.

The lack of accountability that characterised the project meant that quality control both managerially and technically was weakened (Griffiths, 1994). Consultants were hired and changed without adequate consideration for what was being delivered or needed. Decisions were not scrutinised sufficiently, and as a result both time and cost targets were regularly missed. There are well documented dangers in introducing untried or innovative technologies into major projects when they have been insufficiently tested (Bessant, 1993; De Greene, 1991).

The decision to select Vista's high priced global custody system was inappropriate; the core package needed so much customisation that a huge learning process was required on the part of the technologists employed to adapt it. It would have been more suitable to consider a bespoke system, though its development would also have probably run into considerable problems in the circumstances prevailing.

The TAURUS project was characterised by a series of fatal flaws that major projects need to avoid individually, let alone in combination. Many of the fundamental mistakes made throughout the project could have been avoided through learning from major project experiences of other organisations. As at the beginning of 1994, while the settlements crisis had temporarily passed, The Stock Exchange was no nearer to addressing the core issues highlighted in the TAURUS project. The City was still in need of a mechanism for resolving complex inter-company issues which affect the stability of the financial services and securities sectors. The next, more limited City computerisation project has already been planned, although no new management or control structures have been formalised.

10. MANAGING RISK IN MAJOR IT PROJECTS

A comparison of these projects highlights the fact that risk cannot be evaluated and managed as a separate factor but must be handled as an integral component of many aspects of planning and implementation. The areas where differences are most acute illustrate factors which distinguish the good investments from the poor returns. An analysis (Table 10.1) of these major cases against the framework of already described common problems in IT based projects (see above) shows how consideration of certain key areas of management will influence the degree of success achieved. In addition the role of government and quality assessment have been added because these were seen to have a constant and over-riding influence on the outcome of all the projects. In the TradeNet case which overall has been the most successful of the cases investigated, this framework does not appear to have been followed overtly in a strategic way at the outset. However, when compared with the other cases it handled salient issues differently. It nevertheless can be shown that the approach that characterised this project distinguishes it from less successful attempts at major IT project management.

11. TOWARDS A RISK ANALYSIS FRAMEWORK

If risk analysis and evaluation are to become a central part of major IT project development there needs to be a practical framework against which some idea of relevance of risk can be undertaken. Four key aspects derived from an analysis of these major IT cases as well as the risk framework described earlier are proposed

Table 10.1 Managing risk in major IT projects

MAJOR ISSUES	TRADENET	CRISP	MINITEL	TAURUS
Strategic framework	Clear and stable	Regional control	Integral to Government planning	Ill-defined and changing
Role of government	Intervensionist and supportive	Financial support	Financial, and technical co-ordination	'Hands off', legislative restrictions
Organisational adaptation	Redefined trade operations	Stakeholder resistance	New customer/ supplier relationships	Manual processes automated without validation
IT supplier problems	Strong management	Poor contracting and variable standards	Single supplier run by the State	Inconsistent standards unclear terms of reference
Change management	Adaptive	Lack of user participation	Centrally controlled	Organisations resisted procedural changes
Faith in technical fix	Business needs defined first	Underplayed human factors	Evolutionary	Technology driven
Use of relevant technology	Prototyping before major implementation	Systems were too limited for the demands	Used well tried technology	Full implementation of experimental technology
Skills support	Appropriate skills imported	Limited access to skills	Available and used	Relevant skills missing
Educational environment	Consistent and broadly based	Limited and not supported	Specific to project requirements	Inadequate for requirements
Quality assessment	Comprehensive and relevant	Erratic and weak	Limited and focused	Variable and technically directed

as the starting point for controlling risk better within these projects. These are governance, project management, market need and learning.

11.1 Governance

The concept of governance here refers to how the major stakeholders organise themselves to establish objectives, acquire and allocate resources and make decisions. Part of this process can be defined as requiring effective sponsors or champions but governance is seen here as more the overall environment in which a project is conceived and then implemented. It is different from project management, which is here characterised as the critical, but lower level management of the set of activities delivering on decisions arrived at through governance. In the Singapore and Minitel case studies, the strong focus that came from the governments and permeated each tier of the project management is in stark contrast to the approach adopted by the City and the UK government to TAURUS. The attempts made by the Indian government to impose strong control which went against the social, cultural and political structures of the rural communities contributed to a less successful outcome for the CRISP project. The case studies reveal that governance sets the critical parameters in which effective project management can take place. It is the broader framework of operations which ensures some degree of stability. On large-scale projects governance is revealed as particularly difficult because of the involvement of multiple and powerful stakeholders, including governments (Cooke, 1994). The TradeNet case is notable for the high intervention of the Singapore government and the high degree of co-ordination between interest groups permitting the development of clear objectives, strategy and information requirements. This can be contrasted most significantly with the TAURUS arrangements, marked by poor co-ordination within the governance structure.

11.2 Project management: balancing top-down and bottom up

A significant issue faced in all major projects is the degree to which objectives and decisions set at the top are followed through to lower levels. All four projects were threatened by potential displacement of objectives by different interest groups. In the TAURUS project these interest groups continued to resist an overall solution, but in the TradeNet example the focus and urgency of the objectives remained a constant. While it is inherently difficult to prevent these displacement effects, this seems to have been largely achieved in the TradeNet case through balancing defined top-down parameters together with more local involvement in deciding information requirements and project delivery. In India, the strategy was not implementable precisely because of a severe mismatch between the objectives and interests of the different groups. This central issue was never addressed and consequently contributed to the collapse of the initial project.

11.3 Market need/economic survival

Economic survival was a crucial determinant of a project's success. This fact facilitated stabillity and focus. Furthermore, the success of the projects was critically influenced by the degree to which there was an existing market need for what was being delivered. This helps to explain the planning and energy driving the TradeNet system to success; stakeholders were brought together by a clear overriding, salient set of objectives. Minitel offered a service within a very narrowly defined sphere. The success of it has increased its usage and subsequently it has increased market share. In the TAURUS case it is not clear that stakeholders perceived the IT project as determining their economic survival in a significant way, especially once the settlements crisis subsided. On the contrary, it appears that many of the groups viewed TAURUS as job threatening and working against individual economic survival and comfort. CRISP lost its way in regional issues and was viewed by potential recipients as a distributive system for administration rather than delivery of market share or specific benefits.

11.4 Learning

From the cases, there would seem to be two aspects of learning that are particularly significant: learning from experience, and learning something new. The history of IT experience has not been one of evolutionary learning. On the contrary, it has been one of not learning lessons well enough to avoid repeating previous mistakes (Bessant, 1993; Hochstrasser and Griffiths, 1991). This weakness, linked to the fact that major IT projects are often synonymous with charting new learning territory, make them high risk ventures. Under these circumstances, the difficulties of building up appropriate teams with the most relevant experience and skills cannot be underestimated. Collingridge (1992) makes the further point that major projects are too often over-ambitious and over designed at the front end, looking to deliver a completed design fast using a 'big bang' strategy. This would seem particularly risky with technological innovations and the alternative approach he suggests is one of incremental innovation, not least because it allows learning. With the weak framework of control in the TAURUS project, there were only very limited possibilities for building in the necessary learning and effectively using real expertise to great effect. Many of the initial designs for the project had to be continually recast. Planning and implementation often appear to have been done in parallel rather than in a progressive and co-ordinated manner. Much of the project work and programming was pioneering in character and consequently ensured further delays and frustration for end users. In the TradeNet case the supportive educational environment (King and Konsynski, 1990; *Singapore Bulletin*, 1993), and the early prototyping approach were clear factors in using experience and promoting learning within the project.

12. INFLUENCES ON RISK LEVELS

Further analysis of these case studies shows that other factors will have a direct bearing on the levels of risk experienced in major IT projects. The combination of history, context, content and process which was different in each case exerted a significant influence on the eventual outcome of the projects. In Figure 10.5 the development of the cycle is shown to illustrate how these factors interact .

12.1 History

The history of information systems success or failure is seen to directly influence the subsequent risks experienced. The ability to learn from past experience and to apply this knowledge to avoid replicating mistakes appears of crucial importance

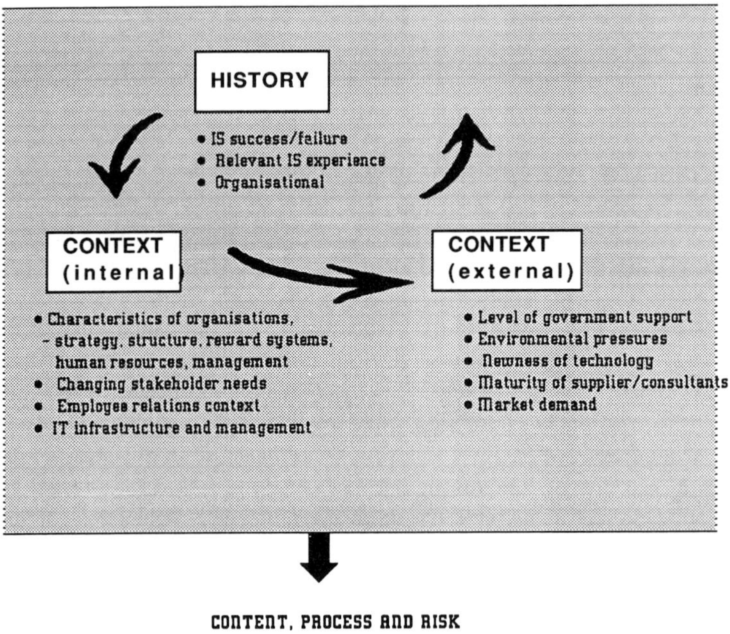

Figure 10.5 Factors affecting risk

in major IT projects. TradeNet could draw upon a supportive educational infrastructure and prior computerisation in government departments. This programme of educational support and technology learning has now become embedded in the attitude and culture of Singapore and is seen as part of a continuous cycle linked to national prestige. Further projects are envisaged and plans and resources are allocated to build on the initial success of TradeNet.

In contrast, the TAURUS project appears to have stemmed from being a good idea at the time to address a temporary but significant problem in London trading operations. The attempts to provide a solution focussed immediately on introducing technology and bringing together a range of personnel who had very limited previous experience of working together. The lack of relevant IS and management skills in the TAURUS case compounded the subsequent risk development. Co-ordination of resources and funding was driven by crisis rather than by knowledge and successful development. Ironically, in the CRISP case there was a history of success on a regional project that could not be repeated when the natinonal scale of the project introduced new risk dimensions and management requirements.

12.2 Context

Both internal and external context strongly influence the outcome of major IT projects. The internal context factors that will affect risk levels are principally managerial, cultural, human resource, evaluation and reward systems issues. Misfits between organisational and IS structure/infrastructure can cause problems as can radical reorganisations and lack of relevant reporting or feedback channels. In TradeNet and to an extent Minitel these reporting structures were clear and provided a continuous means of learning and consequently authorisation of resources when needed. In TAURUS, this internal stablility was lacking and as a result much effort was dissipated unnecessarily in constantly trying to establish control.

The way in which external context factors contribute to the 'riskiness' of computerisation provides one of the hazards which every major IT project experiences. Economic or national interests may cut across original plans and in all four cases it can be demonstrated that the differing levels of government support influenced the outcome; in the case of TAURUS the government was involved but not in particularly helpful ways. The 'newness of technology' factor operated all cases, but was more appropriately handled in some than in the others. Where the project hinged on new technology as with TAURUS it led the organisation to expose itself to the vagaries of the consultancy/supplier markets. As a result the TAURUS project became a laboratory of experimentation for both suppliers and consultants who were often seen to be setting their own objectives and deadlines. In TradeNet new technology formed part of the project but was tested and integrated within a wider context. Control of the project was never neglected. The inherent attractiveness of new technology to the market was a significant factor in the Minitel case. This led to an over-anticipation of market demand which led to a lack of take-up when the project was delivered.

12.3 Content and process

Issues of IT-related change illustrated in Figure 10.6 emerge strongly from all the case studies. Each project was high in terms of size and complexity and number of units being computerised, and both illustrate the risks inherent in 'definitional' and 'technical uncertainty' (see the Parker *et al.* framework above). As can be seen by the scale of both TradeNet and TAURUS, content issues on their own do not determine a successful outcome. The Singapore case was an even larger project than TAURUS which was mainly the attempted computerisation of one type of business operation. The issue that seems significant here is the process itself rather than the scale or complexity of the project.

12.4 Risk outcomes

The combination of the influences and impacts of history, context, content and

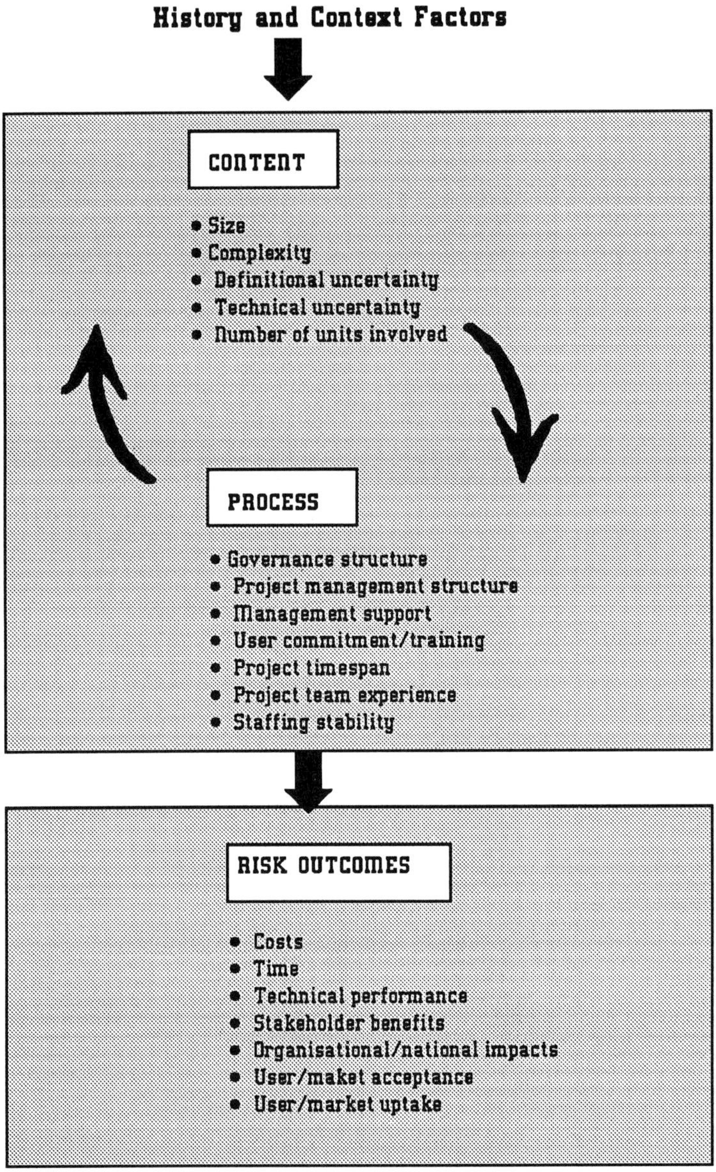

process have a direct bearing on the levels of risk outcomes which characterise major IT projects. The risk outcomes which affected the results of all the projects appear to be principally centred around the key issues of cost, time, technical performance, stakeholder benefits, market interest leading to uptake, and the relevance of the organisational structures involved. These risk areas can only be controlled providing they are perceived to be of importance to all stakeholders involved. If defined outcomes are not representative of the desired objectives of salient stakeholders who can affect the course of computerisation, then this may decrease the likelihood of achieving these outcomes. The dissent among stakeholders in TAURUS and CRISP characterised the projects throughout and were never resolved satisfactorily.

The dominant point that must emerge from this analysis is that it is the relationships between all these factors, the way in which they interconnect to form risk, that deserves more serious attention, particularly before major IT projects are initiated. In TradeNet these links were established early on and were constantly reinforced. In TAURUS, there were initial difficulties establishing these links which continued to plague the entire project. The inability of the project managers to reconcile often conflicting interest groups ensured that the stakeholders were never fully interested in lending their support to the entire project.

13. CONCLUSION

While it is acknowledged that major IT projects are inherently very high risk this risk need not remain a totally unknown variable. In practice, formal risk analysis has often been omitted due to a lack of understanding of the influences that determine successful outcomes of projects. The analysis and comparison of the four case studies discussed shows clearly that any initial explanations of size, complexity and scale are not on their own sufficient to either guarantee or explain success or failure. There are a range of factors covering governance, project management, learning and economic need which are of greater significance to the effective outcome of any project. Evaluation and comprehensive consideration of these issues can provide a practical approach to more effective risk management. New technology in combination with large scale adds dimensions of risk that necessitates an explicit concern for risk profiling to set the risk parameters in which project management can be conducted more successfully.

A framework for defining these risks has been proposed which focuses on the links between history, external and internal context, content, and process. Risk in large-scale IT projects is high, multi-dimensional and can arise from unanticipated combinations of these factors and influences. It is hoped however, that this clearer identification and analysis of the risks and how they can be managed will provide a useful learning tool for future effective investment and management of major IT projects. The indications are that when these areas are addressed major IT projects are worth the risks involved and long term benefits result to stakeholders.

REFERENCES

Appleton, D. 1991 Very Large Projects. *Datamation*, January 15, pp 63-70.

Banerji, S. and Ghosh, D. 1989 Information Technology and Rural Development: A New Harvest, *PC World India*, May 15-26

Bessant, J. 1993 The Lessons of Failure: Learning to Manage New Manufacturing Technology Manufacturing Technology: Diffusion, Implementation and Management, pp 197-214

Bessant, J. 1991 *Managing Advanced Manufacturing Technology: The Challenge of the Fifth Wave*, NCC-Blackwell, Manchester

Cash, J., McFarlan, W. and McKenney, J. 1992 *Corporate Information Systems Management*, Irwin, Boston

Charette, R. 1991 *Application Strategies for Risk Analysis*, McGraw-Hill, New York

Collingridge, D. 1992 *The Management of Scale*, Routledge, London

Cooke, K. 1994 Singapore Finds Quay to Success, *Financial Times*, January 13, p 20

Currie, W. 1994 The Strategic Management of a Large Scale IT Project in the Financial Services Sector, *New Technology, Work and Employment*, 9(1) pp 19-29

Das Gupta 1989 *Computerised Rural Information Systems Project (CRISP) - Some Insights into Information Technology Systems and Development Planning*, Anand, Gujarat, India

Davidson, F. and Huot, J.-C. 1991 Large-scale Projects: Management trends for Major projects, *Cost Engineering*, 33 (2) pp 15-23

De Greene, K. B. 1991 Large Technology-Based Systems and the Need for a Paradigm Shift, *Technological Forecasting and Social Change*, 9, pp 349-362

Donovan, L.1993 Wired for Trade in Singapore, *Financial Times*, July 20, p 9

Dougherty, E. M. and Fragola, J. R. 1988 *Human Relativity Analysis*, Wiley, New York

Douglas, M. and Wildavsky, A. 1983 *Risk and Culture: An Essay on the Selection of Technological and Environmental Dangers*, University of California Press, London

Earl, M. 1989 *Management Strategies for Information Technology*, Prentice Hall, London

Fisher, A. 1994 Good Ideas Stay Out of the Drain, *Financial Times*, June 2

Griffiths, C. 1994 'Responsibility for IT: A Grey Area of Management', in Willcocks, L. ed., *Information Management: The Evaluation of Information Systems Investments*, Chapman and Hall, pp 233-250,

Griffiths, C. and Willcocks, L. 1994 *Beyond 2000: A Source Book for Major Projects*, Major Projects Association, Templeton College

Hay, M. and Williamson, P. 1991 *The Strategy Handbook*, Blackwell, London

Hochstrasser, B. and Griffiths, C. 1991 *Controlling IT Investment: Strategy and Management*, Chapman and Hall, London

Iliff, M. 1994 'The Real Value of Strategy Formulation for Information Technology', in Willcocks, L., ed., *Information Management: The Evaluation of Information Systems Investments*, Chapman and Hall pp 113-130

Kahneman, D. & Lovallo, D. 1993 Timid Choices and Bold Forecasts: A Cognitive Perspective on Risk Taking, *Management Science*, 39(1) January, pp 17-31

Keen, P. 1991 *Shaping the Future*, Harvard Business Press, Boston

King, J. and Konsynski, B. 1990 Singapore Leadership: A Tale of One City, *Harvard Business Case Studies*: Ref: 9-191-025 Harvard Business Press, Boston

Konsynski, B. 1990 Singapore TradeNet (A): A Tale of One City *Harvard Business Case Studies*: Ref: 9-191-009 Harvard Business Press, Boston

Madon, S. 1991 The Impact of Computer-based Information Systems on Rural Development Administration: A Case Study in India. PhD Thesis, Imperial College, London

Madon, S. 1992 Computer-based Information Systems for Decentralised Rural Development Administration, *Journal of Information Technology*, 7(1) March, pp 20-29.

Morris, P. and Hough, G. 1987 The Anatomy of Major Projects, John Wiley, Chichester

OTR Group 1992 Report detailed in *Computer Weekly*, December 12, p 12

Parker, M., Benson, R. and Trainor, E. 1988 *Information Economics: Linking Business Performance to Information Technology*, Prentice Hall, Englewood Cliffs, NJ

Patel, N. 1987 The Impact of Information Technology on Governmental Systems. County Study on India in Searching for a Paddle, *Trends in IT Applications in Asian Government Systems*. 3 APDC, Kuala Lumpur, Malaysia

Pike, R. and Ho, S. 1991 Risk Analysis in Capital Budgeting: Barriers and Benefits, *Omega*, 19(4), pp 235-245

Rapaport, I. 1992 The Technology of the Minitel System, *Harvard Business Case Studies*, Ref:693-006-1, Harvard Business Press, Boston

Rocc Videotex Report Series, London, 1985

Scott Morton, M. (ed.) 1991 *The Corporation of the 1990s*, Oxford University Press, Oxford

Singapore Bulletin 1993 On-job-training for 100,000 workers, 21(7), pp December 7

Sisodia, R. S. 1992 Singapore Invests in the Nation-Corporation, *Harvard Business Review*, May-June, pp 40-50

Strassmann, P. 1985 *Information Payoff: The Transformation of Work in the Electronic Age*, Collier MacMillan, London

Strassmann, P. 1990 *The Business Value of Computers*, Information Economics Press, CT

Waters, R. 1993 The Plan that Fell to Earth, *The Financial Times*, March 12, p 19

Warner, F. *et al.* 1992 *Risk: Analysis, Perception and Management*, The Royal Society, London

Waters, R. and Cane, A. 1993 Sudden Death of a Runaway Bull, *The Financial Times*, March 19, p 11

Willcocks, L. and Griffiths, C. 1994 Predicting Risk in Large-Scale Information Technology Projects, *Technological Forecasting and Social Change* (in print)

Willcocks, L. and Margetts, H. 1993 *Risk and Information Systems: A Case Study Approach*, Oxford Institute of Information Management, Working Paper RDP93/6, Templeton College, Oxford

Willcocks, L. and Margetts, H. 1994 Informatization in Public and Private Sector Settings: Distinctive or Common Risks? *Informatization and the Public Sector* (in print)

11 The evaluation of leading edge technologies

Justin Keen
Health Economics Research Group, Brunel University

1. INTRODUCTION

One of the most striking characteristics of the IT industry is its rapid rate of innovation and development. Organisations have a constantly changing array of new products to choose from. At the same time, organisations are themselves also subject to change, and the general picture is one of a changing and unpredictable world. This is certainly true of health services, which are witnessing remarkable advances in medical technologies, with those technologies being implemented against a turbulent policy background in most developed countries.

Change and uncertainty should, then, be accounted for in evaluation of IT. To ask about the value of a particular technology today is one thing; to ask about its value in a changed climate three or five years hence is quite another. This suggests that the capacity of an IT to respond flexibly to changing circumstances is likely to be crucial. Since both technologies and organisations will change, prediction of costs, risks and benefits is far from straightforward.

This chapter focuses on the problems posed by new technologies, which are often the ones most needing evaluation and yet by their nature are more difficult than other information technologies to evaluate. The next section presents the example of a major new medical technology, digital imaging networks, as a concrete example of a technology that is being evaluated. The middle sections briefly review existing IT evaluation approaches, and the final part of the chapter outlines a new evaluation methodology which can be used to deal with innovative information technologies.

2. STAR TREK COMES A STEP CLOSER

One of the most imaginative devices in the original Star Trek series was Dr McCoy's hand-held body scanner. Not only could it detect abnormalities in humans just through being pointed at them, it could take readings from aliens – though Dr McCoy was often non-plussed by the results ('It's life, Jim, but not as we know it....'). We have not quite caught up with this vision, but innovation in medical imaging is very rapid and it is possible to examine people using a range a technologies without having to break the skin. One of these technologies is familiar to us all – the x-ray machine, which has been with us since the end of the last century. (More recently, systems have become available which take x-ray type films digitally and store them on electronic media.) In the last twenty years this has been joined by ever more sophisticated new technologies such as Computerised Tomography (CT) and Magnetic Resonance Imaging (MRI), many of which have been made possible through the application of microprocessor-based technology. These allow the investigation of different body systems in fine detail. As a result, hospital radiology departments have become very technology-intensive places.

It has been clear for more than a decade that it should be possible to link together digital imaging devices on a network, store and retrieve images, and transmit them to remote locations inside and outside a hospital. For networks within hospitals this technology is usually called a Picture Archiving and Communication System (PACS); outside hospitals wider area networks are called teleradiology systems. A variety of technical obstacles have been overcome, to the point where PACS and teleradiology systems are now technically feasible, and there are examples of both in use around the world. There remain problems, though. For example, not all radiologists are convinced that computer-based images are as good as the conventional x-rays they are designed to replace, and a hospital-wide PACS system costs many millions of pounds, far more than most hospitals are willing or able to invest. At present there is a variety of views as to whether these problems will be overcome in the near future, and digital imaging networks become the normal method of image transmission in hospitals and across communities.

The decision to implement imaging networks is an important one, with implications for the future development of a range of technologies in health service settings. Imaging networks are based on a fusion of diagnostic and information technologies. If medical images – and in particular the conventional x-ray – can be computerised, then so can virtually everything else that is recorded in hospitals and community settings. This might, for example, lead eventually to the 'integrated clinical workstation', where all clinical data is available at a terminal anywhere in the NHS.

Each implementation strategy will have different costs and benefits and different effects on the management of hospitals. This raises the question as to which is the most cost effective strategy. There is a clear need for empirical data on how these systems perform, and for a balanced assessment of the technical, clinical and management risks associated with them.

A PACS is being implemented at Hammersmith Hospital in west London and is being evaluated by the Health Economics Research Group at Brunel University. The evaluation is being conducted over five years. In an ideal world, the principal research design would be a randomised trial of PACS for several different types of medical treatment, but the expense and complexity of PACS means that randomisation is not practicable.

Instead, the evaluation is examining a wide range of specific questions about particular aspects of the technology. In effect, it is a series of linked studies within a case study design (Yin, 1994). One part of the study is designed within a broad cost-effectiveness framework, and will establish the financial costs of PACS and its impact on clinical decision-making using decision-analytic techniques. Another is concerned with changes in the way services are delivered, and is employing a range of process measures for variables such as time taken to retrieve stored images using PACS versus conventional services. A third element is designed to capture subjective views of the impact of PACS on clinical work using cognitive mapping.

In addition, the project management of PACS and changes in wider operational and management processes are being monitored, through interview, observation at meetings and analysis of documentation. The success of the system may depend less on technical factors than on the quality of management processes (Markus, 1983). There is thus a mixture of quantitative and qualitative methods: they are described in more detail elsewhere (Keen *et al.*, 1994). These and other studies will be combined to form an overall judgment at the end of the project.

This is a standard case study evaluation methodology, and should provide useful insights, but it leaves open important questions. How can one account for rapid developments in digital imaging technology, which means that the evaluation may report on a technology which is considered out of date? And, how can one account for changing preferences on the part of users of systems, which may lead to them deciding that substantially different systems are required in the future? These questions point to two fundamental issues. First, is it possible to establish whether PACS or teleradiology technologies – and wider strategies of which they are a part – will be able to respond to changing preferences? That is, are they flexible enough? The other, more general, question is how to address the issue of changing preferences; can evaluation be linked into strategy formulation? It is reasonable to ask, first, whether existing IT evaluation approaches provide any answers to these questions.

3. IT EVALUATION TECHNIQUES

A wide range of evaluation techniques have been proposed for the evaluation of IT. Most are intended to be used for either ex-ante or ex-post evaluation. They vary, however, in the extent to which they can be used by practitioners or require substantial academic backing. This paper focuses on quantitative approaches, though comments in later sections might apply equally to certain types of qualitative evaluation.

Broadly, there are three classes of quantitative evaluation: those based on economic evaluation, on experimental methods and on accounting approaches. The value of cost benefit analysis is asserted by HM Treasury, the Department of Health, and a European Community Advanced Informatics in Medicine (AIM) team. They argue that the costs and benefits of systems can, fairly straightforwardly, be identified, measured and valued. Cost-effectiveness analysis has been used in previous IT evaluations in hospital settings and is being used in the evaluation of PACS. Cost utility analysis involves valuation of different outcomes relative to one another: that is, subjective preferences are elicited for a range of outcomes associated with some intervention (Drummond *et al.*, 1987). The important point here is that these three methods can be used to take account of future changes in patterns of costs and benefits, through techniques such as discounting. However, they cannot by themselves deal with the questions of flexibility and uncertainty associated with IT raised earlier.

Others have used these three 'classical' economic evaluation methods as a basis for new approaches. For example, multi-objective, multi-criteria methods use utility analysis as a starting point. Another, information economics (Parker *et al.*, 1988) is an approach which starts with a broad economic framework but uses it to outline a method for attaching weightings to different, specified types of benefit. Rather than the explicit valuation used in utility analysis, simple weightings are used. The reliance on subjective valuation means that it is not sensible to use this approach in post-implementation evaluation, but it may well be helpful in ex-ante option appraisal. Again, though, it is not clear how the issues raised above can be tackled within this type of framework.

The experimental approach, and specifically the randomised controlled trial (RCT), appears to hold a number of attractions. However, it has only rarely been used in the evaluation of IT. Many health service researchers would argue that it is the only sure means of identifying effects directly to a particular system. The essence of the approach is to control for all variables that are unrelated to the technology itself. This is typically achieved through comparison of a number of experimental sites (with the system) with control sites (without it). Ideally, systems are also randomly allocated to sites, and patients and health professionals to experimental or control groups, so that bias due to site selection is minimised. If 'extraneous' sources of variation can be eliminated, then any remaining differences can be attributed to the system.

In practice, however, this approach is expensive since the number of sites involved may have to be fairly large to demonstrate statistically significant effects. There are also important practical problems with this approach applied to IT, related to the way in which IT is implemented. For systems of even modest complexity, it is likely that they will be modified to suit local needs, making realistic comparison difficult. Sites would in fact be implementing different systems and using them for different purposes. For the points in question in this chapter, a further problem is that RCTs can only establish the value of a system at a particular point in time, and can not easily be used to make projections into the future.

The practical difficulties of using properly controlled trials have led some to adopt quasi-experimental methods (Coffey, 1980); some are being used in the evaluation of PACS. The basic approach is the same, but is used where it is not possible to control for all important variables. Measures are made before and after implementation at a single site, or broad comparisons are made across a number of sites. Of course, this means that any effects observed may be due either to the technology or some other variable, but in practice observation of developments can help to identify major causal relationships. Again, though, these techniques establish the value of a system at a particular point in time, and do not of themselves facilitate projection of future values.

Another set of evaluation techniques can be grouped under the broad heading of accounting approaches. Calculation of Return on Investment is widely known. Another technique is Return on Management (Strassman, 1990), designed specifically to relate IT inputs to outputs. These approaches are useful for making broad estimates of likely costs and benefits of established systems whose impact on organisations is well understood. They are less useful where a technology is new, and so prediction of patterns of costs and benefits difficult.

Finally, there is a basket of methods with different theoretical underpinnings which have been used. These range from technically-oriented performance tests to naturalistic evaluation based on interview and observation. Regarding the latter, it should not be forgotten that many questions can be investigated only through 'soft' methods, and are not amenable to analysis with any of the more quantitative approaches listed here.

The key point about the approaches described here is that they depend on an understanding of the mechanisms whereby IT influences organisation processes; that is, on assumptions about relationships between causes and effects. Knowledge of these relationships is precisely what is missing with leading edge technologies – and arguably also from many others which are apparently well established. The IT evaluation literature does not, then, provide ways of tackling the two key questions and it is necessary to pursue other avenues.

4. ACCOUNTING FOR THE FUTURE

There are a number of possible ways forward. Some would advocate the use of futures exercises in this situation. Extrapolation from the present might be used to peer into the future: predictions might be made about technical, clinical and other developments to build up a picture of the future. Again, however, there are problems in making sensible predictions about the future impact of a system. What is needed, ideally, is a way of moving forward on the basis of concrete information.

Another possibility is to focus on concepts such as flexibility and on the inherent unpredictability of IT-related developments. In principle, it should be possible to develop measures of flexibility (e.g. Jones and Ostroy, 1984; Rosenhead, 1989) and use them to assess the extent to which IT confers or inhibits flexible working practices. At present there are no widely agreed measures of flexibility, though there seems to be no reason in principle why they could not be developed.

A third avenue involves viewing IT implementation as a research and development (R&D) exercise. One could then appeal to the considerable literature on the management of R&D projects, starting with the classic study by Burns and Stalker (1966). This approach stresses the dependence of success on management processes as much as on the product under development; one might examine the relationship between the technology, technologists and wider management processes. The R&D analogy also suggests that it may be necessary to rely on expert judgment about new information technologies, just as companies have to decide which R&D projects to fund on the basis of careful judgment of experts (and admittedly sometimes also on internal politics).

These approaches are very different from those described in the last section, and offer some useful clues. For example, the R&D analogy suggests that it may be important to keep a new system under continuous review, in the same way that new products are reviewed during their R&D phases. The possible importance of evaluating the flexibility of a system suggests that it should be explicitly addressed in any evaluation design. Above all, these approaches emphasise the potential value of evaluation during the implementation of a new system.

5. A DIFFERENT APPROACH TO THE EVALUATION OF IT

Evaluation of IT should possess a number of important characteristics. First, the evaluation must be sensitive to the way in which IT is implemented. It should explicitly recognise the inter-relatedness of project management, performance of a technology and of an organisation (Markus, 1983). It is generally agreed that large systems should be implemented in an iterative fashion, and this offers opportunities for evaluation at different (particularly early) stages of implementation. Evaluation should therefore be integrated into an iterative implementation process.

Second, for a technology of any size or expense, it is important to know its value sooner rather than later. For new systems, there is the additional consideration that it will bring unpredicted risks, which must be tackled before they jeopardise the organisation. Ideally, then, it should be possible to make decisions during implementation, rather than at the end when considerable time and large sums of money may have been committed. An analogy here is a drug trial, where early results are analysed while the trial continues. If these show that (for example) there are unacceptably severe side-effects then the trial is stopped.

It is important to set performance criteria against which the new technology can be judged, particularly to establish whether minimum criteria for continuing with implementation are met. A means must also be found for establishing whether a project is on course for demonstrating sufficient longer-term benefits to justify its costs. Taken together, these two points suggest that an on-going evaluation model would be appropriate.

A third point is that objectives for a new technology are often a mix of the clear and the unknown. One response to mixed or unknown objectives is to keep the right options open (Rosenhead, 1989), so that early decisions do not foreclose on desirable outcomes. (Note that if the evaluation is integrated into an implementation then the evaluator must also keep his or her options open. That is, the evaluation itself needs to be flexible, and respond to results as they become available. It may be that different methods are useful at different stages of an evaluation.)

Taken together, these three points are the basis for Recursive Evaluation, which incorporates evaluation within IT planning and implementation processes. It fits into box D in Figure 11.1. Its theoretical basis lies in constructivist evaluation; that is, evaluation which takes a pluralist, multiple-perspective stance.

Two evaluation methodologies seem particularly valuable. First, Scriven's (1973) concept of goal free evaluation is conceptually important. He contrasts preordinate (goal directed) and goal-free evaluation. Preordinate evaluation is essentially positivist, and concerned with ex-ante specification of objectives - that is, it attempts to 'lock in' an organisation's performance, in order to establish cause and effect. It asks whether an intervention is consistent with *historic* preferences. Preordinate evaluation tends to discourage changing organisational parameters, and is therefore insensitive to changing preferences or needs, and will tend to discourage innovation.

Goal-free evaluation takes the view that the focus of effort should be on establishing current performance. Scriven argues that evaluation should be relatively loosely organised. It should be concerned with establishing what is going on, rather than measurement against historical objectives. Scriven stresses that an

	Objectives specified	Objectives not specified
Prospective evaluation	A	B
On-going evaluation	C	D

Figure 11.1 Broad classification of evaluation approaches.

organisation should be evaluated on the basis of what it has accomplished. This allows for a positive outcome even where original objectives are not achieved, and/or a positive value to be placed on unanticipated achievements (innovations) that are consistent with current preferences. This is important, given the overly ambitious goals that organisations may commit themselves to, often as part of a process of obtaining funds; such goals may be of little practical value to evaluators.

This line of thinking fits reasonably well with the broad points outlined above. By itself, though, goal-free evaluation does not address them completely, not least in failing to offer a means of keeping one's options open, and it does not help to specify what methods might be appropriate.

Second, Guba and Lincoln (1989) have developed fourth generation evaluation (4GE). 4GE acknowledges the importance of responsive modes of inquiry, but develops the ideas of Scriven and others. It starts from the position that it is often difficult or impossible to say what the salient features of a problem are. As a result evaluators must enter into negotiations with stakeholders to establish the scope and nature of the evaluation, and the process of evaluation involves the creation of a consensus around an interpretation of a problem – in this case the possible value of a new information technology.

To trace the possible relevance of 4GE to the evaluation of IT, its four entry options and four inquiry steps are outlined in Figures 11.2 and 11.3. Some of the conditions are uncontroversial and apply in practice to the early stages of many positivist evaluations. However, others are problematic, most obviously the qualitative methods requirement which seems arbitrary. Guba and Lincoln argue that qualitative methods are preferred because most people do not understand numbers; but this is by no means universally true, and is certainly not true in health care. (It could also be argued that there is a premium on quantitative evidence about IT, since qualititative data have clearly not resolved questions about its value in health care and elsewhere.)

Guba and Lincoln also argue for a pluralist rather than a positivist approach to evaluation. For IT, though, it may be that a positivist/cause-effect model is sometimes the best available evaluation design model. This model is simply one among many possible evaluation approaches – but it is still an option. All of this said, the four steps can be helpful if they are interpreted in a particular way. In particular, it is possible to find a way of integrating quantitative methods into the 4GE methodology.

A distinction made by Guba and Lincoln (among many others), between methodology and methods, is crucial. The evaluation of IT should have a responsive/constructivist *methodology*, since the implementation of any large system properly involves negotiation among stakeholders; so evaluation should involve negotiation by the evaluators with stakeholders. The *methods* used can, though, be

ENTRY CONDITION	CONDITION MET?
Study should take place in a natural setting	Yes
At the outset, it is not clear what questions should be asked	Yes
Qualitative methods should be used	Rejected: quantitative methods are the currency of choice in health care research settings
Tacit knowledge can and should be used	Depends on knowledge of evaluator of application area

Figure 11.2 4GE entry conditions: are they met for IT in health care?

STEP	APPLICABLE TO IT?
Purposive (non-experimental) sampling	Yes, likely to use typical or critical cases
Continuous interplay of data collection and analysis	Yes, but evaluators and participants should only talk at the beginning and end of each evaluation step
Findings must be properly grounded	Yes, though results only discussed or negotiated at the end of each evaluation step
Emergent design	Yes, in that the design of the evaluation and the preferred system will emerge over time

Figure 11.3 Four steps in 4GE inquiry.

goal-based for many individual studies. That is, methods should be selected to address relevant questions in whatever way is deemed appropriate.

Sometimes this will result in a decision to design a randomised controlled trial, at others in semi-structured interviews. In some cases a single method may be sufficient. More often, however, multiple methods, each testing specific aspects of the system will be appropriate, and the methods should be coordinated to allow evaluation of the system as a whole. For the measurement and analysis phases the evaluators should act as independent agents, but the various stakeholders will come together to discuss the results (and ideally publish jointly).

6 RECURSIVE EVALUATION

The conduct of a Recursive Evaluation is best explained through an example. The example selected here is the implementation of a network linking a hospital to local general practices and community-based health professionals. One of the key questions is whether or not to include digital images on the network, since inclusion would increase costs by the order of millions of pounds. This is a specific example of a common challenge – the introduction of an expensive information technology into a complex organisation. There is encouraging, if limited, positive evidence in the literature that text-based network links between certain hospital departments may be a worthwhile investment (Tierney *et al.*, 1993; Anderson *et al.*, 1994). It is unclear, however, whether it is worth linking all parts of a hospital on a single system, or hospitals to general practices and other health care providers; and above all the value of imaging networks is simply not known.

Suppose that the hospital's managers feel they have sound arguments for proceeding, including the avoidance of long-term costs of linking disparate systems and the efficiency and quality gains derived from faster and more reliable data communication. The project team set up to manage the project finds that it is faced with some basic questions: is it necessary to link every department? what kinds of data do departments need to exchange? and so on. (It is important to point out that even where a new technology brings great uncertainty with it, it should still be possible to make sensible predictions about the nature of the main costs and benefits which can be used to guide the implementation. For example, it will often make sense to implement first where the greatest benefits are predicted, or perhaps in a department which is felt to be representative of most others.)

They may not know the answers to these questions until the system is fully implemented, when it may be too late; the organisation may have wasted some or all of its investment. They decide, therefore, to adopt a cautious approach, so as to minimise any risks to patients or the organisation as a whole. This involves a stepwise introduction of the system, which allows the managers to review progress at the end of each step. By decomposing the problem into more manageable parts, it also helps managers to identify possible costs and benefits within individual areas, in discussion with local staff.

They pilot the system within one directorate (functional group), general medicine, which is linked to several service departments including radiology and pathology. Beyond the hospital, general practitioners can make referrals to hospital clinicians using the network, and if they wish ask for general advice about patient care. Meetings with professionals suggest that the network might bring efficiency gains and cost savings, but nobody is confident about their scale or timing. Nevertheless, they agree some specific performance targets, and offer their opinions about the ways in which their services will develop over the next few years. These views of future developments are taken into account in designing the system to meet future as well as current requirements.

The project team involve staff from outside the directorate to take baseline measurements, for example of the numbers of patients treated and the resources committed to their care. Since the whole point of the exercise is to quantify the unknown, methods must be chosen which can pick up a wide range of changes. A broad cost-effectiveness framework will often be appropriate, but in principle any method which can pick up unexpected effects can be used. (Also, being statistically aware, they are careful to select a sample size that will give them results at the level of significance they need.) They implement the system, and then the outside staff repeat the measurements. These results give them the short-run costs and benefits of operating the system in the medicine directorate.

The project team also address the question of the likely long-term value of the network. They elect to explore this question in terms of its flexibility – the options kept open or foregone (though note that they might choose another approach if it is deemed more appropriate). After this first step the project team need to establish:

- which initial option has (in retrospect) been taken – this may be very difficult to predict with a new technology;
- which options, particularly desirable ones, remain open.

The evaluative question is whether the new point the organisation has reached is within the 'desirable' range of options. Which options do they need to keep open? The team must be able to identify thresholds, at which flexibility moves from 'desirable' to 'undesirable'. This is a matter of judgment; there is no magic solution to identifying thresholds. Ways in which this might be done are not the focus of this paper, but suffice to say that one possibility is to undertake a robustness analysis (Rosenhead, 1989), which is conceptually simple and easily performed. However, the precise method is less important than the general principle that some assessment of progress towards general long-term goals must be made.

Suppose that it turns out that the first iteration is moderately encouraging. There are some efficiency gains, though overall evidence is mixed. However, the project team find it difficult to decide whether the network should be extended. For example, it is difficult to draw inferences about other functional areas such as surgery, since their work patterns are very different to medicine's; and the costs and benefits of total integration are difficult to estimate from partial exercises. (If an organisation is sufficiently homogeneous, of course, this problem might not be too serious. The results from – say – one building society office could be used to predict the impact of IT in other offices with reasonable confidence. Even here some caution is necessary, though, since cultures can vary greatly from office to office.)

More importantly, it also appears that flexibility is being reduced; for example, the hospital's capacity to respond to changes in admission and discharge practices is reduced, since major system redesign would be required to support it. This emphasises the importance of including flexibility in the evaluation. Positive findings from 'conventional' analysis of the pilot might lead the project team to go ahead, whereas the finding that flexibility is already substantially reduced will at least give pause for thought; the hospital may be going down a route that makes it dangerously vulnerable to changing circumstances.

The project team decides to go ahead, judging that flexibility is not too seriously reduced. They could simply repeat the exercise for the next directorate. Note, though, that things have changed. Additional information has been gained from the pilot, and the passage of time means that information from external sources on new products or management techniques is also available. This allows the project team to redefine long-term objectives and flexibility criteria. That is, the balance of short-term and long-term goals can be re-evaluated. This may lead them to use different measures to pick up different effects during the second implementation step.

This highlights a more general point, namely that the evaluation itself needs to be flexible; it is incorporated within planning and implementation processes, and so must be designed to obtain the results of interest to stakeholders. This picks up the point made earlier that evaluation should be responsive to the changing preferences of internal stakeholders and changes in the external environment.

Let us imagine that they decide to extend the network to the surgery directorate. How they get on in the longer term is not our concern. Two points are, however, worth making. First, the extension to the network may alter its value within the first directorate – it might be that there is substantial data traffic between medicine and surgery. It is important, therefore, to assess the value of the network as a whole rather than in surgery alone. (Put another way, the whole may be greater than the sum of the parts and the evaluation design must take this into account.) Second, there will come a point at which it is sensible to make a judgment about whether to extend the network across the whole area, stop at a specific point or even abandon it (which could occur if extension to surgery is problematic). While this decision will never be easy, the extensive data collected should allow a properly informed decision.

6. CONCLUSION

The iterative process described here is consistent with more sophisticated approaches to planning. Good planning incorporates judgments about flexibility as well as about the more obvious costs and benefits of projects. It is perhaps surprising that so much attention has been paid to planning, and relatively little to evaluation of major plans and projects. Recursive Evaluation offers one way forward which helps to redress the imbalance.

Recursive Evaluation is quite distinct from the conventional approaches listed earlier. Yet the reason for developing it derives from simple observations about the way IT is implemented. We all know that technologies can be rendered redundant by changing circumstances, and that some are easier to adapt than others. Given this, it seems sensible to find ways of taking account of flexibility and unpredictability in evaluations. Recursive Evaluation is one such way.

REFERENCES

Anderson, J *et al.* (1994) *Evaluating health care information systems*, Sage, Newbury Park CA.

Burns, T and Stalker, G (1966) *The management of innovation*, Social Science Paperbacks, London.

Coffey, R. (1980) *How a medical information system affects hospital costs: the El Camino Hospital experience*, Washington DC, US Department of Health, Education and Welfare, National Center for Health Services Research.

Drummond, M, Stoddart, G and Torrance, G. (1987) *Methods for the economic evaluation of health care programmes*, Oxford University Press, Oxford.

Guba, E and Lincoln, Y (1989) *Fourth generation evaluation*, Sage, Newbury Park CA.

Jones, R and Ostroy, J (1984) Flexibility and uncertainty, *Review of Economic Studies*, **51**, 13-32.

Keen, J *et al.* (1994) A model for the evaluation of PACS, Paper presented at SCAR94, Winston-Salem, NC.

Markus, M L (1983) Power, politics and MIS implementation, *Communications of the ACM*, **26**, 430-444.

Parker, M, Benson, R and Trainor, H. (1988) *Information Economics*, Prentice Hall International, Englewood Cliffs, NJ.

Rosenhead, J. (1989) *Rational Analysis for a Problematic World*, Wiley, Chichester.

Scriven, M (1973) Goal-free evaluation. In E House (editor), *School Evaluation: the politics and process*, McCutchan, Berkeley, CA.

Strassman P. (1990) *The Business Value of Computers*, Information Economics Press, New Canaan, CT.

Tierney, W, Miller, M, Overhage, M and McDonald, C. (1993) Physician inpatient order writing on microcomputer workstations, *Journal of the American Medical Association*, **269**, 379-383.

Yin, R (1994) *Case study research*, Second edition, Sage, Newbury Park CA.

12 Information technology outsourcing: economics, contracting and measurement

Leslie Willcocks
Fellow in Information Management, Templeton College, University of Oxford
Mary Lacity
University of Missouri, St Louis, USA and
Visiting Research Fellow, Templeton College, University of Oxford
Guy Fitzgerald
Cable & Wireless Professor of Information Systems, Birkbeck College, University of London

1. INTRODUCTION: THE ASSESSMENT CHALLENGE

This chapter reports the combined findings on major assessment issues in Information Technology (IT) outsourcing practice from two studies conducted in the 1990–93 period (see Lacity and Hirschheim, 1993a; Willcocks and Fitzgerald, 1994a). The studies were conducted in the United States and United Kingdom respectively, and covered 43 case histories of outsourcing assessment and practice. Additionally, we utilise findings from a European survey of IT outsourcing practice conducted in 1993 (Fitzgerald and Willcocks, 1993).

In this chapter, IT outsourcing means handing over to third party management, for required result, some or all of an organisation's Information Technology (IT), systems (IS) and related services. So defined, outsourcing does not exhaust the ways in which the IT services market can be used. Thus we make a key distinction between contracts that specify a service and result which the market is to provide ('outsourcing'), and contracts which call for the market to provide resources to be deployed under the buyer's management and control ('insourcing') Furthermore, contracting under each of these regimes may be on a spot transaction or a longer term ,partnering, basis (Feeny *et al.*, 1993). This chapter is concerned specifically with IT outsourcing arrangements. However, the research covered a spectrum of organisations variously involved in short- and long-term deals, insourcing and outsourcing, and also organisations that had contemplated outsourcing only to reject it in favour of the in-house option. We draw upon this research base throughout the chapter to compare and contrast the economic attractiveness of IT outsourcing against the alternatives.

IT outsourcing is a growing phenomenon in the developed economies. The Yankee Group (1992) estimated global revenues for all types of IT outsourcing as rising to $49.5 billion by 1994. In the UK IT outsourcing spend was £800 million in 1993, and is projected to rise to £1.72 billion by 1998 (Fitzgerald and Willcocks, 1993). What explains this growth? Our own research studies suggest that four general drivers seem to be operating:

1. IT outsourcing is often a response to the hype and publicity surrounding the subject; a bandwagon effect leads to senior executives asking: why don't we outsource IT?
2. Outsourcing may be a response to tough economic and competitive climates and the need to cut, or at least control costs.
3. IT outsourcing may be part of larger and longer term changes in how organisations are structured and managed.
4. Outsourcing may well reflect the desire of senior managers to get rid of a troublesome IT function that finds it difficult to demonstrate its own business value (Lacity and Hirschheim, 1993a; Willcocks and Fitzgerald, 1994a; Lacity, Hirschheim and Willcocks, 1994).

In the cases we have investigated a mix of reasons for IT outsourcing were advanced. These ranged through financial, technical and political objectives to a concern to focus effort on core competences. In the last case, the thinking reflected that espoused by commentators such as Pralahad and Hamel (1990) and Quinn (1992). Either IT was identified as a non-core competence, and so could be outsourced. Alternatively, aspects of the IT function were identified as 'core', for example systems that enabled the organisation to differentiate itself from the competition, while others were identified as 'commodities' that could be more usefully and economically outsourced. In the vast majority of cases, cost savings of between 10–40% were anticipated, and invariably a strong economic logic for outsourcing IT was advanced. However, the economic payoff was not always that anticipated. The European survey found that where lower costs were measured, they were running 19% lower on average, ranging between 5–20% in most cases. However, 18% of organisations surveyed reported higher costs averaging 22% as a result of outsourcing IT. More worryingly, 30% of organisations could not, or had not tried to quantify the costs and benefits of IT outsourcing. A related finding was that when organisations were asked about risks that became reality during outsourcing, the biggest risk was the hidden costs of the contract, closely followed by the credibility of vendor claims (Fitzgerald and Willcocks, 1993).

In all our studies, assessment issues emerged strongly as critically affecting levels of success and failure in IT outsourcing. In particular, many respondents themselves noted four areas of weakness in their practice:

1. Failure to establish adequate measurement of the pre-existing in-house performance.

2. Limitations in the economic assessment of vendor bids.
3. Failures in contracting in sufficient detail.
4. Inadequate attention to setting up measurement systems to monitor vendor performance.

In this chapter we look at the assessment issues in these areas, and provide guidelines to improved assessment practice.

2. ECONOMICS OF THE VENDOR BID

In this section, we look at bids from IT outsourcing vendors mainly from an economic viewpoint. Clearly other factors also influence the degree to which any outsourcing arrangements can be sustained. As some examples, the client organisation will need to assess the technical capability of the vendor to deliver what it promises, the cultural fit between client and vendor, and the quality of the relationship between the relevant staff in both organisations. A full discussion of such factors appears in Willcocks and Fitzgerald (1994a). While such factors are important and invariably have economic consequences, this section focuses on the more directly economic factors in any vendor bid.A proposed outsourcing evaluation process is shown in Figure 13.1.

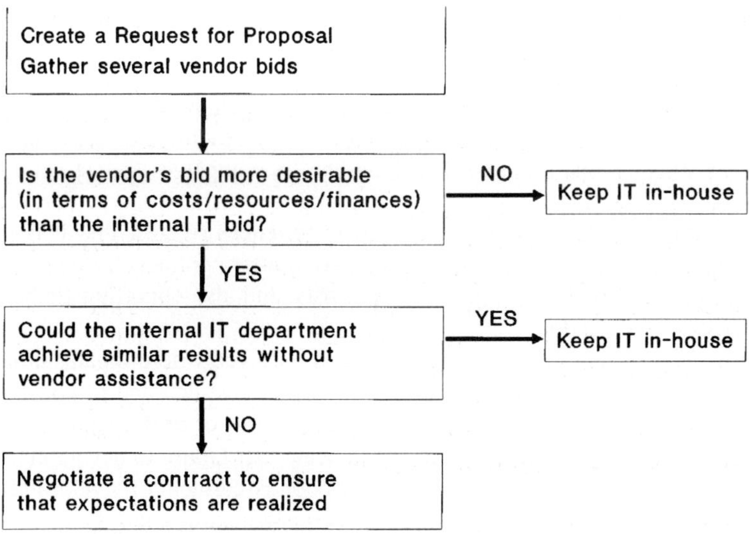

Figure 13.1 Proposed outsourcing evaluation process (Source: Lacity and Hirschheim, 1993a).

This section will use the framework for discussing the importance of the pre-existing evaluation process, the sources of hidden costs, some myths in the economics of IT outsourcing, and the central role of the contract in any outsourcing arrangement.

2.1 Influence of pre-existing evaluation practice

There is already much advice and indeed some prior academic research on the economics of IT outsourcing (e.g. Aucoin *et al.*, 1991; Buck-Lew, 1992; Due, 1992; Gupta and Gupta, 1992; I/S Analyzer, 1990). However, there is little work on how to make detailed comparisons with in-house options. A particularly noticeable gap is the lack of attention given to the relationship between prior IT evaluation practice and ability to assess bids from outsourcing vendors. In fact, a major finding from our research is that organisations find it very difficult to assess properly vendor bids against each other, and against any in-house bid, due to poor pre-existing evaluation practice.

As detailed in Willcocks (1994), typical weaknesses in prior IT evaluation practice include:

- not fully investigating risk and its potential cost;
- understating knock-on operating, maintenance and human and organisational costs; budgeting practices that conceal full costs;
- lack of metrics to assess the business contribution of IT;
- use of inappropriate metrics, given the objectives set for specific IT projects; inadequate approaches to dealing with 'intangible' benefits and for tracking benefits over long time-scales.

For an organisation contemplating outsourcing, such weaknesses mean that a great deal of effort will need to be invested in understanding the costs and benefits of the existing IT operation so that these can be compared against vendor bids. Respondents found this best done in the lead up to the Request For Proposal. Many respondents left it until later; their experiences suggest that it is rarely a good idea to postpone this analysis to the period after contracts have been signed. This can promote both subsequent hidden costs, and also opportunistic behaviour on the part of the vendor.

This detailed analysis needs to be carried out even where organisations have already moved to full in-house charging systems, have detailed in-house service level agreements and/or operate in-house IT as a cost or profit centre (Willcocks and Fitzgerald, 1995). Our own findings indicate that failure to devote managerial effort to this evaluation task means not only poor assessment of vendor bids; there is also a knock-on effect into setting up inadequate measurement systems for subsequent vendor performance. These issues are pursued further in section 13.3.

2.2 Sources of hidden costs

As noted above, a consistent finding across our case studies was that outsourcing frequently carried hidden costs. As one extreme example, Lacity and Hirschheim (1993a) found one petroleum company being charged almost $500,000 in 'excess fees' in the first month into a new contract. More often the hidden costs are less dramatic but accumulate to a significant figure over time. As well as inadequate measurement systems, there seem to be five additional root causes of such hidden costs. They all relate to weaknesses in contracting. These are:

1. Failure to fully define present IT requirements.
2. Failure to define fully future requirements, or failure to create mechanisms for protecting price in the face of contingencies.
3. Loopholes or ambiguities in the contract.
4. Not allowing the vendor a reasonable profit.
5. Unforeseen, rising, in-house contract management costs as a result of weak contracting practice.

Looking at the first three here, we found these weaknesses leaving client organisations open not only to additional costs for services not previously contracted for, but also to higher prices for those services. Loopholes/ambiguities in the contract may also trigger conflicts with, and also opportunistic behaviour by, vendors. As one example, a major US bank in 1992 signed a contract stating that the cost of transferring all software licencing agreements would be borne by the client. The first 30 agreements cost very little to transfer, but the last few involved many thousands of pounds. The contract manager felt that the vendor knew the cost implications of the contract, but had not spelt these out to the client. That said, however, vendor opportunism can also be triggered by not allowing the vendor a reasonable profit. Vendor account managers then come under internal pressure to make their margins from the outsourcing deal.

Finally, we note that in-house management costs in terms of new roles, time and effort are frequently higher than anticipated. IT outsourcing was viewed by some respondents as 'spending rather than managing'. However, our research points out that in all outsourcing arrangements, key management capabilities need to be retained in-house. At a minimum these cover:

- strategic thinking on IT in relation to the business;
- systems integration;
- eliciting business demand for IT;
- spotting business opportunities for the use of IT;
- an 'informed buyer' role;
- contract monitoring, and

- the ability to lever vendor relations to advantage (Willcocks and Fitzgerald, 1994b).

Such costs may not be built into the preliminary assessment of a vendor bid, but we found them to be typical rather than unusual outcomes in most outsourcing arrangements we researched.

2.3 Some economic myths in outsourcing

Detailed analysis of in-house IT performance together with assessing all the likely costs of outsourcing IT helps to establish whether the vendor's bid is more favourable than any likely bid by the internal IT department. To help further in this assessment, some possible sources of additional outsourcing costs are indicated in Figures 13.2 and 13.3. To add to this picture, it is useful to ask whether an internal IT department can achieve similar results without vendor assistance (see Figure 13.1). Our research on this subject indicates that there are two central economic myths propagated by many vendors and trade press sources. One myth is that IT outsourcing vendors are inherently more efficient than internal IT departments. The second myth is that savings of 10–50% can be achieved only through outsourcing (Lacity and Hirschheim, 1993b.; Willcocks and Fitzgerald, 1995). Let us look at these propositions in more detail.

2.3.1 Are IT outsourcing vendors inherently more efficient?

In practice, internal IT departments can be cost competitive with external vendors. The argument that vendors are inherently more efficient is usually based on notions of economies of scale. It is often considered that vendors achieve two types of scale economies over in-house departments: through higher mass production efficiency and through labour specialization efficiencies. In practice, it is difficult to measure such efficiencies in IT settings. However, our evidence is that the advantages vendors bring to bear are generally overstated:

1. Mass production efficiencies will be expressed as lower data processing costs (cost per MIP), and/or lower hardware and software purchasing costs. In practice, a number of our respondents reported operating at high efficiency in-house at the 150–170 MIPs range. Some commentators suggest that after 300 MIPs the benefits of transferring to a larger IT shop are negligible (Bergstrom, 1991; Krass, 1990). Three companies in our studies were running 28, 14 and 17 MIP shops respectively, and all were more efficient in terms of cost-per-MIP than large vendor-run data centres. Real Decisions Corporation have found companies reducing data centre costs by 17–25% a year without outsourcing (Bergstrom, 1991).

   On hardware and software costs, the theory is that buying in bulk allows a vendor to buy at cheaper prices. In practice we found many in-house IT functions receiving discounts similar to outsourcing vendors. Smaller companies can also negotiate cheap hardware leases by using older technology, or by using cheaper networked technology. Software companies are becoming harder on charging for the transfer of software licensing agreements. Furthermore, in several of our cases, contracts stipulated that the costs of transfer of licensing agreements fell on the client company, not the vendor.

2. Labour specialisation efficiencies come from the wider access vendors can have to technical and business talent. In practice many companies outsource to access the vendor's pool of technical talent only to find that (a) they are supported by the same staff, though sometimes at a lower cost, and (b) additional vendor expertise is expensive. As one respondent noted:

   "None of it is cheap. I guess there is a perception that once you have (a vendor) locked in that you have a conduit to all this expertise, but you pay."

   We also found examples where, after the first year of a contract a vendor moved their experienced, skilled staff off on to newer contracts, or where the better transferred staff with critical business knowledge of a company were nevertheless moved to other contracts run by the vendor. On business talent, many participants who outsourced felt a real loss of business expertise, as talented ex-employees were siphoned off by the vendor to assist in attracting other customers from the same industry. However, even where a vendor may be inherently more efficient on labour costs, the natural cost advantage still needs to be significant to cover the vendor's profit margin.

2.3.2 Can savings of 10–50% only be achieved through outsourcing?

We found organisations achieving savings internally through a variety of measures. The organisations that were more hard-headed about IT outsourcing tended to drive down costs as much as possible internally before then considering outsourcing proposals. The alternative approach tended to allow the vendor to 'pick the low lying fruit', that is take, as an additional part of profit on the deal, those cost reductions that could have been achieved internally. As one high profile example, it is probable that this happened in the 1988/9 Eastman Kodak/IBM deal.

Organisations can also drive down internal costs by consolidating data centres. As one example in our sample, Citibank in Europe did this before seeking an outsourcing agreement with a vendor to run those datacentres. In several examples where organisations decided against outsourcing, costs were driven down by optimising resource use, implementing strict cost controls, and by upskilling existing staff rather than seeking access to more expensive technical staff available on the market. Again, even where a vendor may have inherent economies of scale in these areas, these usually still need to be significant in order to offset required profit margins. That said, we found examples where there were political reasons why the IT department could not bring cost savings to bear, or where there were demands to reduce the IT headcount, or where the business required cash from the sale of information assets or needed to move IT from a fixed to a more variable expense. In such cases, the economic logic against outsourcing became intermingled and diverted through a variety of often conflicting stakeholder interests and perspectives.

2.4 The centrality of the contract

A major finding from our research is that, if an organisation outsources IT, the outsourcing contract is the only certain way to ensure that expectations are realized (see Figure 13.1). In practice, weak contracting, based on inadequate assessment of a vendor bid and backed up by poor monitoring systems, not only results in unanticipated, higher costs; it can create major problems for client organisations. In practice it is all too easy for all parties to a contract to agree broadly on what is required from a vendor. We also found parties all too frequently relying on 'partnering' notions to offset any difficulties arising from loose contracting. These rarely proved a sufficient base in themselves from which to run effective outsourcing arrangements (Lacity and Hirschheim, 1993b; Fitzgerald and Willcocks, 1994). The issue is succinctly summarised by one of our respondents:

> "Outsourcing contracts are agreed in concept and delivered in detail, and that's why they break down." (Vendor manager)

When it came to drawing up effective outsourcing contracts we found that indeed the devil is in the detail. Figures 13.2 and 13.3 provide summaries of the typical benefits organisations looked for, and which vendors promised, in the IT outsourcing deals we studied. The anticipated benefits are listed on the left hand side of the Figures. On the right side we list the issues that regularly arose amongst our respondents in the 43 case studies and in the survey.

It became clear from our research that unless, at a minimum, the questions listed here were addressed before IT outsourcing contracts were signed, then unanticipated costs and some significant problems tended to fall upon client organisations. Some more issues on the economic aspects of contracting are pursued in the next section.

3. OUTSOURCING – SETTING UP A MEASUREMENT SYSTEM

Once an organisation has decided to outsource any aspect of its IT function, it

FOR	QUESTIONS
"Cost savings"	BUT: Over what time period? Can you achieve savings on your own?
"Provides scarce IT skills"	At what price? In the contract?
"Better quality service"	A point of no return? Continuity of staff? How measured?
"Assist cash flow problems"	Pay for it later?
"Enables focus on core needs and skills of the business"	Reliability of service Do you need to keep parts of the IS function in-house?

Figure 13.2 Assessing the vendor bid: benefits and issues (1).

FOR	QUESTIONS
"Flexibility to go into advanced/new technologies	In the contract? Price? Available from suppliers? Control?
"Saves money by mopping up excess mainframe capacity	Shared technology? Switching costs if contract is unsatisfactory? Security and contingency issues?
"Clear accountability"	How detailed/sketchy is the contractual relationship?
"Increased management control"	In-house contract management skills?
"Manage demand fluctuations better"	Over what range? At what price?

Figure 13.3 Assessing the vendor bid: benefits and issues (2).

will need to monitor vendor performance. In this section we extend the discussion on the importance of the contract as the fundamental building block for a measurement system, and look at respondents' experiences with different types of outsourcing contracts. We then focus on issues relating to measurement systems and service level agreements, and provide guidelines on these topics.

3.1 Tight and loose contracting

Where organisations are setting up and running measurement systems for vendor performance, the most common potential 'bad practice' areas we have observed in our case studies are:

- over-reliance on the pre-existing standards and measurement systems; and
- failure to define comprehensively in the initial contract the detailed expectations of both sides on standards and how measurement will proceed.

These usually occurred either through time pressures or a belief in the 'good offices' espoused by the vendor. Much depends on the quality of the relationship between vendor and client, of course. Several of our respondent organisations were still actually refining measures during the first six months of the contract. This worked reasonably well where, in the early stages of a contract, the vendor was anxious to demonstrate flexibility and good partnering. One example here in the first year of the contracts was at Pilkington PLC (Figure 13.4).

Note why the Pilkington-EDS approach is working. The previous service levels on the data centre had been largely detailed before outsourcing. Previous service levels delivered were largely what was required of the vendor anyway. The

Pilkington and EDS Scicon form a good example of a successful partnering arrangement allowing some flexibility in how measurement is managed during the contract. In 1992 Pilkingtons outsourced both their Head Office mainframes and also the development of new replacement applications. This was part of a larger HO reorganization with many uncertainties about future needs and direction. According to senior managers at Pilkington they were looking for a minimum fixed price contract with provision to add other things to it as they materialised. They could only define quite high level deliverables because the reorganisation was at an early stage. To put a boundary around the contract Pilkington and EDS Scicon did it by resourcing level. This meant including in the contract a clause that said words to the effect that EDS 'will deliver all of these things or any substitutions thereof by mutual agreement, provided it can be delivered by a maximum complement of 37 people and to defined service levels for the ongoing services.' Pilkington wanted a very flexible arrangement so that it could be changed over time according to their wishes.

On the mainframe side the service level was going to be around existing services. The service level agreement was put in place by the start of the Pilkington financial year 1 April 1992.According to the EDS Account Manager:

> 'We spent the first 3 months of the contract securing the service, settling it down and defining and agreeing service levels with the customer. So they weren't put in the contract on day one, there was like a 90 day period to get the service levels in place. However the development side was largely left to trust.... it was very much around setting the deliverables down, targeting that delivery and having a monthly steering group in place with both parties around each development activity to monitor progress. That would then flag up if we got into contractual problems in terms of deliverables. We set up the management and control mechanisms to monitor progress of projects, to overcome the dilemma of not being able to have properly defined service levels agreements on what is quite a fluid development environment.
>
> We haven't violated a single service level criteria since we started the contract. There were very elaborate calculations as to what it would take to get to a violation, but having said that, it wouldn't take many incidents of down time to actually trigger off a penalty. Thankfully the service has been fine all the way through so far. I think the service was fine before. I don't think Pilkington would have entertained EDS Scicon taking on their people, and delivering those self same things if they weren't satisfied in the first place. If anything probably the service has improved since we moved across because we have been able to put even more technical skill in to help.' (Tony Rickles, EDS Scicon).

Figure 13.4 Case study – measurement on a partnership basis

previous Pilkington IT manager had transferred to the vendor and was managing the contract for them – there was a good vendor-client relationship in place from the beginning. The client knew that it needed a flexible arrangement on vendor performance on the IS development side, and carefully selected the vendor for its ability to deliver this flexibility. Both were clear on the mutual expectations on this point before the contract began. There was also a short-term (3 year) contract to minimise the risk. The means for handling changes in service requirements were specified at the start.

However, in several other contracts we have looked at vendors were more concerned to keep very close to the original contract. This created contract management issues that became exacerbated where the contract was vague or did not cover issues arising. The problem we identified was one of different perceptions by the vendor and client of the meaning and role of the contract. In many cases, the client believed in the rhetoric of partnership much more than the vendor. The emerging lesson was that participants need to be clear as to what the relationship amounts to and how both sides understand it. Another issue arises here. While clients had a tendency to believe that the quality of the vendor-client relationship would see them over limitations of performance measurement arrangements in the contract, in fact the latter could also come to affect the former adversely. In one contract we researched, it took some 18 months of vigorous contract management finally to get the performance measures right and end disputes on service. The contract manager described the situation as follows:

> "There was a contract, a legal one with our signatures on it, with various sections in it, but really it did not define what the service was going to be. And worse still when we invoked penalty clauses, the section in the contract that talked about the penalty clauses was so ambiguously written that we had a bun fight for nearly 6 months over it. It wasn't the question of how much (it turned out to be something like £30,000, which over a multi-million contract was pretty small) but it was the bun fight that was the problem, the fact that they (the vendor) didn't just walk in on the following Monday and say 'we screwed up last week, we were down for three days, and according to the contract this is what you are owed'. I think that all of that proved to me at that stage anyway, that we needed to get out of this partnership issue and back into a proper business contractual relationship and that is what really set us off, I think, down the right road." (Contract manager: UK retail company).

In another case the client was disappointed that the vendor kept rigorously to the contract. The vendor did so because of very slim profit margins but the client felt that something more had been promised. The learning points, according to our respondent, were that the safe option in the period just before signing the contract is to get what is said actually written into the contract; and be prepared to spend time chronicling the agreement in monotonous detail. In all three cases here described the vendor-client relationships became adversely affected because of problems with operationalising the contract.

3.2 Measurement: systems and service levels

We have seen that it is possible to operate on a more flexible partnership basis, and also that some areas to be outsourced may be difficult to specify precisely in terms of service and performance required. However, in outsourcing discretion may be the better part of valour. In reviewing 13 organisations contemplating or undertaking outsourcing, Lacity and Hirschheim (1993a,b) usefully suggested the following safety first guidelines on creating a measurement system:

1. Measure EVERYTHING during the baseline period.
2. Develop service level measures.
3. Develop service level reports.
4. Specify escalation procedures.
5. Include cash penalties for non-performance.
6. Determine growth rates.
7. Adjust charges to changes in business.

The experiences recorded in the UK study fit fairly closely with these guidelines. We will review these in the light of all the cases researched in the two studies. A later section will then deal with additional assessment problem areas we identified as arising during the course of outsourcing contracts.

On the first item listed above, it is useful not to start a contract until current information systems services have been measured in a *baseline period*. There are a number of points here. Some respondents left the contract incomplete with a view to carrying out measurement in a baseline period *after* the contract had started, or trusting to a good relationship with the vendor to deal with problems as they arise. Both approaches are hardly low risk and can leave an organisation as a hostage to fortune. An early 1990s contract between a major UK retail and distribution company and a vendor of telecommunications services was, as at 1994, producing major cost savings but the measurement system still needed tidying up during the course of the contract because of lack of specific targets when it was drawn up:

> "(The vendor) largely wrote it and we signed it. All we were looking for was escalation procedures, what the nap connection charges were, and there was some discussion as to how they would respond and that they wouldn't do this that and the other. Even those comments were ambiguous in the way that they had been written. In undertaking the Service Level Agreement procedure and

the definition of our SLA's I think two things were sorted out. First of all, we then developed a service level agreement that was ours. We went and asked our companies, what do you want. The basis was simply an IT spec. Once we'd done that we then realised that we had no telecommunications targets and strategy relative to the vendor, so we developed them. It was from that point onwards that wrested control from... (the vendor).. of our telecommunications strategy, back to where it should have been, which was here all along. Now everyone understands exactly what their roles and responsibilities are. But we had to learn that." (Contract manager: retail and distribution company).

Secondly, there may be time pressure to get a contract started. This may cut down on the time in which the baseline period for measurement is allowed to run. Lacity and Hirschheim (1993a) recommend a six month period to allow for fluctuations in service levels due to factors like tax season, seasonal business oscillations, and end of year data processing, for example. If service levels are measured monthly and compared, this then allows the setting up of a target variance for each service performance to fluctuate within before 'excess' charges to the vendor will become payable, or underperformance by the vendor can be penalised.

Refining the measurement system after the contract has started can work, provided this was part of the contractual agreement in the first place. Thus a major US-based bank signed an early 1990s outsourcing contract for running its mainframe service. A notable point here is that the pre-existing measurement system was fairly rigorous already.

"Broad inferences were given based upon the service agreements that... (the bank's).. data centre already had on its businesses. They were not really formal service level agreements. They were merely statements of what the online day would be from when to when by service, of all the many different services we have across all the different hardware platforms..... All that was made available to ..(the vendor).., and established as the initial SLA guidelines. The bank then tasked itself with the vendor's agreement to getting much more crisp SLAs and we spent a lot of time with piloting and doing various other things to try and come up with standard, across-the-region support agreements and service level agreements which everyone could sign up to. We are on to reiteration three about now (1993) and close to signing off what will be the final SLA's." (Contract manager, US bank).

A further stipulation about the baseline period is to *measure everything, not just what is easiest to measure.* The problem is less prevalent where what is being outsourced is an area that was being heavily measured before and is on the more traditional 'factory' or production side of IT operations. By this we mean telecommunications and mainframe data centre work. However, there can be a learning curve even here. Thus, WH Smith outsourced telecommunications to DEC, and from the experience was able to formulate much tighter measurement for a 1992 contract between Our Price Records, a company in the group, and the vendor Racal. The sorts of performance items measured in a data centre are well known. Measures on unit cost, efficiency, and availability are required. Typically, there should also be measures of customer service, for example problem resolution time and levels and quality of service required.

A more difficult area to measure, whether outsourced or not, is systems development. Our own view, argued elsewhere, is that these areas are probably best managed on an 'insourcing' rather than on a strict 'outsourcing' basis (Willcocks, Fitzgerald and Feeny, 1994). The problem is that the end goal for systems development, and how to get there, can rarely be well-defined. Some organisations, as in the case of Pilkingtons (Figure 13.4), handle this by stipulating that the vendor will make defined resources available for a defined period. There also need to be in place measures of the productivity of vendor staff. However these should not be based merely on the speed with which development proceeds through a defined methodology and timetable. The outputs of development also need to be measured in terms of business impact – for example improvements in cost, quality and service; systems reliability, ease of use, ease of user learning. The elapsed time to business use is also a useful measure, with financial penalties built in for under-performance. Also how far what is developed conforms to corporate architecture and how far software is and will be re-used.

These are difficult types of measures to formulate unless there are in-house systems people on the team, who already have key targets and measures in place before outsourcing. Thus in 1988 a UK manufacturing company outsourced micro-vax and software development of warehouse and carousel control systems in the factory. There was a lack of in-house expertise in this area. It emerged that there were complex interfaces with the company's mainframe systems and the mainframe development work was outsourced to a further vendor. The company had no complaints about the work of these vendors:

> "It was lack of appreciation of the complexity of the interface early on because of not high enough calibre staff internally to recognise that. Also nearly every department was affected in some way by these systems. Yet despite at the outset it was recognised as a business objective to enhance the capability of the site to deal with orders we found ourselves in a situation where as software was developed and then went to user acceptance testing it was only then that users realised what the system was doing and then raised very real problems....... it has enabled us to rationalise production in Europe but it was longer than it should have been and cost more and it took us longer to become self-sufficient. We were too dependent on a third party for a core,

essential business application." (IT manager: UK manufacturing company)

In later development projects this company successfully operated an 'insourcing' approach, bringing external expertise on to in-house teams to ensure transfer of learning takes place. They have also operated with clearer objectives and measures on development performance, not merely on hours worked and effort expended.

In addition to the above areas there may be a series of services commonly given by the IT department but not documented. Before outsourcing, it is important that these are analysed and included in the service agreement with the vendor along with measures of their delivery. What is not included in baseline period measurement will not be covered by the fixed price offered by the vendor and subsequently may be be open to 'excess charges'. Examples of such services may be consultancy, PC support, installation, training services. An overview of service performance measurement by a manufacturing company we have researched helps to indicate the comprehensiveness needed for a measurement system for in-house and vendor performance. The following are only the higher level measures in place:

- Information processing service performance – % availability; annual rolling availability; unscheduled business interruptions by number of events and time.
- Information processing service to distribution – network and database availability; terminal response times; problems processed within stipulated time
- Information processing service to sales force – successful transmissions at first attempt for salesmen terminals and VANs; successful EDI connections.
- Information processing mainframe capacity – % CPU for personal and operational busy hours for six modes of processing.
- Systems development – % efficiency actual vs. budget; headcount actual vs. budget, monthly project analysis of current and closed projects on time and cost criteria; quality ratios. Detailed monthly project reports.
- Systems support – queries resolved vs. backlog; query analysis by business function type and volume.

Clearly, *specifying service level measures* is critical. Lacity and Hirschheim (1993a) point out that, while this is regularly done a common mistake is to not then stipulate 100% service accountability from the vendor. At one help desk support contract we researched in a major UK-based oil company, 80% of service requests had to be responded to within 20s seconds and 90% within 30 seconds. Financial penalties attached to failure to meet these criteria over a specified time period. However the vendor was also made responsible for reporting in detail on this performance and provide explanations where 100% was not achieved. In a more critical area a measure would also be needed to ensure that the service requests not handled within the stipulated criteria were subsequently dealt with in an agreed reasonable time. Note also in this example the importance of *detailed service level reports.* Also the importance of agreeing in advance what happens where problems escalate, for example providing explanations. This must lead on to *financial penalties for non-performance* as shown in this example from a UK-based bank:

> "It was agreed at contract time there would be financial penalties.... for failure to perform of two kinds. One, if a direct operational loss is caused because of negligence on (the vendor's) part in any one instance and the bank has to pay its clients money in terms of interest charges or penalties, then (the vendor) will indemnify... (the company). up to certain limits, and that's on a one time basis...... Secondly if on an overall average service evaluation, taking its ability to provide a service over the course of a month, it fell below a specified level. So we have two specific financial implications of failure to deliver the service, one over time and one for a particular occasion, and that's well in place." (IT manager: major UK bank)

It is also important to look to the future when negotiating service levels and their price. A particular issue emerging issue from our research was how easy it was to underestimate the rate at which service needs will grow. Based on their own experiences, respondents stressed the need to include realistic growth rates in the contract agreement's fixed price. Specific clauses may also be needed to cover large service volume fluctuations due to merger, acquisitions or sale of parts of the business. Overall, it emerged as important for client organisations to make measurement work for rather than against their interests. Thus in one US manufacturing company the contract specified a two second response time for key applications such as order entry and customer service. It also specified vendor support for up to 20 users at a given time using a 4GL. However during the first week the 11 4GL users were taking up more than 30% of the machine cycles and making response times for critical applications unachievable. The vendor could have been forced to upgrade the technology provided, but the client, in this case, felt the demand would have been unreasonable. A tight contract reasonably handled by both sides was felt to improve the vendor-client relationship and levels of satisfaction all round.

4. ANTICIPATING SOME PROBLEM AREAS

In this section we signpost some further problem areas encountered in our research on economics and measurement during the performance of outsourcing contracts. Some of the following issues are quite widely known about, but nevertheless were still undergone by respondent organisations. Other problem areas identified below would seem to be more difficult to predict. All are very real possibilities of which any organisation contemplating outsourcing should be aware.

4.1 Much effort may be needed to develop an adequate measuring system

This was stressed earlier in the chapter in the context of assessing vendor bids. Here we look at the issue as it faces organisations that have already outsourced. As an example a UK County Council signed a £10 million, five year contract with a major vendor. The contract operated from December 1 1991 and involved mainframe operations and applications service. This was the first major contract of three for the council in the early 1990s. Even though the IT department had been operating largely as a internal trading agency, there was still an immense amount of work needed to get the measurement system in place:

> "There was a lot of information available to the out-sourcing companies about the current equipment, current costs of running equipment, staffing costs. A lot of information from us to them. But although we had been operating as a trading organisation, there weren't any service level agreements in place to build up a business relationship between the departments buying the service and the operations area itself. That was why it took 5 months to get from preferred supplier to contract stage. We actually wanted to have the whole of the contract underpinned by agreed and signed service level agreements before we entered into the contract. Some others choose not to do that, but that's the way we played this one." (IT Director: UK County Council)

It is interesting to note here the desire to get the detailed service level agreements in place before the contract is entered into. The process by which the detailed service measures were arrived at is also worth noting:

> "It was a problem to redefine measurement from scratch. We worked with a preferred supplier to achieve this. The client evaluation team designed the basic service level agreement and then said to the FM (Facilities Management) company does this meet your criteria or is there anything you want to add to this. We had our own staff on the operational side to complete the main part of this document, went to the user departments as receivers of that service to complete their part and then put the documents together to form a single document in initial draft. Then the central client asked the FM company plus the operations staff to meet and thrash out the final versions. We ended up with a mainframe service level agreement, a voice network or telephone service level agreement, and then 97 service department application

type service level agreements. A quantity of paperwork."

From reviewing our research sites it emerged that user involvement in the establishment of SLAs was particularly important, if user needs were going to be properly identified, and if there were to be user buy-in to the measurement activity. However, more detailed service measures and costing procedures can have unanticipated effects on user behaviour as will be discussed below. The sheer detail of the SLAs may also create a monitoring problem. Reflecting on their experiences respondents stressed the importance of focusing on the key measures in any service level agreement.

4.2 Outsourcing can require a culture change on measurement

It is all too easy to underestimate how far outsourcing might require a fundamentally different approach to measurement and control. Many organisations we have researched have not, at least in their early contracts, moved that far away from their existing measures and standards for IT performance. This can leave latent problems and conflicts that will emerge across the life of the outsourcing contract:

> "The performance measures were not strong enough. This was because of the culture we operated in. I think they took us and I don't blame them, we weren't very professional. I think there have been some very good attempts at tightening up performance measurement. But once you've got a contract you've got a contract and if you are dealing with sharp guys like them, then it's very difficult. But it's no surprise to me that the closer we get toward contract renewal, it's amazing what we can get." (IT director: UK public sector organisation)

The fact that the respondent here is getting a better deal on service towards the end of the contract suggests one reason why many organisations might choose to go for contracts of five years or less in length. The prospect of contract renewal reinvigorates vendor motivation to deliver service.

4.3 The possibility of vendor opportunism

This issue is hinted at in the previous point. In the UK study Willcocks and Fitzgerald (1994a) found a number of organisations operating a multi-vendor strategy explicitly to limit vendor opportunism. The Pilkington case, detailed above, also shows how a company can get a vendor working in both organisations' interests. Other organisations often learned over time about vendor opportunism and how to deal with it. One manufacturing company we researched outsourced IT to a major bureau in order to cut costs. A year into the contract they still had no real in-house expertise to manage the contract, and no real IT strategy despite the fact that IT was beginning to impact adversely on the conduct of business. The vendor was providing trainee contractors for systems development but charging top rates. Moreover, the company was having to train vendor staff about the company and the industry it was operating in. Subsequently the company got contract expertise, built up in-house technical staff base and renegotiated the vendor role to a much smaller one.

Two of the case studies researched by Lacity and Hirschheim (1993a) are also very revealing about vendor opportunism. One 10 year contract began in early 1989. It was the product of senior management looking at ways to contain or reduce rising IT costs. A six-month baseline period was measured with the vendor contractually bound to deliver the average service level of this period. However, the contract was signed before the baseline measurement was completed. Therefore, the services covered in the contract were not completely defined. In data centre operations the contract specified a fixed number of resources, e.g. tape mounts, CPU minutes, print lines for a fixed price. On applications development and maintenance the company received a fixed number of man-hours of service. Other utility services are ill-defined in the contract. While the promised 20% reduction off projected in-house IT budgets may be delivered by the vendor on the fixed price, in fact the 'excess' charges as a result of an incomplete contract may well cancel out any benefits. In fact, responses from the operating companies suggest that the vendor reduced its own costs by degradation of service, lack of responsiveness, 'excess' charges, and moving skilled staff transferred from the client on to other contracts. Additionally, despite promises, the vendor failed to develop service levels and performance measures after the contract went into effect. The vendor also took a strict view of the contract's 'change of character' clause, continually interpreting it in its own favour. In a second case there was again failure to negotiate a sound detailed contract:

> "The threat of opportunism was readily apparent in the excess charges, degradation of services, loss of IS expertise, antiquated technology and overworked (vendor) staff." (Lacity and Hirschheim, 1993a)

4.4 Internal charging systems may create problems

Even in a well managed outsourcing contract such, as that between a major brewing company and a UK-based vendor, there can be latent problems between users in business units, the IT people managing the contract, and the vendor. In many examples we have researched the problems built around the charging system as it affected users. In this respect the company's experience in the first year of the contract, signed in the early 1990s, is quite a common one:

> "The problems are around communications with our business which is the bit we are here to manage really. It's all around: are we buying a service level, is this time and materials, can I use X still on this, can I not use X on this, do things change or not? So it's all around communication with the business divisions and their understanding of the agreement. At the end of the day they will be paying, not directly, but I recharge to them. I am taking it into a central pot and reallocating it. Complexity of recharging is what's causing those communications challenges. .... They (the business users) are very wary of it because they now realise that it's an outsider who's charging them and maybe there is a risk they will get charged more and people are going to get more commercial." (Senior manager, UK brewing company)

However, the recharging issue can actually become such a bone of contention as to undermine the whole basis of the contract. One example was an £8 million 5-year contract begun in the mid-1980s. The strategic thrust in this multinational was to get rid of national data centres and devolve IT to business units. The company also wished to rationalise head office computing and save on IT costs. The vendor took over all existing IT work for head office and European companies in the multinational. However, the inadequate initial analysis of IT costs, together with incomplete specification of performance measures and insufficient detail on what services were required fed into creating large-scale problems in recharging users for services:

> "They came to us and said what do you spend on computing at the moment and I'll tell you it was difficult to actually arrive at that figure. There was bits of computing going on all over the place, so that was a stab in the dark. The best educated guess we could make, we think all of that costs us that, and they said right we will give you 15% more." (IT Director: multinational manufacturing company)

The initial difficulties were unbundling exactly what the client was paying for, and then determining when excess charges became payable. Also there were problems over 'change of character' where the hardware base was changing along with the services required:

> "Immediately problems began to occur. How much computing power were we entitled to before we paid any excess charges? .... Of course, there was a billing cost mis-match because they said we will do it for in total about £8M. So we were going to give them £8M and they were going to provide services. That then gave us the problem of actually charging out the £8M so we had to create an arbitrary invoicing system to recover the £8M..... We wondered well

> the £8M has got to come down hasn't it. They were saying but we are having to take a beating on this, it's all swings and roundabouts. Well that's all right, but when you're the guy in the department with a PC, you are thinking its madness. They want to cross-charge me £10,000 for a PC, I can go out and buy it for less."

In one example a personnel system had been put up in by the in-house team and the user department was charged a certain price for IT staff time to run and maintain it. Under the new charging system the user was charged three times as much for the same service. Clearly these problems could have been less contentious if the vendor was making more than a slim margin on the original deal. Here the lack of clarity in measurement at the contract stage led to opportunities for a pressurised vendor to argue legitimately that many of the services were in addition to those covered by the fixed price agreement. This also brought additional cost pressure on the hastily erected recharging system. At the end of three years the vendor cancelled the contract and each user negotiated separately directly with it. Most of those companies stayed with the vendor, initially, but some drifted away.

4.5 Users may become more wary of the IT service

In the cases of charging systems described above, users clearly became much more anxious about the service they were getting for the money they were being charged. In some respects this is often a healthy development, and may lead to users focusing on necessary rather than 'nice-to-have' services. It may also induce a much greater commercial awareness about computer use in their department. On the other hand, there can be some less attractive outcomes in outsourcing situations:

> "I think when you talk about service level agreements and the sorts of terminology you start surrounding a lot of the services with then they tend to get in the way of true fast response, and a question of how much does it cost tends to be an issue. We are already finding that by charging internally for services then the idea that you have to locate a customer who has a budget that can pay, gets in the way of getting a fast response. It shouldn't do but it still does. It's magnified beyond reasonable proportions with an external agency." (Systems Development Manager, manufacturing company)

4.6 IT costs may become too transparent

This would seem to be a contradiction, in the sense that the transparency of costs as a result of outsourcing is usually proclaimed as a desirable outcome. However where there is still a large in-house IT capability there may arise inflexibilities in the ways in which funds can be utilised, and additional IT work achieved:

> "One of the things that some of us were concerned about as part of the deal, but which was overlooked by senior management who signed up to the deal, was the fact that we know the way we operated here in DP. We could always fudge costs.... There's always a little bit of fat in any budget that allows us to take on something unexpected. I am talking about the ability to bring on a new software package which might enhance processing in an area, a systems software package, a new tool, which might cost you a licence fee plus £5000 a year in maintenance costs. We could always do these simple things in-house." (IT Manager – services company)

The irony here is that the in-house IT staff felt that the vendor had done too good a job of analysing costs and establishing what the price for different services would be. The problems are very much for operational IT staff rather than more senior management, who in fact continue to see the non-degradation of contracted service plus large cost savings as very much a good deal:

> "When we transferred across it was on the basis of our (existing IT) budget..... They (the vendor staff) had up front clearly what we were using at the time of the out-sourcing deal. They were very thorough and did their homework. But it's a loss of advantage to us really. We no longer have the ability to demand flexibility of the data centre in the way it manages its cost. We can't force the vendor to find ways to do things on the cheap which is something we would have sat down and found a way of doing, and they feel under no obligation to do this." (IT manager: financial services company)

5. CONCLUSIONS

The economics of IT outsourcing uncovered by our research suggests that organisations need to pursue in-house improvements first, identify full IT costs and establish performance benchmarks, pursue further in-house improvements and only then make in-house vs. outsourcing comparisons. If the outsourcing option is initially rejected, it needs to be revisited at regular intervals, not least because the reassessment can act as an external benchmark on in-house IT performance. However, in practice we found a number of other objectives and interests often cutting across this economic logic.

Organisations found it difficult to assess vendor against in-house bids on a comparable basis, especially where prior evaluation practice exhibited the kinds of weaknesses discussed in other chapters of this book. However, respondent experiences suggested that the time and effort spent on fully assessing in-house performance, and revamping measurement systems proved vital in feeding into more effective contracting. All too often outsourcing deals can be based on varying degrees of 'voodoo economics'. Another finding was that this evaluation work, to enable comparison with and assessment of vendor bids, is best done before any contracts are signed, even where a specific vendor has been chosen. Organisations cannot safely assume that vendor opportunism will not occur. From this perspective, we found the contract to have the central role in determining whether outsourcing expectations would be realized. Hidden costs in outsourcing arrangements were identified, and these were found to be most frequently the outcome of weak contracting. Based on our case study and survey research, the chapter provided guidelines on how to set up and run measurement systems and service level agreements.

It also became clear that even good contracting, based on detailed IT evaluation, and supported by comprehensive service measures and reporting systems, still did not avoid many problems arising during the course of any contract. This stresses again what emerged strongly from all our cases and the European survey: the importance of active monitoring and management of the vendor. As one respondent remarked ruefully about a particularly difficult outsourcing experience: 'The one definite thing I have learned is that it's not like ringing for room service.' On the economics and performance measurement issues in IT outsourcing, truly the buck cannot be contracted out.

REFERENCES

Aucoin, P, Almy, F, Heise, R, Landry, R *et al.* (1991) *Internalizing The Vendor's Resources: Outsourcing In The 1990s*. Report No. C-6-1, Chantico Publishing, Boston.

Bergstrom, L (1991) *The Ins and Outs of Outsourcing*. Real Decisions Corporation, Darien.

Buck-Lew, M (1992) To Outsource Or Not? *International Journal of Information Management*, **12**, pp3-20.

Due, R (1992) The Real Costs of Outsourcing. *Information Systems Management*, Winter, pp78-81.

Feeny, D, Willcocks, L, Rands, T and Fitzgerald, G (1993) Strategies for IT Management – When Outsourcing Equals Rightsourcing. In Rock, S (ed.), *Directors Guide to Outsourcing*, Institute of Directors/IBM, London.

Fitzgerald, G and Willcocks, L (1993) *Information Technology Outsourcing Practice: A UK Survey*. Business Intelligence, London.

Fitzgerald, G and Willcocks, L (1994) Contracts and Partnerships in the Outsourcing of IT. *Proceedings of the Fifteenth Annual International Conference in Information Systems*, Vancouver, December.

Gupta, U and Gupta, A (1992) Outsourcing The IS Function: Is It Necessary For Your Organisation? *Information Systems Management*, Summer, pp44-50.

I/S Analyzer (1990) Taking An Objective Look At Outsourcing. United Communications, Maryland, September.

Krass, P (1990) The Dollars and Sense of Outsourcing. *Information Week*, February 26, pp26-31.

Lacity, M and Hirschheim, R (1993a) *Information Systems Outsourcing*. Wiley, Chichester.

Lacity, M and Hirschheim, R (1993b) The Information Systems Outsourcing Bandwagon. *Sloan Management Review*, **35**(1), pp73-86.

Lacity, M, Hirschheim, R and Willcocks, L (1994) Realizing Outsourcing Expectations: Incredible Expectations, Credible Outcomes. *Information Systems Management*, Fall, **14**, pp7-18.

Pralahad, C and Hamel, G (1990) The Core Competence of the Corporation. *Harvard Business Review*, **63**(3), pp79-91.

Quinn, J (1992) The Intelligent Enterprise: A New Paradigm. *Academy of Management Executive*, **6**(4), pp44-63.

Willcocks, L (ed.) (1994) *Information Management: Evaluation of Information Systems Investments*. Chapman and Hall, London.

Willcocks, L and Fitzgerald, G (1994a) *A Business Guide to Outsourcing IT. A Study of European Best Practice in the Selection, Management and Use of External IT Services*. Business Intelligence, London.

Willcocks, L and Fitzgerald, G (1994b) Towards the Residual IS Organisation? Research on IT Outsourcing Experiences in the United Kingdom. In Baskerville, R *et al.* (eds.), *Transforming Organisations With Information Technology*. IFIP/ North Holland, Amsterdam.

Willcocks, L and Fitzgerald, G (1995) To Outsource IT Or Not? Recent Research on Economics and Evaluation Practice. In Willcocks, L (ed.), *Investing in Information Systems: Evaluation and Management*. Chapman and Hall, London.

Willcocks, L, Fitzgerald, G and Feeny, D (1994) Information Technology Outsourcing: From Incrementalism to Strategic Intent. *Second SISNET Conference*, Barcelona, Spain, 26-28 September.

13 Fuzzy strategy – crisp investment

Philip Powell
Warwick Business School, University of Warwick

1. INTRODUCTION

Numerous commentators have argued that successful business strategy is characterised by flexibility, vagueness and sometimes deliberate ambiguity; that is, strategy is essentially fuzzy. Conversely, the Information Systems (IS) literature is replete with methodologies for system construction which caution developers to specify exactly their system and to bear in mind system objectives; information systems and Information Technology (IT) projects are crisp. This mismatch is not a problem when systems are designed to tackle well-specified, structured tasks, or when the system type is well understood. However, as information technology becomes 'strategic', this problem may assume greater importance.

IS developers have, in recent years, moved away from rigid methodologies typified by the Systems Development Lifecycle (SDLC) approach. Prototyping (Dearnley and Mayhew, 1983), Multiview (Avison and Wood-Harper, 1991) and the like emphasise flexibility in approach. On the face of it, this should close the gap identified above. Yet, these systems usually have, as their *raison d'etre* a vision of the system's output and purpose. The flexibility in these methodologies is in the route taken to achieve the pre-designated purpose, they do not readily allow for fuzzy objectives or flexibility in primary purpose.

Strategy needs to be most flexible when the organisation operates in an unstable or turbulent environment. However, there is evidence that IT increases environmental turbulence (indeed, it could be argued that this may be a primary motive for investment), which, in turn, may cause strategy to be couched in more nebulous terms. The effect of IT on the environment is best summed up by Dussange *et al.* (1992), who feel that IT allows organisations to ask not "what business are we in, but what business could we be in?"

This chapter is organised as follows. First, it assesses the literature on business strategy, concentrating primarily on the identification of the need for flexibility in strategy formulation and articulation, and the conditions under which this is most likely to be necessary. This is partially evidenced by a senior management preference for qualitative information and IT investment as an 'act of faith'. Testimony from the strategy implementation research is reviewed, the link between IT and strategy examined, and a brief review of the systems development literature undertaken. The chapter concentrates on the problems of fuzzy strategy enactment and the implementation or operationalisation of strategy in IT/IS projects.

2. THE NATURE OF STRATEGY

The concept of strategy is well understood; for Jauch and Glueck (1988): "strategic decisions are means to achieve ends. These decisions encompass the definition of the business, products and markets to be served, functions to be performed, and major policies needed for the organisation to execute these decisions to achieve objectives."

These authors draw on the work of Mainer (1968) to differentiate operational management from strategic planning. In essence, Mainer suggests strategic planning is concerned with the identification and evaluation of new objectives and strategies, while operational management is concerned with goals derived from established objectives. In the latter, goals usually have been validated through past experience, but for the former new objectives and strategies can be highly debatable; experience within the organisation may be minimal. Strategic goals are usually evaluated primarily for corporate significance, whereas operational management involves specific sub-goals for functional units. While operational managers tend to identify with functions or professions and to be preoccupied with means, strategic managers need an environment-oriented corporate point of view. Evidence of the merit of new objectives of strategies is often available only after considerable delay. Conversely, operational managers obtain feedback relatively promptly. In the operational setting the 'rules of the game' become well understood. However, in strategic planning new endeavours may be considered and past experience may not provide sufficient competence. Lastly, Mainer feels operational issues are immediate, concrete, and familiar; strategic issues are abstract, possibly deferrable and may be unfamiliar. Chung *et al.* (1989) provide a more succinct set of criteria for identifying strategic decisions. These define the organisation's relationship to its environment; view the whole organisation as the decision unit; the decision is multi-functional, provides direction and, lastly, is important for the success of the enterprise.

Although these differentiating factors are not new or startling, they appear to have been largely forgotten in the rush to embrace IT as a strategic tool. The alignment of IT and corporate strategy is a mantra chanted endlessly in the hope that one day it might come true. Steiner (1979) believes "strategic planning asks fundamental questions" and the purpose of these questions is to change direction of the company, flush out strategic issues for consideration, develop situation analyses of opportunities and threats, gain control of operations, to show where the company is going and how to get there and, to provide awareness of the changing environment so as to adapt better to it. Twiss (1986) identifies the need for strategy as deriving from the inadequacy of the profit maximisation goal. Planning reflects the need to influence not respond to environmental changes and acts as an inspiration to organisational effort.

The question is, can IT projects be formulated and enacted in a way consistent with the attributes of strategic planning as noted above?

3. THE NEED FOR FLEXIBILITY IN STRATEGY

There is evidence, both that successful firms have flexible strategies and, that this stems, to some extent from senior management preference for qualitative (and therefore fuzzy) language. For instance, Lederer and Mendelow (1986) after talking to IS developers, offer the following, "some interviewees maintained that top executives preferred flexibility, which is lost when a plan is written. Written plans are more difficult to change" (p. 259). In similar vein, Harris and Katz (1991) conclude "innovative firms'... management tends to state openly values that would support change and resolve conflicts. As a result, these firms are more willing to modify processes and structures to achieve their goals". Thus flexibility or fuzziness is necessary in a fast changing environment but not in a stable one. The conditions under which fuzziness is valued will be contingent on factors such as the rate of change of the environment and the values held by senior executives.

Part of the need for flexibility arises from the nature of the strategy-making process which contains elements of the objective and the subjective. This arises because such decision making has to fulfil a set of conflicting objectives, including the need to measure and combine objective and subjective aspects, to forecast future uncertain events, and reconcile different interest groups. For example, Reagan-Cirincione *et al.* (1991) comment "strategic decision making is a social and political process, not just an intellectual task" (p. 53), while Schniederjans and Fowler (1989) maintain that "in strategic acquisition analysis, the decision... can be based chiefly on subjective judgement on what are desirable objective factors"; this premise holds as well for IT developments as it does for acquisitions and mergers. Evans and Riha (1989) consider that, in general, efficiency issues are objectively addressed, while effectiveness is subjectively addressed. Problems arise due to the evolutionary nature of systems. If evolutionary systems are difficult to evaluate then it seems likely that evaluation in terms of changing strategy will be even more problematic. However, Broadbent and Weill (1991) identify clarity and consistency of strategic orientation as a critical success factor in aligning IT and business strategy. Clarity and consistency is not ideally commensurate with flexibility. Northcott (1991) criticises capital budgeting research because it has been undertaken from a rational economics perspective which ignores the need to consider social and political modes of decision taking. It is usually viewed as a proactive consideration of known options, given known objectives leading to a rational decision; reality may be much less ordered and systematic. Gordon (1989), claims political rather than 'rational economic' perspectives may dominate decision making and thus no relationship will exist between benefit-cost analysis (BCA) techniques and resource allocation decisions. He feels, however, that such a relationship may exist at higher organisational levels. As such, he is at odds with most commentators who maintain that quantification is employed more at low rather than high levels in the organisation. Gordon partially supports his contention by suggesting that the use of BCA had a significant positive relationship with senior administrators' support for a project, although it had no significant relationship with final funding approval, which presumably came at senior management level. Freeman (1982) sums up the subjective view of evaluation, "the context of estimation will always be one of political advocacy and clash of interest groups, whatever the possibility for sober calculation".

Flexibility has a further role perhaps as a critical success factor in its own right. That is, the vision of senior management, not just their support, may enhance success rates. As Boddy (1989) says, "[researchers] have shown clearly that the results of investing in IT depend on how wide a range of management and organisational issues are dealt with". Walsham (1991) goes further, asserting that all the key issues facing IS executives are organisational not technical. He suggests that IS are a crucial area for the exercise of power in many organisations and the literature on strategic planning of IS unhelpfully takes a formal-rational view of the process. Rather, the formation of IS strategy should be conceived as a process of learning. "Strategic vision and its linking with IS appears... to be an art rather than a science and the `aids' to this process appear rather simplistic and unlikely to provide much help in developing vision" (p. 18). Ginsberg and Venkatraman (1992) show how new technologies and their applications (in their case electronic tax filing) can be viewed differently by different managers.

Ruohonen (1992) accepts that strategic planning, when applied to information systems is ill-structured, "strategic information systems planning is therefore a high level planning activity: it is not well structured and requires considerable creativity and some risk-taking to be successful." Such formulation can be of two types, the first is formulation in advance and allows for planned implementation, the second is difficult to do before the fact and relies on the exploitation of unique firm characteristics (Ciborra, 1991). Since competitive advantage comes from uniqueness, methodologies are likely to be a constraint on identification and exploitation of such attributes. Vitale *et al.* (1986) highlight the lack of practical or theoretical advice on how to identify strategic information systems. They feel that "the most popular anecdotes, like many myths, are often inaccurate and usually exclude details critical to successful imitation" (p. 266). They proffer an alternative, adaptive method for strategy formulation whereby the organisation develops the resources and then identifies feasible strategies flowing from them.

Discussing the nature of high level decision making Te'eni (1990) feels that it is characterised by attending to a set of issues with shifting priorities. Embodied in this process is a shift from a single to a group of interacting decisions, from decision making to attention and agenda, from tactical to strategic, from functional to cross-functional applications, and finally from individual to group consensus. Major policy issues are usually presented to decision makers in the form of recommendations made by subordinates, supported by external opinions. The final decision is the end of a lengthy and iterative process. Smith (1989), considering same issue, feels that it determines the agenda of concerns that problem solving activity addresses. Problems are usually defined as existing-state desired-state gap, but these problems are partially subjective. The causes are intrusive or unusual events. As such, they must be awaited rather than anticipated, and responded to rather than planned.

Little (1990) suggests organisational pathology may account for unintended outcomes and outputs from organisations. This results from two key concepts – over-conformity to regulations and goal displacements (which in turn derive from survival being the organisation's principal concern). This may cause sub-optimisation but it is difficult to see when this occurs, unless decomposed systems are reassembled. Little asserts that "conflict may develop between the technical requirements of support technology and the objectives it is intended to serve at the institutional or organisational level" (p. 31). The key to success is the reconciliation of the technical and the institutional orientation. He points to two conflicting uses of goals, one as motivator, the other as evaluator. Yet, motivation requires broad/vague goals while evaluation usually requires specific ones. This is, however, at odds with the motivation literature (see, for instance, Porter and Lawler, 1986). Evaluation goals are usually quantitative and limited, so goal displacement may arise. Galbraith (1977) suggests that the formalisation of communication channels is offset by a loss of qualitative information. In conditions of high task uncertainty, irrelevant quantitative measures are likely to enjoy an edge over relevant qualitative ones. Similarly, Dreyfus and Dreyfus (1986) argue that there is a predominance of quantitative methods in current management theory. This 'calculative rationality' is likely to degrade expert performance by focussing on quantitative criteria at the expense of experientially-based qualitative understanding. In contrast, Stone (1991) demonstrates that senior management has a preference for qualitative information and that "theories of the role of language in decision making suggest that quantitative languages offer analytical precision but sacrifice descriptive accuracy, while qualitative languages offer descriptive accuracy but sacrifice analytical precision."

3.1 Senior management preference for qualitative analysis

Steiner (1979) provides the first recognition of the fuzzy quality of strategic decisions and the dominance of non-quantitative factors, "many strategic decisions are not readily amenable to quantification... the more important the decision and the higher up in an organisation at which it is made, the less quantitative data influence the outcome", and later, "strategic decision making is very complex and is dominated by non-quantitative factors." This is partially a reflection of the characteristics of senior executives (Zmud, 1986); they manage issues not people or resources, they create decision situations, work with ill-defined qualitative data, work with networks of people not decision models and implement rather than make decisions.

If senior management does have a preference for qualitative data, then a business case formulated in terms of quantitative data may stand little chance of success (Powell, 1992). Perhaps then, the couching of IT activities in qualitative terms is merely an astute political move on the part of IT managers; hence the substantial literature on 'strategic IT' might be viewed as an exercise in attempted legitimation. Sutherland (1991) describes how information systems managers sought to develop the perception among their superiors of IT as 'infrastructure'. The purpose of this was to overcome the 'seemingly insurmountable barriers' imposed by strict cost benefit analysis. Some corroboration for this derives from Stone (1991) who looks at information system assessment models. He finds that relative to information systems students and professionals, senior executives will perceive strategic model methods as more useful in evaluating information systems; and that senior executives will perceive political model methods as more useful in evaluating information systems. Stone notes that strategic and political models rely upon qualitative language whilst the other two models used, fiscal and clinical, employ predominantly quantitative language. A further conclusion proposes that, as the work experience of senior executives increases, they perceive lesser value in quantitative procedures and greater value in qualitative assessment procedures.

Qualitative actions may come to the fore if the organisational processes are so designed. Pinches (1981) identifies the importance of coalitions, interpersonal factors, bargaining and politics in the selection or rejection of capital budgeting projects. He suggests that the reward system has an important impact on the process. Extrapolation suggests that punishment might be more easily avoided if a 'strategy' fails to work, rather than if an evaluated process fails to achieve its aims. Lederer and Mendelow (1988) hypothesize that the concept of strategic information systems might just be a convenient means whereby IS managers can intimidate top management into allocating the desired resources; thus they might be viewed as a 'gimmick for empire building'.

The rejection of quantification is reported by Freeman and Hobbs (1991), who find a high incidence of managers ignoring reject signals given by capital budgeting techniques. They suggest that one plausible reason for this could be that managers are using 'other' techniques to evaluate the strategic value of potential investment opportunities. They claim this is valid if the project is mandatory or if the costs of undertaking an explicit evaluation of strategic benefits is high. Coulson-Thomas (1991) contends that the management issues of technology perceived by IT directors to be important, do not include any idea of return on IT investment. This may, in fact, be sensible since Haka *et al.* (1985) give support to the non-quantification argument, finding no evidence that firms employing sophisticated (i.e. quantifying) project evaluation techniques perform better than firms guided by more naive techniques. Twiss (1986) argues for more formal evaluation, though, in contrast, Lincoln (1990) comments on "the difficulty of developing a conventional business case with a comprehensive cost/benefit analysis". This is primarily due to two factors; first, the difficulty in predicting costs and benefits, and second, the need to go with a hunch or strategic insight due to the speed with which the policy must be implemented. Some support for this comes from Runge and Earl (1988), who claim that 80% of successful competitive-edge applications completely by-passed the normal management approval process. Indeed, senior management are even advised by Swann and O'Keeffe (1990) that "if projects can be classified as 'strategic' they may be excluded from the financial appraisal at the outset rather than being treated in an unsatisfactory method." In contrast, Earl (1989) seems to view IT investment as any other, with the rider that where IT projects are truly strategic, discount rates may need to be modified downwards to encourage bold initiatives. Weill and Olson (1989) and Gunton (1988), amongst others, suggest the use of 'gut feeling' as a method by which IT investment is considered. Perhaps gut feeling is a symptom of an 'act of faith'.

Wassenaar (1988) records how justification of opportunities becomes very arbitrary due to the difficulty of establishing quantitative links between expected benefits like more flexibility, shorter lead time, or better product quality and corporate objectives. Perhaps for this reason, Currie (1989) finds little post implementation analysis of success of information technology investments, and concludes that IT justification is a ritual of legitimacy not an attempt at really assessing benefit, while Baxter and Hirst (1986) characterise it as "self-interested manoeuvres masked in rational rhetoric."

The result of the conflicts between the political aspects of decisions (objectives) and the technical (evaluation of effects) is a tendency towards satisficing (Sharp, 1990). The important criteria for an IT manager to gain approval for a project is the generation of support, but this is difficult in view of past failures. Sharpe, however, makes the bold claim that as decisions are rarely completely novel, authorisation is 'rubber stamping' and only in exceptional cases should the correct decision not be self-evident.

3.2 IT investment as an 'act of faith'

Surprisingly, as competitive pressures increase and there is not only the ability to measure the previously unmeasurable, but also a desire to have more information, 'the act of faith' argument for IT investment surfaces with monotonous frequency. It is not clear, however, what the act of faith actually applies to. It is used in the context of senior managements' faith in their own abilities, their faith in IT professionals both within and without the firm, and in the technology as an entity. This is despite the lack of evidence of real return from IT investment, a lack of quantification and a history of failures of IT applications. Currie (1989), for instance, observes that the introduction of new technology is not generally initiated nor managed by senior management, while Senker and Senker (1992) provide a host of examples demonstrating a lack of managerial understanding of the technology. Dussauge et al. begin with a quote from Chemical Bank which spent over $1bn on IT in the space of three years, yet "its management is still unsure of whether the Bank's investment in IT is too high or too low" (p. 3). This is a substantial act of faith!

The argument is applied across the board in terms of technologies. For instance, Cottrell and Rapley (1990) feel that "since the benefits of an EIS are particularly difficult to quantify the decision to proceed with an executive information system is often an act of faith." While Twiss (1986) insists that "no company is going to invest heavily in technology solely as an act of faith in the hope that by backing the right people 'something will turn up'", Sheppard (1990) counters, that investment evaluation may be measured by staff reduction or by gaining a competitive edge, but more likely it is by 'act of faith'. Lincoln (1990) disagrees: "no longer are (IT) expenditures seen as low and investments 'acts of faith'. Now executives require that their IS are both profitable and can be shown to be profitable."

Williams and Scott (1965) find, not only a tendency to back the judgement of a manager with a successful record in proposing ideas, but also no definitions of objectives that acted as a clear-cut basis for investment decisions. Here the act of faith has two dimensions, one in the reliance on project managers' past records as a guide to the future and secondly in consistency by senior management in the face of unarticulated objectives. Gurnani (1984) reports that 97% of companies approve economically infeasible investments and quotes Petty, 77% of whose sample "acknowledged that though quantitative factors are dominant... qualitative factors do influence the final decision." Sometimes, apparently unprofitable investments are approved because of possible future benefits that cannot be assessed at the time of approval or due to other qualitative considerations. For Ward (1990) there is a tendency that "the greater the trust the management have in their own judgement and the trust they have in the user's understanding of the business and in IS in development effective systems, then the greater the weighting placed on the critical success factors relative to financial aspects." However, Binning (1986) maintains that this is a fundamental misunderstanding of the role of formal analysis which is not that significant, precise quantified results emerge but rather the demonstration that complex situations are capable of logical analysis.

The concept of vision (or what George Bush aptly describes as the 'vision thing') is fine if the organisation has it. Many anecdotal case-studies point to developments based on vision. However, this may just be post-hoc rationalisation. In fact, Runge and Earl (1988) show that many applications which have provided competitive advantage were evolutionary add-ons to existing systems and Runge asserts that in many cases the competitive advantage idea was but a later facility added to an existing system. Thus many strategic systems are evolutionary not revolutionary. Yet, Neo (1988) sees management vision as a major factor facilitating use of IT. The concept of evolution does not sit very happily with vision, though Harris and Katz (1991) review of previous research shows that factors differentiate adopters of technology from non-adopters include the progressiveness of management. Given that Iivari (1986) maintains IS can be characterised by complexity, radicalness and originality, vision is perhaps the only way to address such systems.

Vision or even evolution is subject to change. Parker (1978) contrasts the expected probability of technical success in R&D projects as greater than 80% in 75% of cases with the actual success rate of 44%. Significantly only 16% failed due to unforeseen technical difficulties, the overwhelming majority failed due to company policy. This may be partially put down to experience, which "indicates that the most usual bias in management decision-taking is optimism." Despite this a proper attitude to evaluation is one of scepticism, biased towards an appreciation that quantitative techniques are no more than an aid. Not only does poor judgement play a part, but changes to projects during development is a major cause of problems (Twiss, 1986). Indeed, the BIM (1988) found 40% of its sample had no clearly defined strategy for IT implementation and 43% felt that implementation had not been well integrated with an overall corporate business strategy compared to 36% who did.

A further complication of vision is evidenced by Andreu *et al.* (1991). They find that companies usually put more effort into high level 'strategic systems'" and disregard low level mundane transactional systems, but transactional systems can be used to gain competitive advantage and any system can be of strategic value. As Sol (1991) observes, "it appears unacceptable to look for strategic systems only at strategic organisational levels" (p. 1).

The obverse of vision is what Graham and Jones (1988) identify as a cause of system failure rates as high as 60%. That is, the system is built but never used, indicating that top management are not convinced of the benefit or do not understand how to use the end-product or perhaps the same system makes no contribution to strategic issues. Vision implies originality which, according to Iivari (1986) has a positive effect on uncertainty and the likelihood of the project abortion, a negative effect on commitment and a mixed effect on implementation. One of the roles of vision for strategies is to provide a set of orienting metaphors that enable stakeholders within an organisation to understand that organisation (Ginsberg and Venkatraman, 1992). The strategies reflect rules, routines and metaphors that satisfy stakeholders demands for consistency and reliability, and which determine the legitimacy of different organisational actions. Ginsberg and Venkatraman state "if a technological innovation is legitimate for an organisation, its managers may adopt the new technology with little reflection on the strategic issues it presents" (p. 44). The authors support the importance of strategy in influencing managers' information gathering and sense-making activities and feel that direct influences (for instance, competitive posture) may be more powerful than indirect (interpretation) influences.

Having identified the need for flexibility in strategy formulation it is now necessary to look at models of strategy implementation which allow this.

4. STRATEGY IMPLEMENTATION

Strategy formulation and strategy implementation are clearly connected but a formulated strategy is not an implemented one. As Mockler (1992), comments, "just because overall-company strategy plans have been formulated, it cannot be assumed that operational planning and decision-making and plan implementation, will automatically follow these overall planning patterns" (p. 51). Investigating the process of implementation, Lederer and Mendelow (1987) offer, "for this integration to happen successfully, information systems managers must be aware of top management's objectives" (p. 389). However, there are a number of difficulties encountered by system developers in identifying these, ranging from the organisation having no plan to the IS department being unaware of changes and a lack of communication stemming from confidentiality. The developers' final problem (Lederer and Mendelow, 1986) is maintaining flexibility. In a later paper (Lederer and Mendelow, 1988), the authors feel that top management still needs to be convinced of the potential strategic impact of information systems and that the effort needed to convince top management of strategic impact of IS impeded planning. Top management is seen to lack awareness, view use of computers as strictly operational, perceive a credibility gap, and be action-oriented (rather than to long range planning).

Hart (1992) proposes an integrative framework for the process of strategy formulation and implementation. He identifies four models; the rational model which requires, *inter alia*, explicit goal setting and the use of a formal strategic

planning system; the behavioural model; the organisational model which shows the importance of vision and corporate values; finally the induced and autonomous strategic behaviour model. Hart maintains that the literature suggests rationality is unlikely to be attainable. He derives five modes of action for strategy formulation. The commander relies on strong top management control – strategies are deliberate and fully formed and ready to be implemented; the symbolic which is the creation by top management of a vision of clear corporate mission. The rational mode requires a high level of information processing and formal strategy planning, which is usually written. Here, senior management tries to consider as much data as possible. The transactive mode emphasises interaction and learning and may suggest the inability to separate formulation of strategy from implementation. Finally, the generative mode recognises autonomous behaviour by organisation members; strategy is made via a process of intrapreneurship, hence the there is an on-going adjustment of strategy to reflect the pattern of high potential innovations that emerge from below. Hart feels the command and generative modes are not predictive of high performance and each of the modes has contingency factors attached to them. For instance, the command mode only works in simple situations; the symbolic model works in dynamic, flexible proactive organisations, the rational is best for stable environments, while the transactive is best in situations of high complexity and heterogeneity, finally the generative is best suited to turbulent environments. The conclusion is that organisations may follow a mixed mode of strategy making, for example, middle-up-down and that multiple modes will result in better performance.

IS development is usually conceived in technical terms (Hirschheim *et al.*, 1991). However, it might be appropriate to consider it as a technical process with behavioural consequences or even purely as a social process. Hirschheim *et al.* hypothesise that conflict, resistance and power are all concepts which help to better understand why IS developments fail. Murray and Willmott (1991) concur, "analysing systems development as if it were equivalent to a mechanical or even an organic process is seen to exclude an appreciation of key, constitutive elements; namely meaning and power." Part of the assumption of the strategy implementation literature, particularly when applied to IT, is that the system is a closed entity rather than a vehicle for change. For example, evidence comes from Madden (1992) who quotes a CEO as feeling that IT in his organisation (a utility) is an instrument of cultural change and should be used as such. As such the actual attributes of the systems may be secondary.

Kwon and Zmud (1987) reviewing studies on the absence of a direct, positive effect by IT on organisational performance, emphasise difficulties in the implementation of IT as a potential explanation. The researchers suggest that IT fails to exert a positive influence on organisational performance because of improper implementation procedures, poor administration or abuse. These problems arise because of lack of top leadership or organisational support, poor design of IT, poor alignment of IT with company needs, and organisational political abuses once IT is in place. Das *et al* (1991) highlight these problems with evidence from an A.T. Kearney study showing that firms with integrated business and IS strategic plans outperform those without.

5. IT AND STRATEGY

Although linking IS/T and business strategy is seen as a top concern of management in the US, UK, Australia and Eire (Broadbent and Weill, 1991), the great difficulty of enacting strategy through the use of IT is that sustainable competitive advantage can only be based on differences, and differences are far harder to evaluate and codify within an information technology project. The mere process of codification with its implied rigidity may negate some of the aspects which differentiate the organisation from its competitors. IT strategy researchers are slowly coming to the view that IT *per se* does not confer competitive advantage. For example, Clemons and Kimbrough (1987) differentiate IS that are a strategic necessity and IS that offer sustainable competitive advantage. This competitive advantage derives from improvements in operational efficiency, improvements in managerial effectiveness, product innovations and increased bargaining power of the firm. But, as Finlay (1991) points out, many management tasks are ill-structured, implying that it is the use of information not IT which confers advantage and that there is more value added from IT for unstructured activities because these are organisation specific. Grindley (1991) takes up this point, arguing that it is rare for competitive advantage to be based only on technology, usually what underlies this is an organisational structure which enables the firm to handle implementation of technology more effectively than its competitors. Hence the main difficulties are not technology but its exploitation, and the key to competitive advantage is appropriability, i.e. can other firms easily acquire the technology. Grindley concludes that the problem with a generic strategy is that it tells firms where they would like to be but not how or whether it can get there. Beaumont and Walters (1991) find that payoffs on investments depend on quality of management not quality of investment and that investments are usually *ad hoc* and not linked to organisational goals. It follows that expertise in information management implies the ability to identify and analyse strategic options in depth before competitors and, therefore, on having more precise control over the implementation of selected strategy. A similar point is made by Harris and Katz (1991), "how the technology is used and managed is as important as the level of spending, if not more so" (p. 347). They find that the leadership style in innovative firms tends to be entrepreneurial, less formal and bureaucratic, allowing rapid response.

For certain firms proactive use of IT is built into strategy, they are constantly looking for ways to use the technology to improve their competitive position. Innovators' and CEOs' vision and strategy are often the primary basis for using IT as opposed to environmental pressure or industry structure. In the development of a strategic DSS, Chung *et al.* (1989) maintain that such a system must directly address unstructuredness which in turn implies that such a system must support the intelligence and design phases of decision taking rather than the usually perceived area of choice.

In line with the above, Ciborra (1991) maintains that copyable strategic information systems provide no competitive advantage. So, for instance, co-operative EDI cannot offer individual firm advantages, and developments which use similar frameworks and methodologies will lead to similar systems in firms. Thus strategic information systems which differentiate and give competitive advantage must be built on things such as organisational culture that cannot be imitated. The unarticulated corollary to this is that things such as organisational culture are very hard to distil and support through the use of technology. Dos Santos and Peffers (1991) go further, while stating that there is little empirical evidence that IT investment enables firms to outperform their competitors, in highlighting three requirements for sustained competitive advantage from IT; competitors are unable to respond quickly due to time needed to develop/implement system; differences between firms make response difficult; or competitors can be pre-empted from retaliating. Clemons and Row (1991) make the same point, structural differences – based on resource differences (difficult and expensive to change) not strategic differences (resources the same but strategy different) are important. For them, the factors enabling innovators to defend economic value of innovation include barriers to duplication, significant first mover effects, or that the innovation changes underlying industry characteristics.

The standard view of IT's place in business strategy is well presented by Sheppard (1990). The components of successful use of IT as a strategic weapon are an external focus for its use, technical excellence, value-added justification and a sharing of benefits between organisations. The return on these can be measured by staff reduction or by gaining a competitive edge, but more likely by the act of faith discussed above. This act of faith goes hand-in-hand with Peters' (1990) finding that few organisations measured gains after investment, due either to measurement difficulties, or, more significantly, it "didn't suit their culture". He suggests that organisations should evaluate overall investment in IT in terms of strategy, but individual ones in terms of objectives. How workable this is, is rather debatable. The motivations for new systems might give a clue as to how easy IT/strategy matching might be. The three main motivations Sheppard found were; that the old system was difficult to maintain; a desire to replace the old system with new technology; or to take advantage of an opportunity to expand services. Only the last of these appears to have possible strategic connections. In any case there was little formal evaluation of benefits in nine case studies.

Bergeron *et al.* (1991) maintain that IS for competitive advantage are those that drive or formulate the organisation strategy. Hence, "such systems reflect the fundamental objectives of the firm and may have a significant impact on its success." To provide competitive advantage, IT must modify the structure of the industry, improve the position of the firm or create new business opportunities. Though they recognise that benefits are difficult to quantify, gaining a competitive advantage should result in a long-term added financial return for the organisation. However, these opportunities are rare since imitators often outperform innovators (Teece 1987); IT may be beneficial but not deliver competitive advantage and IT may be a strategic necessity (Clemons and Row 1988). Clemons and Kimbrough (1986) conclude the recent attention given to the strategic use of IS or the priority placed on finding opportunities is not overstressed. The same authors assert that evidence of IS to gain competitive advantage is mostly anecdotal; competitive advantage is more rare than strategic necessity; innovation may change the structure of the industry rather than of individual firms; the role of industry-wide standards may be significant and strategic advantage due to reduced costs is likely to be rare. Bergeron et al. make the point that many information systems for competitive advantage are termed 'strategic' because they result from the formulation and implementation of a competitive strategy based on IT, they generally do not support top management in the process of formulating and implementing strategy. Huff and Beattie (1985) feel that these differ from true strategic information systems.

An additional problem which is likely to result in further uncertainty in strategy and in environmental turbulence is that IT and other technical development provide "new strategic options" (Earl, 1989). Management must perceive and implement these. Perception may be easy *ex post*, it may also be easy as a follower rather than an innovator. Eason (1988) suggests the use of IT to seek new organisational objectives. Such use "depends on conceiving of ways in which the technology can be harnessed to serve major organisational objectives and senior management must be involved in setting these objectives and judging ways of meeting them." While Ives and Jarvenpaa (1991) agree that IT can propagate new business strategies, they feel a more common goal is to effectively harness IT to an existing global business strategy. Earl agrees that, although IT is an enabling technology and capable of yielding sustainable strategic advantage, most will support current business strategy rather than create new strategic options.

Finally, one of the intended purposes of IT investment may be to create change in an industry – that is to initiate environmental turbulence either for competitors or even within the host organisation as a vehicle for cultural change.

6. SYSTEMS DEVELOPMENT

Noble (1991) provides a very comprehensive analysis of a range of office system development methodologies. He identifies two current trends – the use of IT to address business strategy and the recognition that systems development is a process which helps to shape the outcome. The author argues that traditionally IS development methodologies have been very narrow, they are technically oriented and tend to exclude considerations of ways of linking analysis and design with strategic needs. Further, IS development methodologies assume that the boundaries of business needs and functions are well known. Those systems identified as efficiency-oriented take organisational objectives as given, whilst even effectiveness oriented ones have an expectation that there are goals or objectives. Note that Land (1975) suggests that effective systems are more likely if the system is built with flexibility in it. Two methods were seen as being able to take account of change but as Noble points out "the kinds of change considered appear to be relatively minor in the function and activities of the office, rather than strategic." Most methodologies are characterised as cautious and evolutionary and favouring incremental implementation (recall, though that this only refers to office automation). In summary, Noble considers that traditional methodologies reflect uncertainty about the means of development, socio-technical methodologies add uncertainty about effects on people and the organisation, and soft systems reflect uncertainty over the nature of the problem. In the first two methods, goals are given and in the final one no consensus about goals are assumed. Rather the analysis attempts to discover the goals and as such the methodology becomes a vehicle for redefining strategy. This review highlights the direction of much of the systems development work, yet it still assumes that there are goals or strategies waiting to be elicited; no mention is made of the desirability, or indeed the necessity, for nebulous, fuzzy strategy. As stated, the methodologies do not allow for the type of radical changes that would be required to cope with a constantly evolving but often unarticulated strategy.

The very purpose of methodologies is to bring order and consistency to a system development process. Conversely the trend in strategy is to retreat from rigorous definition and to avoid imposing such constraints. Avison and Wood-Harper (1991) identify weakness of conventional approaches to system development; these include failure to meet the needs of management, unambitious systems design, inherent instability of the models of process and inflexibility due to output driven design. They suggest that a planning approach "can involve strategic management in information systems work so that their needs are analysed and that information systems are implemented which do more than computerise the operations level applications" (p. 99). However, later planning approaches are criticised since they "tend to be mechanical and inflexible following the identification of strategic needs" (p.100). Again, strategies are there awaiting discovery. Avison and Wood-Harper argue for a contingency framework and proffer Multiview as a step in this direction. Such a framework will allow an attack on a number of fronts of the fuzziness of some applications. Finally, Herring (1991) argues for a convergence of skills in the information system developer, which, in turn, may lead to holistic information strategies in organisations.

7. CONCLUSIONS

Organisations need to be aware of the difference between using IT to assist in implementing corporate strategy and the formulation of IT strategy. However, this chapter has highlighted the difficulties of strategy formulation and enactment as applied to information technology projects. There is ample evidence of strategy not only being expressed in a nebulous way, but also that this formulation type is consistent with organisational success. Implementing any fuzzy strategy is likely to be difficult, implementing IT projects, given their need for more complete specifications and their lower tolerance of flexibility will be even more problematic.

REFERENCES

Andreu, R, Ricart, J and Valor, J (1991) The Strategic Dimension of Transactional Information Systems: Some Organisational Implications, *Journal of Information Systems*, **1**(4), pp. 223-232.

Avison, D and Wood-Harper, A (1991) Information Systems Development Research: An Exploration of Ideas in Practice, *The Computer Journal*, **34**(2), pp. 98-112.

Baxter, J and Hirst, M (1986) *A Capital Budgeting Case Study: An Analysis of a Choice Process and the Role of Information*, University of NSW, Department of Accounting Working Paper Series, No. 58, January.

Beaumont, J and Walters, D (1991) Information Management in Service Industries: Towards a Strategic Framework, *Journal of Information Systems*, **1**(3), pp. 155-172.

Bergeron, F, Buteau, C and Raymond, L (1991) Identification of Strategic Information Systems Opportunities: Applying and Comparing Two Methodologies, *MIS Quarterly*, **14**(1), March, pp. 88-101.

British Institute of Management (1988) *Managers and IT Competence*, London.

Binning, K (cited in Twiss) (1986) *Managing Technological Innovation*, Longman, Harlow.

Boddy, D (1988) in Boddy, D, McCalaman, J and Buchanan, D (Eds), *The New Management Challenge: Information Systems for Improved Performance*, Croom Helm, London.

Broadbent, M and Weill, P (1991) Developing Business and IS Strategy Alignment: A Study in the Banking Industry, *Proceedings of the 12th Annual Conference on Information Systems*, New York, pp. 293-306.

Chung, C, Lang, J and Shaw, K (1989) An Approach for Developing Support Systems for Strategic Decision Making in Business, *Omega*, **17**(2).

Ciborra, C (1991) From Thinking to Tinkering: The Grass Roots of Strategic IS, *Proceedings of the 12th Annual Conference on Information Systems*, New York, pp. 283-301.

Clemons, E and Kimbrough, S (1986) Information Systems, Telecommunications and their Effects on Individual Organisations, *Proceedings of the 7th Annual Conference on Information Systems*, San Diego, pp. 99-108.

Clemons, E and Row, M (1991) Sustaining IT Advantage: The Role of Structural Differences, *MIS Quarterly*, **15**(3), September, pp. 275-292.

Cottrell, N and Rapley, K (1990) Critical Success Factors in Developing an Executive Information System in BA, *European Journal of Information Systems*, **1**(1).

Coulson-Thomas, C (1991) Directors and I.T., and I.T. Directors, *European Journal of Information Systems*, **1**(1), pp. 45-53.

Currie, W (1989) The Art of Justifying New Technology to Top Management, *Omega*, **17**(5), pp. 409-418.

Das, S, Zahra, S and Warkentin, M (1991) Integrating the Content and Process of Strategic MIS Planning with Competitive Strategy, *Decision Sciences*, **22**, Winter, pp. 953-984.

Dearnley, P and Mayhew, P (1983) In Favour of System Prototypes and Their Integration into the Systems Development Lifecycle, *The Computer Journal*, **26**(1), pp. 36-42.

Dos Santos, B and Peffers, K (1991) The Effects of Early Adoption of IT: An Empirical Study, *Proceedings of the 12th Annual Conference on Information Systems*, New York, pp. 127-140.

Dreyfus, H and Dreyfus, S (1986) Why expert systems do not exhibit expertise, *IEEE Expert*, Summer.

Dussauge, P, Hart, S and Ramanantsoa (1992) *Strategic Technology Management*, Wiley, Chichester.

Earl, M (1989) *Management Strategies For Information Technology*, Prentice Hall, Hemel Hempstead.

Eason, K (1988) *Information Technology and Organisational Change*, Taylor and Francis, London.

Evans, G and Riha, J (1989) Assessing DSS Effectiveness Using Evaluation Research Methods, *Information and Management*, **16**, pp. 197-206.

Findlay, P (1991) IT and Sustainable Strategic Advantage Within the Competitive Area, *Proceedings of the British Academy of Management Conference*, Bath, pp. 165-168.

Floyd, S and Zahra, S (1991) The Effect of Fit between Corporate Strategy and IT Adoption on Organisational Performance in Small Banks, *Technology Analysis and Strategic Management*, **2**(4), pp. 357-373.

Freeman, C (1982) *The Economics of Industrial Innovation*, Frances Pinter, London.

Freeman, M and Hobbs, G (1991) Costly Information, Informed Investors and the Use of Sophisticated Capital Budgeting Techniques, *Proceedings of the AAANZ Conference*, pp. 68-74.

Galbraith, J (1977) *Organisational Design*, Addison-Wesley, Reading, MA.

Ginsberg, A and Venkatraman, N (1992) Investing in New IT: The Role of Competitive Posture and Issue Diagnosis, *Strategic Management Journal*, **13**, pp. 37-53.

Gordon, L (1989) Benefit-Cost Analysis and Resource Allocation of Decisions, Accounting, *Organisations and Society*, **14**(3), pp. 247-258.

Graham, I and Jones, P (1988) *Expert Systems, Knowledge, Uncertainty and Decision*, Chapman and Hall, London.

Grindley, P (1991) Why is Technology Hard to Manage? *Proceedings of the British Association of Management Conference*, Bath, August, pp. 165-169.

Gunton, T (1988) *End User Focus*, Prentice Hall, New York.

Gurnani, C (1984) Capital Budgeting: Theory and Practice, *The Engineering Economist*, **30**(2), Fall.

Haka, S, Gordon, L and Pinches, C (1985) Sophisticated Capital Budgeting Selection Techniques and Firm Performance, *Accounting Review*, **60**(4), pp. 651-669.

Harris, S and Katz, J (1991) Firm Size and the IT Investment Intensity of Life Insurers, *MIS Quarterly*, **15**(3), September, pp. 333-352.

Hart, S (1992) An Integrative Framework for Strategy-Making Processes, *Academy of Management Review*, **17**(2), pp. 327-351.

Herring, J (1991) Information Management – The Convergence of Professions, *International Journal of Information Management*, **11**, pp. 144-155.

Hirschheim, R, Klein, H and Newman, M (1991) Information Systems Development as Social Action: Theoretical Perspective and Practice, *Omega*, **19**(6), pp. 587-608.

Huff, S and Beattie, S (1985) Strategic Versus Competitive Information Systems, *Business Quarterly*, **50**(4), pp. 25-30.

Iivari, J (1986) Implementability of In-house vs. Application Package-based Information Systems, *Proceedings of the 7th Annual Conference on Information Systems*, San Diego, pp. 67-80.

Ives, B and Jarvenpaa, S (1991) Applications of Global IT: Key Issues for Management, *MIS Quarterly*, **15**(1), March, pp. 33-49.

Jauch, L and Glueck, W (1988) *Business Policy and Strategic Management*, McGraw-Hill, New York.

Kwon, T and Zmud, R (1987) Unifying the Fragmented Models of Information Systems Implementation, in Boland, R and Hirschheim, R (Eds), *Critical Issues in Information Systems Research*, Wiley, New York.

Land, F (1975) Criteria for the Evaluation and Design of Effective Systems, In Frielink, A (Ed.), *Economics of Informatics*, North Holland, Amsterdam, pp. 239-250.

Lederer, A and Medelow, A (1987) Information Resource Planning: Overcoming Difficulties in Identifying Top Management's Objectives, *MIS Quarterly*, **11**(3), September, pp. 388-399.

Lederer, A and Medelow, A (1988) Convincing Top Management of the Strategic Potential of Information Systems, *MIS Quarterly*, **12**(4), December, pp. 524-534.

Lederer, A and Medelow, A (1989) Coordination of Information Systems Plans with Business Plans, *Journal of Management Information Systems*, **6**(2), Fall, pp. 5-19.

Lincoln, T (1990) *Managing Information Systems for Profit*, Wiley, Chichester.

Little, S (1990) Task Environment Versus Institutional Environment: Understanding the Context of Design Decision-Making, *Design Studies*, **11**(1), January, pp. 29-42.

Madden, D (1992) Light at the End of the Tunnel, *Financial Times*, 30 January, p. 12.

Mainer, R (1968) *The Impact of Strategic Planning on Executive Behavior*, Boston Consulting Group, Boston, pp. 4-5.

Mockler, R (1992) Systematically Implementing Enterprise-Wide Strategies: Integrating Enabling Planning, *Journal of Strategic Change*, **1**(1), pp. 51-57.

Murray, F and Willmott, H (1991) The Communications Problem in IS Development: Towards a Rational Approach, *Proceedings of the 12th Annual Conference on Information Systems*, New York, pp. 339-349.

Neo, B (1988) Factors Facilitating the Use of IT for Competitive Advantage, *Information and Management*, **15**, pp. 191-201.

Noble, F (1991) Seven Ways to Develop Office Systems: A Managerial Comparison of Office System Development Methodologies, *The Computer Journal*, **34**(2), pp. 113-121.

Northcott, D (1991) Rationality and Decision Making in Capital Budgeting, *British Accounting Review*, **23**, pp. 219-233.

Parker, J E S (1978) *The Economics of Innovation*, Longman, London.

Peters, G (1990) Beyond Strategy – Benefit Indentification and Management of Specific IT Investment, *Journal of Information Technology*, **5**, pp. 205-214.

Pike, R (1983) The Capital Budgeting Behaviour and Corporate Characteristics of Capital-Constrained Firms, *Journal of Business Finance and Accounting*, **10**(4), pp. 663-671.

Pinches, G (1981) Myopia, Capital Budgeting and Decision Making, *Proceedings of the 11th Annual Meeting of the Financial Management Association*, Cincinnati, Ohio, pp. 6-19.

Porter, L and Lawler, E (1986) *Managerial Attitudes and Performance*, Irwin, Homewood, IL.

Powell, P L (1992) Information Technology and Business Strategy: A Synthesis of the Case for Reverse Causality, *Proceedings of the 13th Annual Conference on Information Systems*, Dallas, Texas, December.

Reagan-Cirincione, P, Schuman, S, Richardson, G and Dorf, S (1991) Decision Modelling: Tools for Strategic Thinking, *Interfaces*, **21**(6), November, pp. 52-65.

Runge, D and Earl, M (1988) Gaining Competitive Advantage from Telecommunications, In Earl, M (Ed), *Information Management: The Strategic Dimension*, Oxford University Press, Oxford.

Ruohonen, M (1991) Stakeholders of Strategic Information Systems Planning: Theoretical Concepts and Empirical Examples, *Journal of Strategic Information Systems*, **1**(1), pp. 15-28.

Schneiderjans, M and Fowler, K (1989) Strategic Acquisition Management: A Multi-Objective Synergistic Approach, *Journal of the Operational Research Society*, **40**(4), pp. 333-345.

Senker, J and Senker, P (1992) Gaining Competitive Advantage from IT, *Journal of General Management*, **17**(3), pp. 31-45.

Sharp, J (1990) Capital Investment – An Optimal Control Perspective, *Journal of the Operational Research Society*, **41**(11), pp. 1053-1063.

Sheppard, J (1990) The Strategic Management of I.T. Investment Decisions: A Research Note, *British Journal of Management*, **1**(1), pp. 171-181.

Smith, G (1989) Managerial Problem Identification, *Omega*, **17**(1).

Sol, H (1991) *Information Systems to Support Decision Processes*, NATO Advanced Study Institute on DSS: Theory and Applications, Italy, June 16-28.

Steiner, G (1979) *Strategic Planning*, Free Press, New York.

Stone, D (1991) Language, Training and Information Systems Assessment, *Accounting, Management and Information Technologies*, **1**(1), pp. 91-108.

Sutherland, E (1991) Strategic Management and Information Systems – An Ambiguous Relationship, *Proceedings of the British Academy of Management Conference*, Bath, August, pp. 169-173.

Swann, K and O'Keefe, W (1990) Advanced Manufacturing Technology: Investment Decision Process, *Management Decision*, **28**(3), pp. 27-34.

Teece, D (1987) *The Competitive Challenge*, Ballinger Publishing Co., Cambridge, MA.

Te'eni, D (1990) Support Systems for High Level Policy Making: What Makes Them Special, *Information and Management*, **19**(1).

Twiss, B (1986) *Managing Technological Innovation*, Longman, Harlow.

Vitale, M (1986) The Growing Risks of Information System Success, *MIS Quarterly*, **10**(3), pp. 327-334.

Walsham, G (1991) *Reading the Organisation: Metaphors and Information Management*, University of Cambridge, Dept. of Engineering Research Paper, 15/91.

Ward, J (1990) A Portfolio Approach to Evaluation Information Systems Investment and Setting Priorities, *Journal of Information Technology*, **5**, pp. 222-231.

Wassenaar, A (1988) Information Management in an Industrial Environment - An Education Perspective, In Boddy, D, McCalman, J and Buchanan, D (Eds), *The New Management*

Challenge: Information Systems for Improved Performance, Croom Helm, London, pp. 49-57.
Weill, P and Olson, M (1989) Managing Investment In I.T., *MIS Quarterly*, **13**(1), March, pp. 3-17.
Williams B R and Scott W P (1965) *Investment Proposals and Decisions*, George Allan and Unwin, London.
Zmud, R (1986) Supporting Senior Executives through Decision Support Technologies, In McLean, E and Sol, H (Eds), *Decision Support Systems: A Decade in Perspective*, Elsevier, Amsterdam.

14 IS evaluation: the hard centre and soft shell

David Targett
University of Bath

1. INTRODUCTION

The dictionary definition of 'evaluate' is to 'find the value of' or, more narrowly, 'give numerical expression to'. The former definition is broader since it does not necessarily imply quantification and therefore has a wider scope. However, the latter definition seems more applicable to the use of the word 'evaluate' in the context of IS (information systems) investments in business.

Within organisations 'evaluation' is usually employed when the effect of an IS project on income and cost streams is being quantified. Less often is it taken to mean that its wider impacts – strategies, organisational, social and financial – are being assessed, quantitatively or qualitatively. Two broad interpretations of the narrow definition can be observed when the term 'IS evaluation' is used in organisations. Sir Denys Henderson gave expression to them when he was quoted as saying:

> "I still worry enormously, both about the amount we spend on IT and the increasing difficulty of justifying that expense in terms of the bottom line." (Henderson, 1990)

The first interpretation is when, at an aggregate level, an attempt is made to determine whether investments in IS have given a satisfactory return. This type of evaluation might be carried out when a Chief Executive asks whether he is getting value for money from the organisation's IS spending. He or she may want to compare the organisation's IS spending with that of competitors, and then techniques such as Boundary Values (Martin, 1989) can be used.

Aggregating still further, attempts have also been made to ascertain the value of IS at a national level. Such research usually leads to the conclusion that IS investment has not resulted in any significant financial returns (See, for example, the work of Loveman, 1991, and Hochstrasser, 1987.) There is much debate about such studies and it is difficult to see their findings as conclusive.

The second interpretation, which is the starting point of this chapter, is when evaluation is taken to mean the process of justifying a project. In other words the worth of an IS investment or project is assessed as part of the decision whether or not to proceed with it. This is usually done by measuring the business benefits and costs of an IS project. So, for example, the benefits might be a 20% reduction in clerical staff and a 10% reduction in professional staff. Techniques such as Return on Investment (Radcliffe, 1982) are used. Where some benefits are difficult to quantify, techniques such as Cost Benefit Analysis (Emery, 1973) may help. However, the nature of many IS investments means that not all benefits can be quantified. An evaluation might have to include, as well as the clerical staff reduction, the argument that there is an unquantifiable improvement in customer service which, it might be added, is a strategic goal. Likewise the costs of the system will be measured where possible and, where not possible, listed. Organisations therefore do not and cannot adhere strictly to the 'give numerical expression to' definition of evaluation although they may try to do so whenever possible.

The interpretation of 'evaluation' is usually extended to include the process by which benefits and costs are balanced against one another, culminating in a decision to go ahead with the investment, or reassess it, or stop it. The range of evaluation techniques from Return on Investment for quantifiable financial benefits and costs to Information Economics for wider types of benefits are all intended for this purpose (Parker *et al.*, 1987).

This 'mainly quantification/should we go ahead' approach to evaluation is the hard centre. It thrives on accounting data, rigorous processes, and formal procedures. Research, however, is showing that evaluation cannot and should not be so constrained. An earlier research project (Farbey *et al.*, 1992) focused on the way organisations evaluated IS investments as part of the decision whether to proceed, i.e. how they put into practice the hard centre concept of evaluation. But the research also touched upon many broader issues which, the research showed, were inevitably and inextricably intertwined with hard centre evaluation (Farbey *et al.*, 1993, Ch. 5). These issues constitute the soft shell which is wrapped around the hard centre. The shell may be thicker than the centre.

The purpose of this chapter is to pinpoint and amplify these soft shell issues. Since the earlier research referred to above had its focus elsewhere – on the hard centre – the results presented here are a case-based platform for further work rather than a rigorous study in themselves.

2. EARLIER RESEARCH

The earlier research investigated sixteen IS projects, all of which had just been implemented or were in the process of being implemented. The main focus of the research was to study how the projects had been evaluated and justified as part of the decision to go ahead. The systems were management-related and in the area of office automation. Broadly, eleven of the sixteen were specific applications, three provided infrastructure and two were senior management support systems. A brief summary of the research is given below. For a fuller description see Farbey *et al.* (1993).

2.1 The organisations

The projects were located in a wide range of organisations which are categorised in Table 14.1.

2.2 Research method

Evidence about each of these systems, from the original conception through to the latest position, was collected from relevant documentation and from interviews with the people involved in the development and running of the systems. In particular the research sought to interview those stakeholders who had had a major influence in getting the project accepted.

The interviews were structured to ensure that the correct topics were covered. Table 14.2 summarises the questions asked.

2.3 Benefits achieved

The interviews revealed that organisations had achieved a wide range of benefits, both anticipated and unexpected. The benefits could be classified into five main groups which were, in order of increasing impact:

(a) Efficiency: saving (or avoiding) time, manpower and money.
(b) Functionality: being able to carry out either new activities or existing ones at a higher quality level.

Table 14.1 Organisations where the sixteen projects were located

Business Sector	*No. projects*
Consultancy	2
Defence	2
Financial Services	3
Industrial	2
IT	3
Pharmaceutical	1
Public Sector	2
Publishing	1
Total	16

Table 14.2 Interview structure

Topic	*Questions*
System context	What the company did Whether it had an IT strategy Where the system was to be located.
Motivation	When the system was proposed What the anticipated benefits were How they were cost justified What the nature of the decision-making process was
System	Description What the implementation process was
Achieved benefits	Whether the anticipated benefits were achieved Whether other benefits were achieved
Review	Achieved vs. expected benefits Whether a post-implementation evaluation had been carried out Changes to the system Future plans

(c) Communications: linking different systems and exchanging information.
(d) Management: improving the quality of management and enhancing individual jobs.
(e) Strategy: enabling corporate objectives to be met or gaining competitive advantage.

2.4 Evaluation methods used

Figure 14.1 illustrates how the justification issue was handled in the sixteen cases. The projects can be categorised according to whether a standard justification technique or an *ad hoc* procedure was used or whether no justification was carried out.

1. *Standard technique (four projects).* For three projects the technique was Return on Investment, for one it was Cost Benefit Analysis. In all these cases the organisation insisted on this type of cash flow analysis. For only one of the projects were the main benefits of the efficiency type that could easily be quantified. The other three projects were justified via efficiency benefits even though the main benefits were of a higher order.
2. *Ad hoc procedure (five projects*). These projects went through a justification procedure based on arguments about expected benefits presented in a report.

In three cases the argument was that present systems were obsolescent and needed to be improved; in one case the argument was that corporate headquarters (overseas) required that the investment was made to conform to worldwide company standards; in one case the argument was that the investment would contribute to the corporate strategy.

3. *No justification (seven projects).* The decisions to go ahead with these projects were taken at a high level without any detailed attempt to analyse expected benefits. In four cases the project was approved because it was an essential part of the corporate strategy; in one case the project was approved because corporate headquarters insisted that a functional division went ahead with it; in two cases the project was agreed on a 'got to do' basis because without it the organisation would lose out to the competition. In five of these seven projects the organisation had a formal justification procedure which was by-passed because the project could not fit into it.

Overall, about half the organisations had a formal justification procedure but most of them found that for some reason it could not be applied to the IT project satisfactorily and did not use it. Even when a formal prescribed method was used, it was sometimes modified in an *ad hoc* way to suit the exigencies of a particular situation. Consequently the overwhelming majority of the organisations in practice justified the investment by some *ad hoc* procedure (12 projects in all, categories 2 and 3 above).

The rationales behind these ad hoc procedures can be classified under the following headings:

1. Top-Down Strategic: senior management believes that IT is fundamental to the success of the organisation. ('Act of faith' in Figure 14.1).
2. Top-Down by Dictat: regulatory requirements dictate what must be done or corporate headquarters make rules on what divisions can do. ('Dictat').
3. Incremental Change: the project is determined by technological change or obsolescence. ('Step by step').
4. Competitive Imperative: the organisation must use IT to survive. ('Got to do').

3. THE SOFT SHELL

Although it was not part of the original objectives of the research, it became clear as the investigation progressed that it was not possible to separate, or sometimes even distinguish, evaluation from the general IS decision-making processes and a wide range of other important organisational factors otherwise unconnected to IT. While evaluation is taking place a variety of decisions are being taken and many other issues are influencing events. For example, the exact scope and definition of

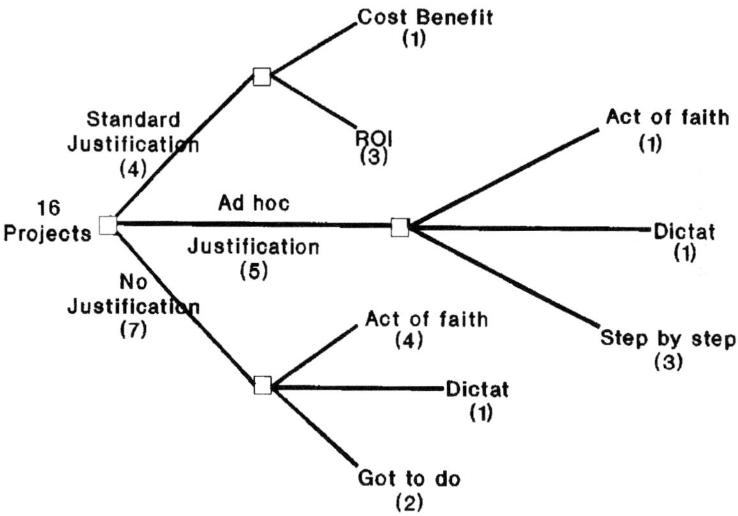

Figure 14.1 IT investments justification methods

the projects is being decided; the project management teams are being assembled; the roles of the users are changing; the roles of other stakeholders are also changing and the nature of their stakes becoming clear; differences between formal and informal agendas widen, and between formal and informal meetings; organisational politics start to play their part.

All these are major issues which are intertwined with the evaluation of the investment. Nor are the decisions about the project usually one-off decisions: more often they are rolling decisions which emerge over time as experience is gained and new information becomes available. As more stakeholders enter the decision-making process the dimensions of the project change, sometimes gradually, sometimes explosively.

These dimensions constitute the large – extremely large – soft shell which surrounds the apparently hard centre of evaluation. The shell does not get as much attention as the centre yet the research suggests that it is extremely influential in determining the eventual success or failure of the investment. Follow up research, in the style of longitudinal 'action research' (ESRC, 1993) has recently commenced and is now starting to pinpoint the soft shell more clearly. This has led to a re-examination of the earlier research. Further consideration of interview transcripts and documentation has produced evidence of the close links between evaluation and associated organisational factors and other influences within the IS decision-making process.

These dimensions are many, and in view of the true objectives of the research, it has not been possible to produce validated evidence of the nature of the links. The findings presented here are case-based and anecdotal rather than rigorous. A particular difficulty is that IS decision-making processes differ from organisation to organisation and comparisons are difficult.

However, as any IS decision-making process continues, and in consequence of it, the IS projects/investments involved are either chopped, delayed, or moved into the implementation phase. In re-examining the earlier research attention has focused on this common point – the channel between evaluation and final implementation – and concentrated on discerning how the hard centre and soft shell have reacted together to influence the projects' progress through the channel.

4. HARD CENTRE VS. SOFT SHELL

Re-examination of the sixteen projects produced the results summarised in Table 14.3. It shows the soft shell issues that arose together with the consequences for implementation.

Four of the projects are classified as 'straightforward', in that evaluation went ahead as planned and the projects were implemented, at least partially successfully. In two of the four (IT 2 and Industrial 2) the expected benefits were of the cost reduction/efficiency type and Return on Investment methods captured the economics of the investment accurately. In the other two (Publishing and Industrial 1) evaluation was not a major issue because the IS was forced upon the

Table 14.3 Soft shell issues

Organisation	*Justification*	*Issues arising*	*Consequences*
Pharmaceutical	Standard	Restricted eval; HQ politics	Missed benefits?
Defence 1	Standard	Massaging data	Delayed benefits
Defence 2	Ad hoc	Management communication	No alignment
IT 1	No just.	Stakeholders neglected	Slow take-up
IT 2	Standard	Straightforward	
IT 3	No just.	Stakeholder uncertainty	Benefits limited
Financial Ser 1	Ad hoc	Champion role decisive	B.P.R.
Financial Ser 2	No just.	Business pressure; audit	B.P.R./inefficient
Financial Ser 3	Ad hoc	Business pressure	Uncertainty/risk
Publications	No just.	Business pressure	
Public sector 1	Ad hoc	Corp. procedures	Unnecessary delay
Public sector 2	No just.	Senior management drive	Resistance/delay
Consultancy 1	No just.	Unstructured	Poor take-up
Consultancy 2	No just.	Formal; wrong stakeholders	Disaster
Industrial 1	Ad hoc	Straightforward	
Industrial 2	Standard	Straightforward	

organisation, one by a large customer stating how it wanted to do business and the second by head office decreeing which new systems should be used. The evaluation was limited in one case, non-existent in the other. In all four cases the context in which the investment was being made was tightly defined and implementation went down the appointed track, with or without evaluation.

In the latter two cases the fact that the organisations' fates were determined from outside meant that the way forward was clear and narrow. In two other cases, however, (IT 3 and Financial Services 3) outside pressures to 'do something' were equally strong but in a rapidly changing competitive situation the options of what to do were many. The outside pressures resulted in fast and limited evaluations. The outcome was a great deal of uncertainty about what the IS were intended to do, culminating in confused and much delayed implementations. Evaluation would not have helped in deciding to go ahead but it might have contributed to resolving the uncertainty.

In two cases (Pharmaceuticals and Defence 1) organisational procedures and culture required that all benefits and costs be quantified. This created difficulties and turned evaluation into an obstacle to be surmounted, in the eyes of the managers concerned. In one case the main benefit was getting a product to market sooner which would, it was estimated, mean a daily increase in revenue greater than the capital cost of the system. However, this benefit was so hard to quantify exactly that it was omitted from the evaluation which relied on minor cost cutting benefits. The minor benefits were sufficient to get the project past the corporate hurdle rate but the only strategic benefit, getting the product to market sooner, and other benefits omitted for similar reasons, were delayed in their realisation and could have been missed altogether. In the other case the return on Investment approach led to a IRR (Internal Rate of Return) which was less than the corporate hurdle rate. The data was then massaged until an answer was produced which exceeded the hurdle rate. In both cases evaluation seemed to be a corporate ritual to be got through as quickly as possible, rather than a true evaluation.

The corporate ritual was also the problem for public Sector 1. However, in this case the procedures were so tightly drawn that re-defining the case or massaging the data was not possible. The result was an unnecessarily drawn out decision-making process and a much delayed implementation. In a private sector organisation the length of the delay could have been strategically damaging.

Including an incomplete set of stakeholders in the evaluation process was a major source of difficulty in four cases (IT 1, Public Sector 2, Consultancy 1 and Consultancy 2). In each case the IS was undertaken as an 'act of faith', strongly led by senior management. While many studies (Galliers, 1991) have concluded that senior management commitment is necessary for the success of IS projects, if that commitment is not accompanied by the involvement of a full set of stakeholders then, according to these cases, it is not sufficient. This conclusion may be especially relevant if, as in these cases, the excluded stakeholders are mainly professionals with substantial autonomy and control over their working practices. These stakeholders wielded enough corporate power to resist and ultimately block the projects they did not understand and felt threatened by. As described by interviewees, one of these cases was a major disaster, two were major disappointments and one was a minor disappointment in terms of the take-up of the technology by the intended users and the achievement of business benefits by the organisation.

In a further case (Defence 2) the set of stakeholders was comprehensive but communications amongst them poor. The IS had originally been undertaken as a standard cost reduction system. It later emerged as a major strategic system (Runge and Earl, 1988) but the senior management was not aware of this role. Consequently there were misunderstandings within the organisation about the role of IS at a strategic level.

'Champions' played an important part in two projects (Financial Services 1 and Financial Services 2). In one case a champion who was a functional manager fought the board and IT committee over the adoption of generic personal com puter solution to an IS need when, she believed, a specific solution was essential. Her championship overturned corporate evaluation and approval procedures and secured the implementation of the system of her choice. The 'ownership' that this success engendered led to the system being further exploited and substantial business process engineering was undertaken successfully. In the second case competitive pressures were keenly felt by a business group and they forced through a project which they regarded as a business winning system but which the rest of the organisation regarded as an unnecessary expense. The system was a success, so obviously so that the organisation felt no need to monitor or audit the business outcome. When an outside body carried out an audit they confirmed the success but found great inefficiencies. For example, workstations had been ordered, paid for and delivered, but never used.

5. RISK VS. SOFT SHELL

The research indicated that a prime contribution made by evaluation was that it produced new information about the project (beyond the financial implications) and about stakeholder perspectives on the project and its implications. Information reduces uncertainty and therefore it could be expected that evaluation is linked to risk.

To investigate this association some method of classifying the projects according to risk is needed. One of the best known and most pragmatic classification methods is that devised by McFarlan (1981). Although too simple and lacking in precision for detailed research, his framework is appropriate here because McFarlan's matrix classifies projects according to implementation risk.

The axes of the 2 × 2 matrix are, first, the level of company-relative technology of a project and, second, its inherent structuredness. The former means whether the project involves levels of technology outside the organisation's current experience. The 'company-relative' part of the definition is important since what is sophisticated for one organisation may be basic for another. The latter means whether the output of the IS – its information content, scope, style, screens and documents – is clearly determined at the outset or whether it is expected that it will come to be defined or to emerge as the project progresses. McFarlan allocates different risk levels to the different cells as shown in Figure 14.2.

In Figure 14.3 the sixteen projects have been allocated to the cells. The allocation was subjective, based on the information gleaned in the research.

There is some pattern in the spread of the projects. In general the high risk projects were the ones for which no justification was carried out, the lowest risk projects used Return on Investment methods. This is of course not surprising since the existence of intangible, non-quantifiable benefits will both make evaluation difficult and contribute to the uncertainty and risk surrounding the project.

Although understandable this nevertheless appears to be the wrong way round. Risky projects with uncertain benefits should be the ones that most need the additional information that evaluation can provide. Indeed of the four projects perceived by stakeholders as falling somewhere between disappointing and disastrous (IT 1, Public Sector 2, Consultancy 1 and Consultancy 2), three had had no justification. The fourth had had an *ad hoc* justification but it had excluded the majority of the stakholders from any meaningful involvement.

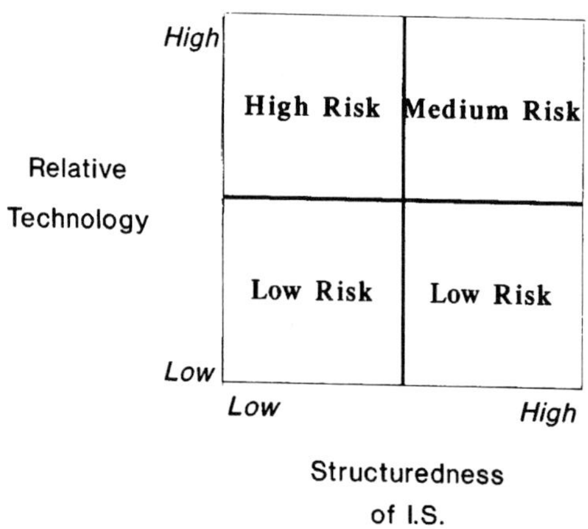

Figure 14.2 The McFarlan Implementation Risk Grid.

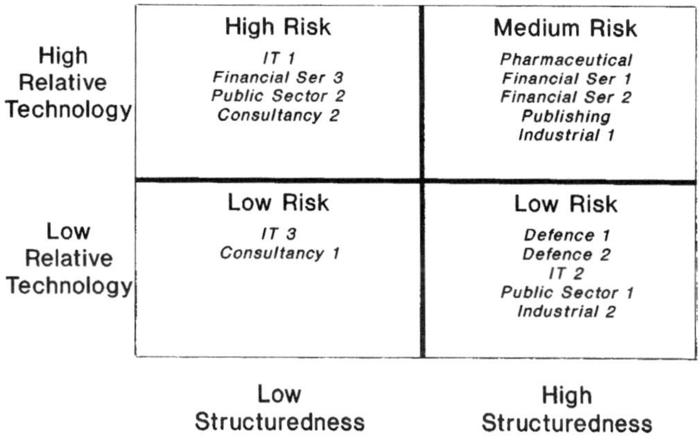

Figure 14.3 Risk levels of the sixteen projects.

Three of the four were also in the 'high risk' cell. The only other project in the 'high risk' cell had also had no justification and its final success or failure, as known at the time of the research, was highly uncertain.

The problem with the sixteen projects seemed to be that evaluation was interpreted in a narrow sense – a quantification of costs and benefits sufficient only to allow the project to overcome an organisational appraisal hurdle. The wider and more flexible interpretation of evaluation, as an assessment of the overall impact of the project, would have been more helpful at least in terms of risk. The straightforward projects would have received minimal evaluations while the risky ones would have had comprehensive evaluations, albeit at greater cost. Comprehensive evaluation would have required the use of sophisticated evaluation techniques, for example Information Economics and MOMC (Multiple Objective, Multiple Criteria) (Chandler, 1982) which, as their names suggest, are specifically intended to handle complex projects.

6. CONCLUSION

The research findings, although far from rigorous, permit some speculation about the links between evaluation, implementation and the final success or failure of a project.

Evaluation has too narrow an interpretation in many organisations, being taken to refer to the quantification of well-defined benefits with the sole objective of getting the project over organisational fences. The inevitable result is that clear-cut projects are evaluated more or less according to the textbook whilst fuzzy, possibly strategic, projects are evaluated in cursory fashion or not evaluated at all because many of the benefits do not match the requirements of standard accounting techniques such as Return on Investment. If, as seems probable, evaluation influences implementation success then it may also be inevitable that without evaluation projects are more likely to fail.

What is needed is, first, a wider interpretation of evaluation, closer to the dictionary definition of 'assessing the value of', and interpreted as meaning an overall assessment, by whatever means, encompassing the full impacts of the system, financial, strategic, social and so on. This wider interpretation would imply that evaluation should involve non-quantitative benefits however unwieldy. This process should then in itself tease out any latent benefits and catalyse an investigation into the full range of impacts of all types within the organisation.

As IS cover greater areas of the organisation and have impacts at all levels ranging from strategic to tactical, the problems of evaluation and implementation success are going to increase. In particular as empowered organisations become more common, situations parallel to those involving the management of professionals described in several of the projects will arise more often and the importance of soft shell evaluation increase.

REFERENCES

Chandler, J S, A multiple criteria approach for evaluating IS, *MIS Quarterly*, **6**(1), 1982.

Emery, J, Cost Benefit Analysis in IS , *SMIS Workshop no.1*, 1973.

ESRC research project, *Evaluating IT Investments.*

Farbey, B, Land, F and Targett, D, Evaluating IT Investments, *Journal of Information Technology*, 1992.

Farbey, B, Land, F and Targett, D, 1993, *How to Assess your IT Investment: a study of methods and practice*, Butterworth Heinemann, Oxford, 1993.

Galliers, R D, Strategic IS Planning: myths, Realities and guidelines for successful implementation, *European Journal of IS*, **1**(1), 1991.

Henderson, D Quoted in the Price Waterhouse Information Technology Review, 1991.

Hochstrasser, B, *Does IT slow you down?*, Kobler Unit, Imperial College, London, 1987.

Loveman, G, The Productivity of IT Capital, in *The Corporation of the 1990s* (Scott Morton, MS, editor), Oxford University Press, 1991.

Martin, R, *The Utilisation and Efficiency of IT: a comparative study*, Oxford Institute of Information Management, Templeton College, Oxford, 1989.

McFarlan, W, Portfolio Approach to Information Systems, *Harvard Business Review*, September/October 1981.

Parker, M M, Benson R J and Trainor, H E, *Information Economics*, Prentice Hall, NJ, 1987.

Radcliffe, R C, *Investment: Concepts, Analysis, Strategy*, Foreman, Glenview, IL, 1982.

Runge, D and Earl, M, 1988, Gaining Competitive Advantage from Telecommunications, in Earl, M, *Information Management: the Strategic Dimension*,Oxford University Press, 1988.

15 Barking up the wrong tree

Barbara Farbey
Centre for Research into Strategic Information Systems, School of Management, University of Bath, UK[1]

1. INTRODUCTION

Assessing the costs, benefits and risks associated with IT investment has never been easy. Justifying proposed expenditure, assessing the benefits that will accrue from a proposed investment or appraising the worth of a project that has been implemented are topics which have been high on the management and research agenda for a very long time. In the 1990s, nearly fifty years after the advent of computers there are very few signs that the problems are yielding gracefully either to research-based ideas or to pragmatic, heuristically derived methodologies.

One reason for this impasse is that the issues keep changing. The technologies, the organisations and the uses of technology today are different from what they were yesterday. Characteristically, today's new systems are integrative, mopping up older systems, upgrading them, replacing them and joining them together. They are closer to the heart of the value-chain. Frequently the declared aim is not automation *per se*, it is nothing less than the transformation of the business itself. Without making any judgement as to how far such transformations are actually achieved or even desirable, it is clear that methods designed to evaluate large calculating machines are unlikely to accommodate the new aspirations. We are in uncharted waters.

Nevertheless people do evaluate IT investment. They must. IT is central to the strategic agenda, offers great potential for supporting radical change in the organisation and very costly. Not to attempt a proper evaluation would be foolhardy.

It would also give greater currency to the informal evaluation of IT. This is a process which will always happen anyway, but if there are no commonly agreed and accepted processes, the evaluations people make will reflect only their own limited view and may be seriously biased. And without a recognised process there is no common basis for managers to achieve agreement on what actions are appropriate for the enterprise.

The papers in this book provide many insights into these problems. Several propose new methods or extend and update older ones to cover the new agenda.

[1]Research conducted by the Centre into the evaluation of IT investment is sponsored by the Economic and Social Research Council, UK. We are most grateful for their support.

Jones[2] for example offers a technique for focusing and prioritising IT investment which contributes to the surfacing of issues and the generation of opportunities; Leyton sets out a framework for evaluation which includes developing a closer understanding of the environment, of the relevant activities, of the investment itself and of the impact the investment may have; Birch and McEvoy deal with systematic calculation of risk and Coleman too takes on risk as well as providing a way of dealing with intangibles. Connolly attacks the problem of understanding the overhead cost base, certainly a pressing contemporary problem for management.

Some authors address the organisational and political issues which underlie the whole notion of evaluation. As much as the more methodological papers, these too are looking at the problems of today, thrown up as Coombs writes by IT's move from a supporting to a 'starring' role. Targett sets out some of the managerial issues which follow from the new role, issues which are now central to IT management as well as general management. Powell confronts a very modern agenda when he contrasts the demands of strategy and fuzziness with the need in IT for more complete specifications and the difficulty for IT projects in coping with requirements flexibility.

Two papers capture problems of change and novelty, albeit from rather different perspectives. Both are case studies. Heduan examines the role of IT as a vehicle for change in an organisation which is itself undergoing fundamental and continuous change. The project itself is standard; it is the context which is swirling round. He sees process and process management as key to the successful outcome of such projects. Keen by contrast, looks at a leading edge technology. For him the difficulties of evaluation come from an unknown, unknowable future impact of the technology. He suggests a method of recursive evaluation.

The authors are unanimous on one point: IT investment decisions are rarely taken solely on the basis of financial calculations. Partly this may be due to IT's new starring role: in this role the ultimate evaluation and decision-making is in the hands of very senior executives and, as Powell points out, senior executives show a preference for non-quantitative data. But partly it must be that the ordinary financial tests applied to capital investment are not regarded as sufficient to reveal the full significance of the investment. Financial calculations form only a part of what goes into making the decision to proceed or continue with an IT investment. As Galliers succinctly has it, there are too many contradictions in focusing too narrowly on IT and on financial calculation. That way '(w)e are barking up the wrong tree.'

So we need to rethink. In the remainder of this final chapter we take a slightly different tack: instead of concentrating on the individual contributions we look

[2] All references in this chapter are to the papers in this book.

across the book as a whole, tracking a few key themes and questions which are common to many papers and which we believe will help us move forward. These are:

- Purpose: What are the commonly understood purposes of evaluation? What other purposes do these papers reveal?
- Objects: most methodologies are designed to evaluate an individual IT project. Do these papers suggest we should be focusing our attention elsewhere? Where (IT) projects create value together, what is the appropriate level of evaluation? Changes to the Information System may be part of a wider change. What then are we evaluating?
- Methods: do current methods address the right issues? Do they tell us what we need to know? How does the balance fall between hard and soft issues?

2. THE PURPOSE OF EVALUATION

The 'hard' purposes of evaluation are clear. Evaluation is used as a basis for decision-making: to decide, for example whether to initiate a project or continue it. It is also used as a basis for control and accountability: to ask, for example, whether the project has lived up to expectations or to ascertain who is responsible for its impact. But as these papers show, there are other, softer uses too. In the papers we find references to:

- *legitimisation*
  Much IT appraisal is, as Powell reports 'a ritual of legitimacy not an attempt at really assessing benefit.' In other words the purpose of an evaluation may be to legitimise a decision already taken on other grounds. Or it may be that it is not the project itself which is being legitimised so much as the position and actions of the people involved. In recent years, as Powell notes, projects have gained legitimacy by being positioned as 'strategic'. Cynically one might observe that this frequently means 'big', 'expensive' or 'unable to pass the hurdle rate.'

- *gaining commitment*
  It is a feature of many of the methods proposed in the book that they expressly emphasize the importance of getting and retaining commitment to the investment and its outcomes. The success of a project depends crucially on a sense of ownership and commitment from all the interested parties – managers, developers and users. Both commitment to the project and the sense of shared ownership can be made stronger through careful management of the control structures of the project, for example the composition and

procedures of a Project Board, and through careful attention to the process of evaluation. Specifically, process and structure must be designed as far as possible to bring to the surface the differing motivations and expectations of those involved, clarify business goals and capture different political 'readings' of the situation. (Galliers, Coombs, Leyton, Jones, Keen, Heduan, Targett).

These proposals for new methods implicitly or explicitly acknowledge the importance of evaluation as a tool for persuasion. Powell makes a challenging point. Observing that there is research to show that senior management characteristically has a preference for qualitative data he remarks that 'a business case formulated in quantitative data may stand little chance of success ... Perhaps then, the couching of IT activities in qualitative terms is merely an astute political move on the part of IT managers'. Popular opinion of course has it that, especially in the cost-conscious, 'lean and mean' 1990s, senior management is demanding hard facts. There is a contradiction here between the hard and the soft which is worth exploring.

- *learning*
  In surfacing the assumptions and expectations of the key stakeholders, evaluation can be a learning process. Targett explicitly remarks that '[the process of doing an evaluation] produced new information about the project and about stakeholder perspectives on the project and its implications'. Methodologies such as Business Systems Strategy (Galliers); Investment Evaluation Methodology (Leyton); the three phase process proposed by Jones; recursive evaluation (Keen) and others all carry the implication that the organisation can, indeed must, learn and respond to a changing environment.

- *as a starting point for negotiation*
  All the papers which emphasize the political nature of IT development, evaluation and management recognise that 'the actual numbers are only one of the inputs into the process of judgement and bargaining which eventually makes the decisions' (Coombs).

3. THE OBJECTS OF EVALUATION

Most writing on the evaluation of IT is concerned with the evaluation of individual systems or projects. This would appear to be problematic on three counts.

First, as Galliers points out, there may be synergy between projects, the value of the whole being more than the sum of the parts. For such investments it makes sense to consider them as a 'bundle' and as he says, quoting Hendricks, this idea is gaining ground in accounting circles as well as in IS.

Second, as he and several other authors point out (Galliers, Coombs, Connolly, Leyton, Heduan and Powell), systems cannot be divorced from their context. For Galliers the particular error is not to see systems planning and strategy as intimately tied to business planning and strategy. It follows that the basis for evaluation is much broader than the system *per se* and must take account of business targets and the differing motivations and expectations of different stakeholders.

Third, as Coombs argues convincingly, changing the IT systems often signals a much wider change in the organisation. Such changes may be to the structure, a change from hierarchical to flat organisations for example, or to the culture.

To illustrate the argument Coombs recounts the story of a pensions company, intent on developing its administrative systems on the one hand, and new products on the other. This led to a battle between the IT department on the one hand and also between the two sponsoring departments. Behind this battle, on the surface an argument about capacity and priorities for IT, lay a deeper debate. What was at stake was no less than a strategic and cultural change: the change from a traditional administratively-led company to a modern market-oriented company. In these circumstance, the value of the IS investment emanates from the value of the wider change. As Coombs says 'get people to focus on that, and measure the benefits in those terms rather than through some proxy cost-benefit analysis of the IT system!'

4. THE METHOD OF EVALUATION

Many papers in this book suggest new methods for evaluating and managing the IT investment, or substantial modifications to existing ones. Explicitly or implicitly they point to the fault-lines in our current methods. From what has been written, these would appear to be:

- most existing methods fail to deal adequately with non-financial, non-quantifiable aspects of IT investment. Many derive from the prescriptions of micro-economic theory which give rise to decision-making processes which in turn require hard measures. This has led to the development of hard techniques. Because these methods do not address the softer issues, they tend to accentuate the hard ones, by default. It is easier to see what is being spent in hard money, than what is gained or lost through the non-quantified aspects of the proposed system. If, as often seems to be the case, it is the latter which are the more important, neglecting the soft issues can so skew the evaluation as to make it more or less meaningless. Worse, it can actually get in the way of proper management.
- the content of evaluations, even the hard, quantitative elements, is too narrow.

Organisations need to calculate not only the capital spend, but the running costs: the total cost of ownership (Leyton). They need to include a systematic assessment of risk (Birch and McEvoy).

- as the ways in which we use IT become more strategic, the methods we use need to be more inclusive. Current developments affect a wide range of stakeholders at many levels in the organisation and beyond it. Their interests need to be included in the calculations. Moreover, methods need to take account of the fuzziness which, as Powell says, is characteristic of strategy a the higher levels. Galliers presents a method which is inclusive in this sense. Its strong emphasis on process and on continuing review, a theme also very much part of Keen's suggestion for recursive evaluation, are designed to address these softer points.
- change is a defining feature of modern corporate existence. Technologies change as do organisations and their environments. Even our view of what business we are in changes. Evaluation methods have to cope with this: they need to be flexible (Targett and Powell), on-going and iterative (Keen and Galliers). Keen's paper on evaluating leading edge technologies shows the problem at its most acute. Everything is moving and the impact is impossible to predict. He makes a strong plea for the evaluation itself to be flexible, responding to the shifting need of stakeholders as well as the environment. Not all cases are as hard as the one he tackles, but in understanding the extreme cases it becomes easier to recognise the outstanding issues which beset even the more conventional ones.

5. A LAST WORD

Information Systems stand at a confluence of two streams of thought. The first is technical – computers including hardware and software are immensely complex and wonderful machines. Making the machines work effectively in a business context requires a great deal of creative thought, disciplined by incisive logic. The second is human – the systems serve the purposes of people as individuals, in teams and in organisations. People too are complex and wonderful, but they are not machines. Making the systems work obviously requires creativity and analytical logic in good measure but must rest also on a deep understanding of individual psychology and of team and organisational behaviour. The logic of the machine must be tempered by the logics of power, negotiation, group norms and personal responses.

So, as the title of the book implies, there is an inherent paradox. One part of the equation – the money spent and the money saved – is reckoned in hard numbers. The other – the changes to organisational structure and culture – emerges via many complex social and political processes. The outcomes are soft.

In summarising the chapters of this book we have chosen to stress the intangible, the fuzzy and the soft. We have made much of the dangers of over-rationalising and of not paying enough attention to the social and political aspects of evaluation and management.

This is not to say that we do not see a place for calculation and rational argument in evaluation. We do. Indeed, as many of the authors in this book, we would argue for extending reasoned, quantitative,'hard' techniques so that they do tell us more of what we need to know. Our contention is rather that in dealing with information systems we have to do well at both.

The papers themselves reflect both the 'hard' and the 'soft'. They are inspired by modern developments in Information Systems, catching very clearly the dilemma of having to justify hard money in hard times, spent on projects which inevitably have soft outcomes. The authors offer a range of sound approaches, ideas and ways to go. The issues they present are important. We hope that the readers of the book will take them up, and 'think on'.